Where I Fell to Earth

A Life in Four Cities

PETER CONRAD

POSEIDON PRESS

New York   London   Toronto   Sydney   Tokyo   Singapore

Poseidon Press
Simon & Schuster Building
Rockefeller Center
1230 Avenue of the Americas
New York, New York 10020

Originally published in Great Britain by Chatto & Windus Ltd.
POSEIDON PRESS is a registered trademark
of Simon & Schuster Inc.

POSEIDON PRESS colophon is a trademark
of Simon & Schuster Inc.

Manufactured in the United States of America

1   3   5   7   9   10   8   6   4   2

Library of Congress Cataloging in Publication Data
Conrad, Peter.
Where I fell to earth: a life in four cities/Peter Conrad.
p.   cm.
British ed. has subtitle: A life in four places.
"Originally published in Great Britain by Chatto & Windus, Ltd."—
T.p. verso.
1. Conrad, Peter.—Homes and haunts.   2. Critics—Great Britain—
Biography.   3. English teachers—Great Britain—Biography.   4. London
(England)—Description—1981-   5. Oxford (England)—
Description.   6. Lisbon (Portugal)—Description—1981-
7. New York (N.Y.)—Description—1981-   I. Title.
PR55.C66A3   1990
820.9—dc20
[B]   90-33021
CIP
ISBN 0-671-68233-4

First Poseidon Press Edition May 1990

Contents

I

The View from Four Windows

E VERY MORNING STARTS WITH A MOMENT OF TRUTH, AN
instant of terror. You can't remember who you are supposed to
be, and therefore can't separate left-over dreams from reality. A life
waits to be resumed. The empty clothes on the backs of chairs tell
you that. But whose life is it, how did it get to the point where it was
broken off yesterday, and does the muddle of sensations in bed,
gradually cohering into a person, fit whatever fragment of world
might be outside the window?

Later, there will be a stranger to stare at in the mirror, behind
whose face you can retire for another day; first – never quite sure
what I will find, as if going back to the mystified beginning – I pull
the curtains open and look out. What I see should tell me who, or
perhaps only where, I am.

What I see is this: a blank brick wall, its paint smeared by rivulets
of rain. The rain gurgles down drainpipes, spits from the leaves,
dents a blossom, bubbles on the tiled floor. A letter, pushed under
the door into my yard by a neighbour, grows limp and slurred on
the wet step. Vines dig suckers into the wall, or twist round the
pipe. The sky pours into this square of space, then runs away down
gullets between the tiles.

Rain drills on the roof, as if entreating entry. When I go downstairs, the floor intestinally grumbles: a train tunnels through
bedrock far beneath. I hop across the splashing yard to rescue the
letter and wring it out. Bread I have left out to bribe the birds is
soggy on the tiles. Above, in the colourless oblong which is my
allotment of sky, a plane screams and snarls through fuzzy limbo.

This is London, sullen and cowering under its caul of drizzle. At least if I unlock that door, go down a passage beneath the house in front, unlock another door and climb a coiled iron stair into the street, I can enter the city. The rain-lashed street becomes a square which grows into a circle. From this point I can start a journey to anywhere. Solitariness will soon be merged, like uncountable rain drops, in the welter of other lives.

Back here, retreating down the stairs and along the passage and across the yard, with three doors and four locks intervening, it is not London yet. It is just as much space as a life needs: a bare necessity of white walls, undefended from the rain, suspended like a cage between the machines which shriek in the clouds and those which rumble in the rock.

Upstairs, my desk faces the back wall of the house across the yard. The wall used to be ashen, stained by the city's marinade of soot; I have had it painted white. Sitting down, I look at the featureless, polar zone of bricks, and hope that images will start to flicker on them. Sometimes they do.

Or I open other curtains, and sample a different day.

It is another place. A four-leaf clover of lawn rather than those questing tendrils on the pipe. The lawn has been clipped and rolled in stripes; in patches it is dry, yellow, like the dusty glowing stone of the walls around it. Four paths between the sections of lawn converge on a pond.

This time the scene is peopled. There are two characters in prospect – a scurrying old man in a white shift with a black book under his arm, and a lean youth poised in the middle of the pond. The old man has emerged from a cavernous door in one corner; he scuttles along the stone rampart above the lawn, and is gone under an arch. The youth stays where he is, improbably angled over the water, on one bare foot with a hand raised to exhort the air. He is holding a wand. All he wears is a peaked cap.

He is a Greek god, or the statue of one: Mercury the messenger, springing forward to levitate on some Olympian mission. The old man is another kind of fixture: a canon of the cathedral which opens up behind that gaping door, on his way back to breakfast after matins. Mercury's errands used to be those of a divine go-between, before he was tethered on his pedestal; the old man's business is the daily routine of giving thanks to other gods. Both pantheons find house-room here.

I am in Oxford, looking out on the quadrangle of Christ Church, named Tom after a dolorous clock which bangs out the hour above me. This set of rooms counts as my office. The tax inspector considers it the equivalent of the tied cottage which an agricultural labourer occupies. Soon, resuming another life, I will have to teach.

First I check the view to see that nothing has changed. The canon can be relied on, but the athlete cast in metal is not altogether resigned to his grounding. He still manages occasional metamorphoses. Some mornings he will be wearing a toilet-roll for a bangle on that thin wrist, sometimes a chamber-pot or a mortar-board on top of his winged cap. He has had, over the years, quite a wardrobe of T-shirts. If it is icy, he might wrap a striped college scarf round his midriff like a loin-cloth. Once he took flight altogether, to be recast. When I opened the curtains that morning the pond was drained, his pedestal empty, with a scaffold of trestles around it. The men in overalls glumly explained his removal. 'We're going to hang a few students, sir,' they said. 'Didn't you know?'

Returning from the foundry, Mercury went back to his career as a photographic model. He spends the day brandishing his wand over orderly troops of Japanese, Americans in pastel leisure wear, and English trippers with their umbrellas. Everyone wants to be associated with him, and to attitudinise in imitation of him. The Japanese humbly giggle at their own presumption, the Americans clown and hold up imaginary torches like the Statue of Liberty, the English are stiff in the presence of a monument.

He is an image – of what? For visitors, of the quaint and obsolete deities honoured here. For students, of an ancestry to be debunked by chamber-pots and noisily ideological T-shirts. But also of the speed of thought and its fleet-footed changefulness. He is mercurial. Or he would be, if he could wriggle out of his cerement of metal.

Behind other curtains, at the beginning of other days, a screen is lowered over the window. Its horizontal bands are divided by pin-holes, through which brightness, heat and bird song already leak into the room. If I put my eye to one of the holes, screwed tight like the eye's own pupil, a dot of world appears. It holds brushes of pine needles, or orange roofs and white chimneys, or a patch of sky as blue as the glaze on pottery. The screen is raised by tugging a canvas pulley; it is like standing in the wings and hauling up a theatrical curtain on the view.

At first there is only the bombardment of light, which stuns the eye. Then, with no barrier like the brick wall in London or the stone façade completing the Oxford quadrangle, sight measures space until the horizon. Outside the balcony, the tops of trees: bristles of pine, cones cracking open in the sun, the birds picking and probing. Below, a garden of lemons, yellow weights tugging the twigs to earth; a trellis of grape vines. Other houses slide down the hill, blurring into haze. Then the river, which rounds corners and widens towards the ocean.

This scene belongs in Lisbon. Beyond the glinting cliffs of apartments – along a last stretch of levelled scrub, rolled boulders and suicidal surf which I can't see from here – is the cape where Europe ends, or begins. I am on holiday, staying in the house of friends.

The window looks directly west, at the point where the sun submerges – white-hot in summer, making the sea seethe; in winter falling through gashed clouds and a smouldering sky. On the coastal beaches you can stand in the surf at nightfall with breakers crashing onto you like masonry; as they crumble, you watch the sun set through them from underwater. It gains heaviness and volume as it is lowered clumsily down the sky. Once the sea takes it, solidity drains away. From beneath the breakers, it is a ripple of melted bronze, shedding form, dissipating its fire. The object, drowning, is now an impression. During the day, it can't be looked at. Slipping towards the water, it declines into sight. We can see it only in the act of losing it. The image is an afterthought.

From the window, when the trees, houses and interposing earth run out, I try to find the disputed border between sea and sky. A knife-edge sometimes, an incision on glass to separate one blue from another: purple above, gleaming polished silver below. But the strips can overlap, or blend into the same grey. With land rolled up like a carpet and put away, the weather stages dramas out there. Storms in skeins unfurl from the clouds. Rain like tilted columns walks across water towards the continent. Or the sun is crimson when it sets, furious, as if this were its last inundation. In earth's absence, the world belongs to water, evaporating air and fire.

At one of the headlands a sand-bar juts out, and a lighthouse beam winks; beyond it is the point where all lines of perspective conjoin and vanish, where the sun commutes between hemispheres and where the planes which howl overhead disappear, where the whole radiant box-shaped panorama – which can be squeezed into a dot on that metal screen over the window, or fitted into my eye – dwindles again to a blip and blinks off, like the lighthouse beam.

Along the street from this house, a chapel is propped on a bluff. It is a cube of yellow plaster, with curlicued flames of stone around its roof. Here the Portuguese navigators in the fifteenth century paused to pray, before they rode down the hill to the river and sailed off the edge of the earth. A plaque salutes Pedro Álvares Cabral, who bumped into Brazil at the bottom end of this unmappable ocean. I often walk along to the chapel: it gives me the sensation of going to the end of my tether, and of the land's (and then of being able to reach home again in five minutes). Once I brought a child along, the housekeeper's grandson. I asked him what they had taught him at school about the place, and as we stood on the steps of the locked chapel and shaded our eyes to see that spot out at sea where you fall over the precipice, he explained that this was the last stop of the explorers before they went off to discover the worlds.

'*Os mundos*', he said: the worlds; the multiple universes he would learn how to imagine, and which for him still awaited discovery.

In January, these worlds of potentiality withdraw. When I pull up the screen in the morning, nothing exists. The river has breathed a pale fog over the hills. The air is a choking mesh around the house. The street beneath us smudges and is blotted out. The invisible river moans. Planes drone in circles above, since there is no land to alight on. Only in the afternoon does the mist relent, and worlds become possible again.

If the mind pushes beyond the vanishing point, and draws a line for three thousand miles across the ocean along the same latitude, it arrives at another continent, where there is one more window: a place from which to peer back east at the other places left behind.

Here, noise penetrates the slats of blinds long before they are opened. Trucks lurching between pot-holes concuss the air, and the building spasmodically quakes. Unloaded crates clatter onto the sidewalk outside the supermarket, rattling like skeletons. Fire-engines clang past in full cry all night long. Darkness belongs to the sirens, sketching loopy, alarming parabolas of visible sound above the streets. Police cars scream blue murder – and violet murder, and indigo, and hot pink. This city doesn't murmur, its alimentary pipes complaining discreetly like London's as the tube trains circulate; it is a brass band of crashes, screeches, shots, eruptions, all the frenzy of fatigued metal, frayed rubber, brittle glass and scraped, abraded nerves. New York, the last of my outposts, scene of another occasional life, fitted in between terms in Oxford and Christmases or summers in Lisbon.

Voices hurl themselves against the closed windows like panicking birds. 'Move it out!' – a megaphonic growl at two in the morning; a patrol car has spotted skulduggery in the park opposite, and turned its loud speaker on. An hour later, an unseen woman on the corner broadcasting her complaint against a silent partner: 'Why are you so ob*nox*ious? Do we have a relationship or *what*?' Later still, a squabble between the black men who sleep, guarding their pyramids of redeemable tin cans, in the park: 'I'm gonna kick you ass, nigger. You keep you hands offa my cans.' At weekends, jeers for the adolescents from across the river who kerb-crawl in their parents' cars, radios blasting with the force of grenades: 'Go back to Jersey, fucking jerks!' Once in a while, a single syllable which subsides into heedless silence or heedless uproar: 'Help.' Always, the mumbled repetitious litany of the pan-handlers. One of them used to pace back and forth, as if on a leash of his own imagining, along a few chosen feet of sidewalk outside the supermarket beneath me. He varied his refrain as he shuttled to and fro throughout the day: 'Just making a living in America. Just hustling along in America. Just passing time in America. Just living my life in America.' After a few hours, the 'America' developed a tic, a pulse, the beat of blood in an overcharged artery. By the afternoon it alternately tootled, brayed or twanged like a plucked string, all its separate syllables bouncing acrobatically on the trampoline of the thick reverberant air: 'A-me-ri-caa!!!'

This window obliquely overlooks a street corner, where a one-way traffic of life hurtles past. The stream of tin and chrome and aluminium flows uptown, never looking back and never returning. People perch impatiently on the verge of it, appealing to be carried along. Their arms jerk out at right angles, while the rest of the body reads the newspaper or runs on the spot, like a car reluctantly pausing at a stop-light; when taxis swerve alongside, they throw themselves in and are projected into space around the corner where the avenue begins.

The street, upwardly mobile, is a ladder to the sky. Buildings have the same destination: at night in the window two towers at the bottom of the island pile up electric pillars of jewels; others aim nose-cones at the clouds, wear wreaths of lightning-bolts, or launch steel gargoyles into the air. Each building is a beacon, a torch-bearer like the adamantine lady standing in the bay. Together they make up a collective fantasy, a horizon of entrancing artificial light. Below in the streets, everyone is pursuing some dream or other, even the pan-handler whose few measured feet of pavement were his limitless America; the concentrated energy of so many hopes switches the buildings on like bulbs, and writes messages on the underside of scudding clouds.

In this place of rapid transit, everything will eventually come to pass, and will pass by at speed. If I keep my eye on this corner, all human possibilities will be acted out, though in no particular order, and perhaps even all at once. I will certainly see death. (Indeed I already have done so: the woman removed from the café on a stretcher, with only her expensive shoes peeping out from under a sheet; the corpse sprawled as if dozing across a chequers table in the park.) Likewise copulation. Maybe – if I maintain the vigil long enough – birth. In my sliver of space, glancing diagonally through the trees to another row of red and brown houses with the uplands of jagged, luminous illusion behind them, the revved-up globe revolves, and lives are abbreviated to a second. The slice of street I can see between my building and the one opposite is a place, like the world, for accidents to happen in.

Looking down at the yellow missiles of taxis or at the people straying across the street and lingering briefly on the sidewalk, I wonder if this corner might not measure out all there is: all the time we are allowed for our journey, all the space we are permitted to spread into. Life, as the local T-shirt doomily declares, is not a rehearsal. Which may be why the cars move so fast, and why the people, terrified in case the city does not notice their existence, attitudinise so loudly. New York is a contraption for accelerating and intensifying experience. As raucous and restless as childhood, it exists to dispense energy, with no thought of conserving or re-plenishing it. I suspect, seeing my own reflection in the window, that I am the only stationary object in the place.

It is like sentry duty, looking out of the window: observation as a discipline. The pane of glass, the screens and shades and curtains are the barriers, varyingly transparent, which intercede between life and me. Bounded by the frame, sight is organised into vision; looking out, I persuade myself I have composed a picture.

A blank wall is not a view. Nothing happens, in my London yard below street level, except the angled passage of the sun and the growth of creepers. The day contracts inside this sunken square, even more summarily than those lives hastening across the few yards between buildings in New York. The sun pivots over in a semicircle, washing the tops of the walls. My tree cries out to it, growing on one side only in its keenness to reach up, so it has to be circulated in its tub; the flowers on the wall gather strength to defy gravity and thrust in hair-pin bends towards it. As clouds cross, the light flicks off, and the shadowed leaves and branches fade; they reappear on the white ground like images materialising from oblivion on photographic paper. The light seems to throb from that source above, out of sight. It is furry, sharp, or wiped away altogether, depending on the thickness of clouds and the intervals between them: I have learned to interpret affairs in the sky at second-hand. By mid-afternoon it has gone, brushing the yard in a painfully puny synopsis of its daily circuit.

Unable to face the blank wall, I rigged up a system of reflectors to relay news of events above and outside: a mirror in the corridor beneath the house which stands between me and the street, so I can spy on comings and goings from a flat which opens onto the passage; another mirror screwed to an outside wall, which when I look at it from upstairs reports on the sky above the houses behind me. As if through a periscope, images are handed down to me. But indistinctly, unfocussed. The most information I ever get from the mirror in the passage is a swish of skirt or the spray from an umbrella; I am left to deduce the mood of my neighbours from the way they bang their door.

For a while, when the tenant was a girl called Denise, there was a good deal of eloquent banging. She was a nocturnal creature, with a frizz of black hair and eyes which swam in painted pools of black and purplish lava. Her boyfriend Greg, a pouting, slack-jawed youth in a leather jacket, practised subtle kinds of mental cruelty, such as not turning up for their anniversary dinner, when she had defrosted something special. The anniversary, she told me when she came in sniffling to ask me to dinner instead, was of their second month; the decision to celebrate so prematurely told all. She waited for his visits in dread, terrified that he would never turn up, afraid to go out shopping in case she missed him (he always dropped in unannounced). Generally he would leave in a tantrum after a few hours, kicking the door behind him. Sometimes they both exited, one after the other, with two grand slams of that put-upon door: the flat was not large enough to fight in, since he needed to do a lot of hunched, pantherish pacing, and they transferred their battle to the street. Once they had a lengthy reconciliation in the telephone box, which inconvenienced no one because it was permanently out of order.

Then, overnight, Denise disappeared, leaving only unpaid bills, final notices, eventually threats of disconnection and distraint to remember her by. Peace returned to the passage, and most days the mirror has nothing to look at but the slow crumbling of plaster or a spider's finicky errands up and down the wall. And the outdoor mirror has blistered in the rain, its silver corroding. Now it looks glaucous and overcast, even if the sky it's supposed to reflect is clear.

In Oxford, there is no need for espionage. Here, architecture does the framing for me. The four raised sides of the quadrangle and the four clover leaves of lawn around the pool rule the space into a picture. Those who enter have either come to see it, or must consent to being seen in it. Students shout to test the acoustics, my colleagues pause to confer or intrigue in corners. Our erstwhile college Steward – a pint-sized martinet who had been a naval commander, and still brandished both the title and the manner – would emerge from his office to pace the rampart above the lawn at moments of crisis or weighty deliberation. What punishment did the chef deserve for cold toast sent to High Table? Was the supply of swarthy Spanish matrons who made the beds running out? How to account for the pilferage of toilet rolls? Having promenaded on his would-be deck, he could then strut back inside and resume barking orders or blowing an imaginary whistle. The quad is a great ego-enhancer. By contrast with my blind, recessive yard, it is the most ostentatious space in Oxford, a palatial room without a roof. Cardinal Wolsey, for whom it was all laid out, was of course a politician not a scholar.

The scene outside this window asks to be observed profession-ally. As I write, at a desk in a window seat during the summer, an amateur artist at her easel is sketching the bell tower designed by Christopher Wren, and is being photographed at work by a curious tourist. On a sortie into the quad, I noticed as I passed that the woman was using charcoal crayons. The bell tower is actually golden-brown, like sunned flesh against a leaden sky. In her version it looked spooky, as sooty as crows' feathers, with a streak of white pencil around it which suggested the halation of a full moon. Meanwhile, the tourist who snapped her had changed this black and white back into the cheery coloured chemistry of the photo-lab. Having reoccupied the window seat, I could add my own variation. The woman at the easel wished the place a ruin, in the interests of picturesqueness; the man with the camera treated it as a place peopled by anecdotal figures, the kind prized by photographers. She had left the tower disabled, inkily grim, a Gothic prop for some unscripted drama; the photographer snapped her as a quaint, patient specimen of Englishness, like the anglers you see shivering all day beneath their umbrellas on the river bank.

The woman wore a straw hat, the man a sweat suit: for both of them, representation – on the pinned sheet of paper or the roll of film – was what happened on holiday, when you stepped aside from your own life to study the lives of others. They were happy with single frames, inside which nothing happened. But at my window seat I wanted to organise all the things that could and would and did happen in this arena. For them, the image was a souvenir, some-thing to outlast the event. Couldn't language do more than that, accompanying events, miming their motions, bringing them to a full stop only when it chose?

The quadrangle, after all, tells a story. Narrative here does not have to be guessed at from glimpses of retreating figures in a mirror. The lie of the land dictates formality. Happenings outside this window, by contrast with New York's accidents, take on the predictability of ritual. Inside the battlemented square with its raised paths, the lawn is girdled by a circular drive; this in its turn frames the pond and its statue; steps in one corner lead from the drive up to the door of the cathedral. Mercury, seen this way, is the hub of a wheel, fixed while the circular path rotates. The ages of man advance clockwise round the circle: punctually every morning and evening a double file of choirboys; black cars on Saturday carrying frilly brides; gallantly thinning troupes from the British Legion once a year, their spirits rallied by banners and a brass band; some days, other black cars carrying oblong boxes. Everyone enters, completes this circle and (after a sanctifying send-off from the cathedral) reverts to non-existence by departing under the bell tower. Even Mercury is not immutable, and has to be taken off every now and then to be given a new body in the foundry.

The frame compresses mortal beginnings, middles and ends. We all tread the same track, at the same idling, shuffling pace, like the hearses careful to avoid unseemly haste or the arthritic legionaries. The quadrangle narrates our traipsing round the clock face, while the bell tolls above to order us from one age to the next.

On summer evenings, when the path and the pond are blotted out, the low range of spires, belfries, domes, flag-poles and chimney-pots around the square is redefined as another frame. Now the indented border contains the sky. Inside it are clouds scaled green and yellow, like sleek aerial fish in an upside-down ocean, through whose darkening layers you can see to the bottom. Only the rim of silhouetted buildings saves you from dizzily tumbling in. Out at sea in Lisbon, when the sky is torn by those tilted shafts of rain, you seem through the fissure to catch sight of a white, glaring world beyond ours, separated from us by the skin of damp air: offshore, where the continent ends, this next dimension of cold stormy light takes over. The quadrangle, head over heels at dusk, hints at other infinities. The routine of tramping clockwise round the path from choirboy to old soldier is suspended. We are skidding across the surface of the sky; we don't drown in it because we are too immaterial to sink.

When day returns, the sky becomes opaque again, like Mercury's pond when it ices over in the winter; the inverse world rights itself and the view once more marshals a society, tricked out in cassocks, mortar boards, bowler hats, overalls, blue jeans, rowing gear.

17

The Lisbon view tells another story, which unravels backwards in time and maps the history of Portugal. Along the street is the chapel where the navigators bargained for favourable winds. Beneath it, in the district called Belem (the local Bethlehem) is the tower from which they set sail. The tower is tethered to the bank, in case it drifts back into the river where it stood in the sixteenth century; a carved rhinoceros romps, in anticipation of the exotic worlds across the ocean, above the water on one of its sides. Behind the tower with its balconies and balustrades of twining stone is the clammy monastery in which the epic poet Camões and the explorer Vasco da Gama, the bard and his hero, have their tombs. Over to the west, on top of the mountains, are the jumbled turrets and minarets of the palace above Sintra, where Adamastor (the monster dreamed up from the deep by Camões to warn the voyagers against continuing their journey) grips an arch with his rubbery feelers and greedily leers at the Atlantic.

The estuary used to be a window which no one could see through. It framed a notional, visionary view: the map of a world already conceived of but not yet found. The Portuguese have always credited their empire to the fantasy, to discontent with a literal allotment of facts and with this narrow littoral between the mountains and the ocean. At school, children are told that the explorers 'gave new worlds to the world'. Isn't that the proper business of poets, not spice- and gold-seeking sailors? The empire might have been acquired so Camões could write about it in *Os Lusíadas*, enlisting Vasco da Gama as his custom-made Ulysses. Lisbon too likes to derive itself from the exploits of a fictional hero. It claims to have started as Olissipo, a town Ulysses paused to build on his circumlocutory voyage home.

Here is narrative at its most audacious and illusory. It is never enough for any place merely to exist. It must be imagined – supplied with legendary ancestors, inscribed with stories. We invent our origins in retrospect, and beget a god who repays the compliment by begetting us. I am looking out, down these hills which slither into the river which spills into the ocean, on the ground-plan of a myth.

The Oxford quadrangle has its own symbolic parents. Mercury on his plinth flaps his wrist in the direction of Queen Anne. Pompously wigged and tasselled, wearing a bulky gown of metallic plush, she looms in a niche of the bell tower above my roof. He kicks up his winged heels as if about to enter orbit, and excites a circle of water-spouts at his feet. She, weighted down by her staid clothes, signals condescendingly. The skipping Renaissance androgyne and the matriarchal baroque legislator are an odd pair. But the space owes its authority to their presence in it, even if he is looking over his shoulder and away from her while she stares haughtily above his head and addresses her salute to the middle distance.

In fact, they are both as much interlopers here as Ulysses in Lisbon. Our real founding father is Wolsey, the prelate felled by Henry VIII, whose insignia pervade the college. His cardinal's hat – wide-brimmed, designed to protect the sly pious face from a sun fiercer than the local one, with trailing fringes like hassidic side-curls – is printed on our stationery, and even stamped on the coin-sized portions of butter they serve to us at dinner.

Society elects the progenitors honoured in the Oxford quadrangle or along the river in Lisbon. New York doesn't have a long enough memory to bother with its elders. They hang about, dejected, in brawling parks where they know they no longer belong. Father Duffy's statue is over-run by the crowds buying half-price theatre tickets on Broadway. Everyone has forgotten who he was; ditto Father Demo, who lends his name to a triangular square at the point where Bleecker Street crosses Sixth Avenue. Opposite Lincoln Center, the widow of the tenor Richard Tucker set up a bust of him between the lanes of traffic on Broadway. The pigeons shampoo his toupee daily, but no one else knows he is there.

Here if you want patrons and protectors you must find them for yourself, and since they will probably be machines you then have the trouble of changing them to human form before you can pay them your respects. The skyline is an assembly of monoliths in need of an imagination to give them identities.

At either end of my short street I have a choice. From the corner where Eighth Avenue begins, there is a clear view across to the Empire State Building. Long since rid of lovesick apes and crashed planes, it is now a sympathetic ancestor, festively flashing with seasonal colours. Its shaft was yellow when the Iranian hostages came home; for Hallowe'en it is as orange as pumpkin pulp; on St

Patrick's Day it is mentholated green. At the other end of the street, if I look down into the bay, the Statue of Liberty waves her cudgel-like torch.

Across the river in New Jersey is a third emblem, in many ways my favourite. At dusk, on the lowly shore of Hoboken, a single red tear wells up and weeps all night. It plops from the edge of a tilted cup into a saucer, testifying as it falls that Maxwell House coffee is good to the last drop. At daybreak it mops itself up, looks on the bright side, and disappears.

A totem-pole carved with candied light, or the starchy giantess with the illiberal scowl? The New Jersey communion cup, shedding the same tear in perpetuity for the sins of its neighbour Manhattan?

To tell the truth, they are not available. From my window, the options are more limited; the first rule for constructing the world is that you must start strictly from what you are given. The art of the procedure, after all, is to convert your deprivations and inadequacies into advantages.

The window looks downtown, and what it consents to frame are a stump of the World Trade Center and the Woolworth Building. The Trade Center cannot always be relied on, since low-flying clouds regularly decapitate it. By day it is two grey filing cabinets. I like it best at night, when it dematerialises. All that remains is a vertical avenue paved with bulbs, the tapering island's continuation into the sky. Now it's a galaxy compressed into a spindly tray, duplicating itself to make a binary partner; the planes which glint past it are breakaway novas. I feel directly allied to it, by lines of force through the air. The lighted rod which juts from one of the towers is my local source of images, bouncing invisible pictures over the intervening roofs and into my television set. Beside it is the lair for some prehensile demon: the Woolworth Building with its green spiked crown, thorny pinnacles and plummeting slopes, jaundiced by floodlights.

My excerpt from the city is enough. The frame finds room for a compact cosmos. When the two flat-topped towers in one window wink and scintillate while the horned pyramid in the other gives off a green stain of sickly copper, while sirens and caterwauling car alarms make the street scream below me and the blades of helicopters thresh and slice above, I have a whole planet of heights and abysses, false dawns and mechanised rapids, to play in. The view from this window is supernatural.

Of course it is never quite like that. The reality outside is haphazard, chaotic, insignificant. The eye flickers here and there to arrange a view and ordain a composition. Unless we do so, how can we tolerate the randomness and indifference of things?

Before my mirror rotted, all it had to show for itself was the vagaries of the London sky. The clouds are a sequence of happenings, never an event – frayed like tattered fabric as the wind tugs at them, thick and curdling on other days, very occasionally rubbed away by the sun. Stray tribute drifts down into the yard, like wreckage washed up from this evaporated sea. A single feather, or a balloon which the breeze has robbed from a child somewhere over the wall; once, after a storm, a blue tarpaulin, jerked from its moorings on top of a building, which lunged to earth and propped itself up outside my front door; always the pigmentation of black dust.

These accidents can't be chronicled. It is only in novels that things happen with a purpose. Maybe it is the very purpose of novels to ensure that they do. In them, the sky is accountable to human joys and miseries, like the sympathetic magic of the Empire State Building's lighting-plan. When Emma is downcast and repentant after her social error at Box Hill, the barometer obliges Jane Austen the moralist by promptly dropping: 'the weather added what it could of gloom'; a cold rain sets in, uncharacteristic of July.

Art promises to discern a logic in the world: it claims that causes inside the window have effects outside. If the sun had continued shining, might Emma have spared herself the effort of suffering to secure redemption? My mirror on an average morning disproved fiction's argument from design, with its inconsequential snatches of ragged vapour, its pepperings of hail, or its blithe, mocking brilliance; I was not sorry when the mercury tarnished and its fragmentary evidence was effaced.

The Oxford quadrangle – apparently eternal, with everything in it precisely calculated – is in its own way as impromptu as the weather. The eye, scratching at seams and joins, can easily unpick it. In the first place, it is unfinished. Arches cling to the walls, with clusters of amputated columns set to spring through the air. But they go nowhere, and have no weight to support: Wolsey wanted a cloister, then didn't get round to constructing it. Every time the stonework was restored, the outlined arches were mistakenly emphasised. By now, it looks as if the useless bows above the doors and windows were meant to be that way.

Nor do the classical god and the baroque monarch belong here. Wren, having erected the bell tower, left niches which should have held statues of Charles II and Wolsey. His plan was vetoed; Queen Anne filled the gap as a later compromise. Mercury came to rest even more chancily, as if forced into an emergency landing on the pond. For its first hundred years, the centre of the space was an unkempt pasture. Then a pit was dug for a reservoir; in it was placed a globe, with a serpent twisted round it hissing water. Before the end of the seventeenth century, the leaden planet and the aquatic snake were supplanted by Mercury. But still not in his present incarnation. The original was damaged during a prank in the nineteenth century; the current incumbent – copied from an original by Giovanni di Bologna (who was actually Flemish, lived in Florence, had nothing to do with Bologna, and got his soubriquet from a translation of Boulogne) – turned up in 1928. Since then he has been recast, just as the stones are replaced when they crumble. Everything is a copy of something it once was, or might have been.

Nothing here is rooted. It has all plunged as fortuitously from the sky as that blown-away tarpaulin. No identity is constant. The bell we nickname Tom because of its booming summonses began its life as Mary, and changed its gender some time in the seventeenth century. Having had its photograph taken so often, the quadrangle affects inevitability. Still, its contents are contingent, getting on with each other as best they can like an ill-assorted band of travellers: the monarch reduced to stowage in a vacant niche; the naked athlete; the bisexual bell; and a stone convocation of prelates, dangling above doorways as if suspended on a gibbet.

The history proclaimed by the picture I see from the Lisbon window doesn't withstand inspection either. Inside it, the heroic past jostles with a present which can't afford lofty ambitions. An avenue named after those Renaissance discoveries runs through the suburb down to the river. In hard times, it is the parade-ground of timid teenage prostitutes, whose grey-suited clients shuttle up and down choosily in their cars. The villas of the plutocrats are embassies now, with rooftop batteries of snooping equipment and flags in brash primary colours flapping from balconies. Outside the gates, the girls from the slums clutch their handbags, and give a brave imitation of depravity as they swivel on high heels they aren't old enough to manage. Business is conducted on the hills behind the houses, among a litter of pine needles and sardine spines.

The Portuguese, generously giving new worlds to the world, gave those worlds away. The descendants of the discoverers who rode down from the chapel to their caravels are the dismayed reluctant migrants you see on every flight out of Lisbon with their flagons of inky red wine, off to clean bathrooms in London, to work on building sites in Paris, or to catch fish in Providence.

The river, slicing the country across the middle like a sandwich as it passes through Lisbon, separates past from present. On the northern bank, monuments stand to attention – the monastery, the flamboyant tower, a pink rococo palace in an orange grove, a museum of coaches like cakes on wheels. On the southern bank there is only a line-up of sullied hills and spoiled beaches, with a trail of silos, gas tanks, cranes and wharves. The northern headland, breaking up into boulders as Europe makes its last stand, at least has a blow-hole, where the ocean throws up spouts of spray. It is known as the mouth of hell, and the necromancer Aleister Crowley chose to disappear there in 1930. But the southern headland – just before the vanishing-point of geographical conjecture – is the roost of a crab-shaped factory, extending a dozen arms to loading bays on the water.

Beside the factory, in a cove, a village lurks out of sight around a corner. This settlement mystified and tantalised me for years. Seen from the window, it was too far off, or too protected by haze, to disclose itself. It even resisted binoculars. I was sure I had found the secretive inlet to one more world: beached fishing-boats, cobbled alleys where women balanced trays on their heads, shutters open in the white houses onto rooms like black cool crypts; behind the cliff above the village, Morocco might begin. Once, recklessly, I took the ferry across the river and walked into my fantasy. It was a tactical error. The streets stank of cod and cabbage; mongrel dogs fought with the flies over scraps; the beach was a warren of hovels made from pilfered planks, squares of rusted iron and counterpanes of plastic, trustingly capped by rocks; children squealed among the fish-heads. The view was best left unvisited. I have learned to keep my distance.

In New York, I know, I have permission to look, not to touch. All love for this city must get by without requital. My towers are owned by others. The upright blocks exist to be used, and if they bother with beauty, it is only to glorify the entrepreneur who raised them. Their height doesn't aim to be sublime; it is just the banal calculation of accountancy, piling up rentable floors on the lucrative granite of Manhattan. The city is divided between those who look down on it from corner offices to appraise a diagram of real estate, and those who look up at the rungs of steel and glass climbing out of reality and imagine angels gliding smoothly to a halt on the Trade Center or a coven of verdigris witches scrambling over the Woolworth's prongs and hurling thunderclaps or empty Coke cans down into the street. Our wistful revenge, confined as we are to ground level (or at least the lower floors), is to see what is not there.

The view is accidental; so is whoever looks at it. I often feel myself fragmenting, like a body warped in a hall of mirrors, as I wander to and fro between my four landscapes. The figure moping across the Oxford quadrangle can't be the same as the one who enjoys the jiving ballet of the New York pavements. How it is that the internee of the wet, isolated London yard belongs in Lisbon to someone else's family?

We try all our lives to match the stray scene outside the window and the person who happens to be watching it – to control the contingencies, make meaning accord with appearance. By doing so we might arrange our distracted selves into a character, or discern a plot in our discontinuous actions. Perhaps we finally learn how to read the scenes and see ourselves in them when the moment comes to lower the screen, pull down the blinds, draw the curtains.

Meanwhile, we have only this aperture: a window with a frame to fix the speeding chances into form; a pane of glass which overlays the watcher's reflection, like a ghost, on the indifferent outdoors.

2

Crossing the Bridge

I CAN REMEMBER THE EXACT MOMENT OF MY BIRTH. IT happened on Waterloo Bridge, on a morning in August 1968; I was twenty years old at the time.

Those previous twenty years were, however, cancelled at that moment, relegated to a phase of pre-existence. I had spent them in Tasmania, reading about what my life would be like when I was reborn in the northern hemisphere. I was inclined to see this term of years as one of those penitential, ignominious lives you have to toil through in order to atone for crimes in some other incarnation – except that I was doing my penance in advance, and once I'd got it over could expect release, perhaps, into a new existence.

The rite of passage from one identity to the next happened in the middle of that bridge, as I walked out of Waterloo Station, down a tunnel, up into the air and across towards London. I paused halfway across, to look at the curve of the river from St Paul's to Westminster: the dome, the carved range of towers, the ranks of steeples and columns between them, the growling streets beyond.

Could any of the walkers plodding their habitual courses have known what I felt, or have cared? I had no camera, but even at this distance in time I don't need a photograph to recover my sensations. My body remembers in every fibre the charge which went through it, like electrocution. Ahead, where the bridge ran out into the Aldwych in a sunny crux of blue dust, was the door through which, innocuously, I would step into life.

I think I slowed down as I approached it. If this was the

beginning, that meant it was also the beginning of the end. The years of waiting in the antechamber suddenly seemed precious: everything was to come; nothing had been risked or expended yet; all that stored experience was held in reserve, like a heaving, brimming sea.

I enjoyed the tedium of the journey this far, because it postponed the desired, dreaded outcome. I had spent a month on a liner, ploughing over two featureless oceans. The English retirees, on board for the round trip, died every once in a while, and coffins sometimes thudded into the wake at sundown. One of the Liverpudlian stewards developed cabin fever on the way to Cape Town and pulled a knife on an Irish colleague while dishing out fried breakfasts. Occasionally there were reports of events in the nonwatery world: deaths in Vietnam, Nixon's nomination as presidential candidate. Pretending deliciously to inertia, making believe that we were travelling in the wrong direction, we put our watches back half an hour a day.

Then, on the boat train from Southampton, there was the low, drab, grimy endlessness of the London suburbs, just as sweet in its teasing protraction. I hadn't checked when the train would reach Waterloo; I wanted it to surprise me. But as it jerked through the yards of soiled brick, I made the mistake of glancing out the window and saw for a second, in the crevice between two office blocks, the thin pencil of Big Ben (whose chimes I knew by heart, since they announced the television news in Tasmania). Too soon! I wasn't ready. I hated myself for having spoiled it, and got out of the train in a flush of annoyance. Arrival was a premature climax, rather than a deflating anticlimax.

Once on the bridge, with the sun managing to bless the moment, I found that my untimely glimpse didn't matter. It was simply the last of those anticipatory dreams with which I had passed the time inside my head for so many years. Here was the truth, to which I had finally awoken. Light had polished the dome of St Paul's, the crockets and gewgaws of Westminster were sharp against the sky. Blackfriars Station and Charing Cross gobbled and regurgitated trains, just as Waterloo behind me was doing; all journeys ended or began here, as mine – both ending and beginning – had just done. The scene seemed so ancient and thick with life that Cleopatra might have left her needle on the embankment personally. The gulls swooped after garbage below the bridge for joy not hunger. The sun, I knew, was out as a personal favour to me. Across the river, the city faintly roared, in what I hoped was exultation.

I didn't walk the rest of the way to that open door alone. My preconceptions kept me company. I knew these things already, because I had fed myself on descriptions of them. To the left of me was Wordsworth's Westminster Bridge, from which London, earlier in the morning than this, seemed as fair and slumbrous as Eden; to the right was de Quincey's St Paul's, whose whispering gallery kept secrets circling in the haunted house of the brain; underneath was the Thames, softly melodious for Spenser, grimly chartered for Blake. For Waterloo Bridge itself my only pretext was a bad old film in which Vivien Leigh, having failed to meet Robert Taylor in the railway station behind me, slunk off into the fog to sell her body, before arriving at judgement or redemption under a convenient bus. I recalled Robert Taylor, his hair immaculately aged, leaning on the balustrade as an air-raid ripped the sky and looking down at all the water which had flowed under the bridge since then. I walked on and left him there in his mist of retrospection. I had, as yet, no memories of my own, only hopes.

In front, as the bridge ended and London began, were the streets where Dickens claimed that dinosaurs lumbered through primeval pea-soupers, where Virginia Woolf saw buses dipping on a glittery tide like bright red yachts, and where Henry James, in the squares around the British Museum, overheard the hive-like hum of cogitation. This place had been a many-mansioned house of fiction for its imaginative tenants. Anything could be done in it, or to it; it was the heaped-up sum of human possibility, indexing experience like the volumes of its telephone directory. When I reached the corner of the Strand, the traffic stopped for me (though only because the lights told it to).

I didn't feel any obligation, on that day, to see all the paintings in the National Gallery, or trudge round the tablets in Poets' Corner. If this was the inception of a life, I had a lifetime's leisure – I supposed – in which to annex this inheritance. I wandered about aimlessly, making sure that it all did exist: Nelson commanding his flotilla of pigeons, Queen Victoria dourly enthroned in front of Buckingham Palace, the stately battalions of trees in the parks, the roll-call of legendary names outside the theatres on Shaftesbury Avenue.

Everything I saw seemed authoritarian, a reminder of my own insignificance. But that was what I had counted on, in my colonial fantasies about it all. The ancestors on their columns and the ancient trees had to deny any knowledge of me, or of where I had come from. It was only by a haughty act of elimination that they could help me to begin afresh.

My new-born elation lasted until night. I sat at dusk on a bench in Leicester Square, listening to the sparrows squabble for space on the branches above. The metallic jangle of their competition for room to live was thrilling, not yet a cause for fear.

By the next morning, I noticed with a spasm of shame that I had begun to take everything for granted. Yes, of course the buses were red: so what? The long, stealthy, mortal process of diminution was under way. I knew I would probably never be as happy again as I was the day before.

The promise of London was absorption. It took you in, once you reached the gate of entry to it at the end of Waterloo Bridge, and then promptly forgot that it had done so. Among all those millions of people tabulated in the phone books – which I leafed through in the cubicles, making no calls but enjoying my first encounter with infinity – I knew not a single one. The awareness didn't daunt me; it was the austere proof of my liberty. After all, I had come from a town so small that there was a cousin behind every shop counter, an auntie on every street corner. The few total strangers you passed on the pavement there smiled at you in recognition, because they had seen you every day of their lives and would probably turn out – if you swapped stories with them – to be distant cousins too. London was my licence to be nothing, nobody, and therefore anybody I liked.

Oxford was a different matter. I would have to function there, own to an identity and submit to its verdict on me. I had come all this way so it could tell me whether I was any good – or not, as the case might be. I rejoiced in London's indifference, and didn't even mind when a shrewish bus conductress scolded me for pressing the bell to start the bus rather than the cord to stop it. After all, whom was she addressing? Someone she didn't know, someone who didn't know himself. But Oxford was to exercise a more alarming power over my life: disapproval, which meant disqualification.

Crossing Waterloo Bridge, I had sauntered into a place documented in dreams, pieced together from images. About Oxford I had no advance notions. It wasn't really my ambition to go there; the scholarship I had won was simply the first available exit visa from my previous life. I chose my college at random. I found an alphabetical list of the English Faculty. Before I got to the letter D, I had recognised three names, all teaching at the same college. For the rest, all I knew of the university was an intimidating volume I had been sent in Tasmania, elaborating the examination statutes (subtitle: STATT. UNIV. OXON. TIT. VI) and the rules which governed the process cringingly called 'Supplication for degrees'. There was even a section itemising the costume you had to wear when being examined. I would need, sooner or later, a white bow tie.

After a week, I travelled up by train to look over this supreme tribunal. I began my life there at a disadvantage. On the journey, the zipper on my trousers jammed, and for all my frantic tugging in the lavatory it wouldn't travel any further up its little twisted railway track. My first act in the city was to buy a newspaper, to angle in front of my embarrassment; my next, on a long and haphazard search through the trench-like streets with the paper clutched tautly to the fore, was to find a shop which sold safety-pins. I'd never had occasion to buy one of these (or anything else except books, if the truth be told: that was why you had parents, surely – to provision you). My half-hour pursuing the pin which would hold me together and make existence possible once more was my first miserable dose of self-reliance. Why, I wondered, did I ever leave home?

And what kind of place was this, where Latin grammars, pots of a concoction called Gentleman's Relish, mugs crusted with gargoyles in high relief like grimacing barnacles and striped scarves several yards long were easier to find than a life-saving pin? Once I'd laid hands on one – or rather a single hand, having to conduct the transaction in the shop without letting slip my cod-piece of news-print – I took refuge in a lavatory under the town hall, where I managed to suture my yawning fly.

I have never, in the twenty years since then, been back down those steps, but I often walk along the alley and think, as I hear the taps in the urinals hiss in exasperation, of that first furtive hour in

Oxford. The body's memory is as exact as of that earlier moment on Waterloo Bridge: this time not shuddering excitement but lamed humiliation, as I stumbled about with one arm clamped where it shouldn't have been, the other three limbs unsure what to do and banging into each other in their addled indecision.

Pinned up, I went off to see my college and meet my tutor. I am chronically early everywhere – does this come from impatience at having to run on the spot for twenty years before life started? – so my mishap with the zip at least hadn't made me late. The tutor had a study beside the college garden, the scoopings of earth from whose sunken lawn were piled into a shaggy mound: a comically savage hump of mountain jutting through the plain of shaved, pomaded grass. The lawn was as smooth as a green baize tablecloth on top of which decisions are made. From it, the peak of brambles, shrubs and tottering horizontal trees rose like a sudden, disruptive geyser of wildness. It made no sense. It was, in fact, nonsensical. I spent a long time after that pondering the English combination of propriety and folly, conformism and oddity.

Meanwhile, I knocked on my tutor's door. He had a pair of them, the outer one of rough varnished timber, the inner one delicately panelled. He answered, and I went in. There were two men in the room. Not sure to whom to address the information, I told them both my name.

'I know who you are', said one of them. 'Would you mind waiting outside?'

He and I became good friends later, but as I closed both of the doors behind me – another solecism, since the outer one was a symbolic drawbridge, a slab of oak used only to announce that thought was occurring inside (or that no one was home) – it occurred to me that a single safety-pin wasn't enough to secure one's self-possession. By the time I was readmitted and told him my name again, I no longer believed in the person it had once, somewhere else, labelled.

Back in the street, blinking, I found myself on a dislocated planet. The passers-by were of a kind I'd never encountered before. London was humanity aggregated, the march-past of types as if on floats in the Lord Mayor's Parade: doctor, lawyer, beggar-man, thief; grey-striped Anglo-Saxons (with none of the weathered ruddiness of my own compatriots), burnished West Indians, Asians with their saffron-coloured fabrics and red stigmata; examples of every mutation, filing in and out of the ark. Oxford contained one genus only, and its individual specimens looked unrepeatably weird. Men trod the pavement like praying-mantises on frail, spindly legs. The women had dishevelled birds' nests for hair. Everyone rode bicycles, with an air of elderly childishness. This was a zone where brains scarcely bothered about embodying themselves. How did these lofty, unanchored minds contrive to stay astride their bikes? I began to understand why a safety-pin had been so hard to hunt down. Keeping the scarecrow's rags fastened together was not a priority here.

The young passed through Oxford on their way to join one of those corporate throngs I had seen in the streets of London. They allowed it three years, which they spent hallooing or beagling or rowing or breaking furniture. Their loud and drawlingly languid sense of entitlement amazed me. But then they were English, aware (as my benefactor Cecil Rhodes declared) that this meant they had drawn first prize in the lottery of life. I didn't dispute it, and stood back to let them pass. I had some marginal purchase on their literature, no claim at all on their society. The choral voices which whispered quotations as I crossed Waterloo Bridge had misled me. England belonged, by right, to these young men, who were forever calling things super or splendid; the writers just described it. And at an extra remove of dispossession there were those, like me, who described the writers' descriptions.

After their three years, each consignment of undergraduates vanished to London. They would reappear every decade or so for feasts, bloated with distinction. On those who stayed behind, Oxford began to make indelible marks. Here in this moist, stifling labyrinth between two rivers and inside a circle of hills, people were turned inside out by thinking. Brains as squashy and unarmoured and tentacular as jellyfish dodged in front of buses on the High Street or furiously pedalled those wobbling bikes. Before I had been very long in Oxford, I began to recognise some of these rarefied beings. Later still, I got to know a few. Was it my fate to become one of them?

There was the philosopher of identity, perplexed all his mental life by the conundrum of the self. If it defined us, where did it inhere? If we couldn't identify its location, how could it identify us?

He was often to be seen puzzling out this mystery while jolting unsteadily over the cobbles in the square beside the Bodleian Library or cleaving with a spark of understanding in his eye through the aisles of the covered market, between butchers' shops where the hares wore donnish bifocals and mortar boards had been placed on the heads of stuffed sheep. You could tell he was intent on the issue because his neck would jerk sideways in a sudden wrench, as if he wanted to unscrew his brain from its rusty socket, the better to inspect the automatised antics of that body which somewhere concealed the self. His backward glances suggested the hauntings inside his head: identity had become his spectral double pursuing him and, as it closed in, threatening to take over. Perhaps he has already been replaced by this other, conceptual ego; perhaps it's a *doppelgänger* which now roams the streets. Last time I saw him, his hair had turned white.

Then there was the eminent mathematician who for twenty years has been taking a succession of identical dogs on nocturnal outings around Christ Church meadow. The dogs are always overgrown poodles, which tread as haughtily as if they were riding. For them the purpose of the jaunt seems more like intellection than urination. They canter along, intent on loftier things than the connoisseurship of bushes, followed by a master who seems to be growing more like them every time I pass him on these repetitious circuits: high-stepping, emaciated, eyes on stalks under the bramble of unkempt curls, propelled by the urging of an idea. His body is spiral-shaped, and bounces down the path like a coiled spring or self-operating pogo stick. While the legs strut ahead, one arm pivots sideways, breasting the wind; his chest arches outwards with the profile of a billowing sail. The landscape doesn't exist for him, I am sure – the volumes of drifting papery leaves which clog the river in autumn, the fields sagging under floods during winter, the clammy cocooning mists of spring. He stares through it all to some starker terrain where the scenery is burned or bleached away and thought can scribble its theorems on the sand or ice. He walks anti-clockwise round the meadow, whereas I soon got into the habit of going clockwise. When he and the current dog pass me, they seem to leave a violent draught behind them, a vapour-trail of mental force. In summer the gnats which hang over the path like hair nets are scattered by this transitory gale.

A third solitary haunted the reading rooms of the Bodleian, whose resident tatterdemalion ghost he was, wrapped in a disintegrating academic gown, its silky black sickening to a mottled green, its sleeves unravelling in spiders' webs of thread. With a crest of black ruffled hair and spectacles behind which his eyes retracted into lustreless beads, he would often perch on a ladder above the desks, clawing through texts in medieval Latin. Looking up from my cubicle, with the sky dying outside the window, I always expected him to unfurl that flaring gown into wings and circle the room above our heads: Minerva's owl on the rampage. When the library closed for the night at ten o'clock he took it personally, like an eviction notice served by a heartless landlord. I followed him once down one of the dog-legged ancient alleys between the colleges which led him . . . where? To some room built from books on the other side of the river, where he no doubt slept in that wrinkled gown under counterpanes of inky paper. I remember him disappearing round the last angle of the alley, among a brief flash of white flakes. Pages which dropped from the folders clutched under his arms? Dandruff? Snow?

The introversion of the place proved contagious. Before I had been in Oxford a year, I developed a limp. It was no affectation: I now walked lop-sidedly. Unco-ordination came with the territory. I wandered about with one leg suddenly shorter than the other, in a misery of self-mistrust. At the age of twenty, I felt more adolescent and inadequate than ever before. I recall the occasion when I risked my first joke in the arch, unforgiving city. Mercifully, I have forgotten what it was. But I do remember the fact that no one laughed. It happened in the beer cellar of my college. Afterwards, walking back through the garden under the medieval wall beside the crazily rampant mound, a friend put me right. 'This *is* Oxford', he said; 'you'll have to do better than that.'

Every weekend I caught the train to London, and enjoyed an interim of non-existence. A city was for me, by definition, a place where you could cease to be yourself, or become someone else at will. Getting out onto the platform at Paddington, I found my limp had gone into remission.

A year after that untimely sideways glimpse of Big Ben, I set eyes on the next of my cities. Here too, my first sight was of its triumphal flag-pole: the Empire State Building, first seen from the blue, simmering highway through Queens, its spire wilting like a candle in the moist, orange air.

The clock tower at Westminster and this sharpened rod marked two different realms of fantasy. One was familiar long before I had seen it, the other was a frontier of the unknown. The clock's governessy call to order had resounded through my childhood. When its chimes on the radio announced the news to my parents, they sent me to bed. The chimes spoke directly – or so I thought until I began to hear static on the tape – from the other side of the world; from the world where news happened, and where it was now day although for me it was prematurely night and bedtime. Like Tom in the Oxford quadrangle reverting to Mary, I always heard the chimes as a woman's voice: the mother's, stern but comfortable. The building now ahead of me and the mythological America it introduced were a later state of mind, roughly dating from the era of my first erection.

Around the time that event took place, an uncle of mine had left Tasmania to go on a world tour. He was the only member of the family who could afford it, having managed to rise above his assigned social class. He died of a heart attack not long afterwards, and there were those who saw this as a judgement on such presumption. That world tour, the clucking tongues said, must have tired him out. He was a radio ham, who communicated with other amateurs around the globe: it was like a séance in his den, with strange voices which came and went through crackling ether as lights winked on his switchboard. He had gone off, finally, to stay with all of these absent, unseen friends. When he returned, he dropped in one evening to tell us about the world over a cup of tea. I had two questions for him. Was everything in England old, I wanted to know, and was everything in America big? He reassured me on both counts; I went to bed happy.

England with its crumbling stone and its bad weather and crinoline-shaped, unstringy trees was my chosen alternative to my current world, and therefore seemed so ancient that I could remember it from dreams without ever needing to set eyes on it. (And when I did finally see it, the very first glimpse contained all of the above elements. I came out on deck as the liner drifted up the Solent on its last morning and there across on a corner of the Isle of Wight

34

was Osborne House, where Queen Victoria lived out her bomba-zined widowhood. The scene had everything: the grey, crested pile; pearly mist; wet lawns and oak trees.) But this alternative in time begot its own alternative. All the rage and aggression and wilful determination to make my own world which I couldn't find room for in my imagined England I transferred to America. The Empire State Building had no sentimental piety, and no roots in any past. It declared that you didn't need to believe in a god, only in your own rebellious, self-generated power.

Already England and America were different loves – separate but simultaneous; a case of cultural bigamy. Or perhaps England was a love, America an infatuation. The affection for England went back to childhood, the obsession with America was a product of ado-lescence, rather like acne (and probably, like that, of hormonal origin). For England, my emotion was a faith; I had to believe in it, because I had lived off its consoling image for so long. My attraction to America, happening later, always seemed to imply an infidelity.

As well, its imagery was shameful, like the usurping scenarios of adolescence. Opposed to the sedate, grandmotherly palace among the oaks were all the assassinations of the 1960s. When Martin Luther King was shot, I recall a friend in Tasmania – who had been to the United States, and brought back (along with his own magnified, radiant aura) some florid pink hippy kitsch from Haight-Ashbury – prophesying, 'They'll have *winter* riots over there this year.' I admired the worldly wisdom of the remark, but more than that I found the idea wickedly thrilling. Riot seemed preferable to the bucolic peace I saw outside the window. We were in the university refectory, looking at the somnolent car park. Protests against the Vietnam war brightened up our lives. But when LBJ came to Australia for the funeral of Harold Holt (the Prime Minister, who was swept away in the surf as he swam) I couldn't help being excited by the arrogance and panoply of American power as I watched him on television. The motorcade – a new word, very 1960s – of black Batmobiles, with crew-cut youths in mirrored shades running along beside; the travelling hospital further back in the procession, in case our own peaceable land should be livened up by violence; the craggy war-monger who resembled an eagle. I felt like a simple, woad-daubed ancient Briton crawling out of a midden to watch Julius Caesar ride by, his breast-plate shining and his harness belligerently jangling. For me, the Empire State Building was an apex of empire.

I saw it clearly on that first night in New York, free of the glutinous summer murk of the afternoon, from on top of a building in Chelsea. A white flare polished its steel sides; its needle prodded a passing cloud, scrubbed white by the upturned floodlights. Beneath it, seen up the narrowing tunnel of Seventh Avenue, neon galaxies sparked, exploded and joined together again in a saga of harmless planetary catastrophe. The avenue itself evacuated steam, as if beneath the skin of tar and concrete, beneath the veins of pipe and wire, there were rivers of sulphur and bubbly pools of lava.

I soon learned the story of the albino alligators, flushed down toilets when children tired of keeping them as pets in the 1950s, left to snap and grope and procreate in the sewers. I believed it, of course; about this place I could believe anything. The clean metal spire, pointing out the non-existence of God, grew from a swamp which heaved with sound and throbbed with light. I was surveying human history in synopsis. From the rank jungle floor with its clotted tendrils and rotting leaves and smelly rivers of saurians, a ladder is raised; up it, the ape can clamber back to the forfeited penthouse of the angels.

The tale of the blind, pink-eyed alligators convinced me, because a scene like this needed myths and monsters. Next morning I saw the ape reclaim the Empire State. *King Kong* was being shown that day in a flea-pit round the corner on Eighth Avenue. The old film summarised New York for me, in a diagram of evolutionary over-reaching and beastly regression. The gorilla heaved himself up the ladder, but on the summit didn't change into a human being. He slavered, growled, thumped his chest and swatted planes like hornets. Soon he was knocked from the ledge and thudded heavily back into the trough where he began.

New York with its rhinestone skyline was an image of perfectibility, but so far it had not managed to make anyone perfect. On my brief acquaintance, it seemed to turn men into animals, not the reverse. Along 23rd Street there were people who bayed and barked, assembled their meals from bags of garbage or the corner trash-cans, and slept – to no one's surprise but mine – on the sidewalk. Perhaps Kong was right to confuse the streamlined, aeronautical Empire State with the superstitious pinnacle on Skull Island. Was it just, after all, an excrescence of the jungle?

London, as I had seen and overheard it from Waterloo Bridge, was a world: an encyclopaedia of experience; perhaps an anthology of quotations. New York was a universe. There were heavens here, and hells. Times Square switched on its own solar system every evening. Rats scampered and sniffled along the subway tracks between stale puddles. In Central Park, tusks of granite tilted out of the soil; a polar bear lumbered round its pool a few yards from Fifth Avenue. Helicopters vibrated upwards from pads in the East River, like dragonflies lifting off from water-lilies in a pond.

I even saw the present emperor up close. Nixon came to town one day to speak at the United Nations. I was sure, in my innocence, that there must be a public gallery from which one could listen to him. But the barricades were up when I arrived. The streets had been cleared of traffic, and the pavements filled with the people over whom he presided, who screamed curses at him as he drove past. Inside their car, Pat, like a wan, weary glove-puppet waved her acknowledgements to the mob abusing her husband. Above us was Tudor City, a manor-house of rustic brick and quaint half-timbering, elasticised to reach the sky. The crevasse beneath echoed with accusations of murder.

At the other end of 42nd Street, which in trudging its couple of miles between rivers circumnavigated the world and traversed all its highs and lows, a dazed youth once swayed towards me late at night and asked in utter seriousness if I could help him get to Babylon. The usual star-bursts and maelstroms were happening behind his head, and probably inside it. 'You're there already', I unhelpfully answered. The city could even supply hanging gardens; I had seen them from on top of the RCA Building, flowering on parapets over the gulch of Fifth Avenue.

Disillusioningly, I later learned that Babylon was a dormitory town on Long Island. The boy only wanted money for his bus fare. But truth seemed feeble when set against New York's lurid fictions.

It is one of literature's oldest and most reliable plots. The young man from the provinces goes on his hopeful, fearful pilgrimage to the city – David Copperfield to London, the obscure Jude to Oxford, Midwestern Nick Carraway to New York. Sometimes there are declarations of war, Napoleonic vows like that of Balzac's hero Vautrin, who shakes his fist at Paris from the slopes of Montmartre and swears he will conquer it. More often, the story ends in a sadder, wiser return home.

I was, I suppose, the ultimate provincial, finding out how to cope with three different but equally ultimate cities. Back in Tasmania, they kept a light in the window for me. When I left, a girl I was fond of told me what home meant: 'Home is where, when you have to go there, they have to take you in.' The trite little verse contained a warning, maybe a prediction. Would I stumble back from my new life or lives as a demoralised refugee, and be grateful that they had kept my bed made? Would I take to muttering, as my relations testily did whenever other worlds were invoked, 'Well, *I'm* happy enough here'?

Oxford's verdict was deferred for two years, until I sat for those fancy-dress examinations. Meanwhile, before the trip to New York, I spent my first northern Christmas in London, wondering how I would survive, afraid of not loving the city as fiercely as I had convinced myself I would.

I slept on the floor of some old friends, fugitives from Tasmania. Jean had taught me at high school, where she was a great heroine because she made mildly improper jokes in mathematics classes. (She explained logarithms, for instance, with reference to the exponential curve of the rabbit population.) Her husband Gordon, a physics tutor at the university, was an old-time radical, who belonged to the Communist Party a generation before we set about execrating LBJ. They left Tasmania because they were too comfortable. London would rescue them from the corrupt, cosy flabbiness of middle age. It did so at once by demoting them a social class or two: she got a job as a book-keeper; he couldn't get a job at all and instead researched revolution in the British Museum, watching as he walked the damp pavements among the shuffling crowds for cracks in the social fabric, signs of avenging anger.

They occupied half a flat in a sooty Highbury crescent. The flat itself was rented by a troglodyte couple, randomly sampled from the millions of Londoners tabulated in the phone book (except that they weren't in it, not having the phone on, as they put it). The woman was Maria, dusky and unspecifically Latin, a Soho waitress who worked at a hissing espresso machine and ferried cakes to tables in a café which was once someone's corridor. She had met Jean and Gordon in a pub, and took them home with her to live. Her husband Les looked ever so slightly taken aback when they arrived; when I followed, he scarcely blinked, having prepared himself for any eventuality.

Most days Maria was bustlingly good-humoured, and ranted merrily. There were also occasional verbose rages with kitchen knives. Les, who kept well clear of her temperament, slouched by the gas fire in a cardigan and scrutinised his football pools. He had an academic knowledge of Australia, because he bet on down-under teams during the local off-season. We sometimes compared fictions: names of teams, which to me connoted only dull Melbourne suburbs – Carlton, St Kilda, Footscray – were to him as unfactually enchanting as the improbable outposts of the London which bored and dispirited him – Seven Sisters, Isle of Dogs, Elephant and Castle – were to me. He neither knew nor cared, he told me grumpily one day, who the seven sisters were. He'd been brought up in the suburb named for them, and that was enough. When Maria juggled the knives and began to keen in a shrill upper register she reserved for tantrums, he hunched his shoulders, bowed his head and appeared to fold up into his ill-fitting, mis-buttoned cardigan. Gordon took notes on the demoralisation of the proletariat.

With its whistling draughts, its patches of boggy plaster, its back garden of shivering twigs, the place was squalid enough, but it didn't depress me. I had passed most of my conscious life thus far translating words about London into pictures of it, and trying then to project myself into those fuzzy, foggy images. The very word which named it, the twin syllables orotundly booming like Big Ben or Robert Morley, had the power to speed up my heartbeat. I was prepared to forgive the city anything.

I eagerly believed its lies. I had two favourite frauds: the Old Curiosity Shop in the tortuous lanes and legalistic by-ways off Lincoln's Inn Fields, and a pub in the East End called Dirty Dick's.

The shop was a ramshackle cabin with floors which creaked, a staircase which canted, and a roof like a gnome's cap. It contained a job-lot of icons: china figurines of Henry VIII and his line-up of pasty-faced wives, Sherlock Holmes sucking his pipe, Winston

39

Churchill glowering on the lid of a biscuit tin. A printed notice signed 'Charles Dickens' asked you to replace his works on the shelf where you found them. England happily summed itself up as a scrap-heap of damaged ancestors.

The pub took a special pride in its filth, a privilege of antiquity. I remember encrustations of greasy dirt which changed the bar to a gloomy cavern, and cobwebs clinging to the upturned, glugging bottles of spirits; underfoot, a quicksand of grubby sawdust. Dirt was its tradition. At least that's how I think it used to be. I went back recently, to be confronted by a placard on the door forbidding soiled clothing. Inside, brokers concluded deals at wine kegs doubling as tables; on the street, a gang of construction workers excluded by their overalls ate some sandwiches which one of their number had been allowed inside to buy. I suspect myself of having muddied it in recollection.

Why was I so determined to be impressed and consoled by the age of everything, and to accept dirt as the prerogative of history? In order, I suppose, to spite the freshly-made, planed-down, vacuum-cleaned world I had grown up in. Instead of the barbered weather-board carton with its ply-board partitions and its corrugated iron roof which my father had helped to build, the lop-sided hutch of curios; instead of my mother's militant scrubbing, polishing, dusting and swabbing, the pub which succumbed to the coagulation of grime.

That same winter I discovered Highgate Cemetery. I intended to visit Marx, poking through the top of his monument like a bushy patriarchal Jack-in-the-box; waylaid by an iron gate on the other side of Swain's Lane, the stubby Egyptian columns on duty around it strangled by ivy, its arch dented, I wandered up an avenue of thorns into the wrong part of the boneyard.

I had walked back by accident into the nineteenth century. Victorian worthies, with Egyptian swank, had designed their own after-lives here. A Jewish financier consigned his remains to a mausoleum aping that of King Mausolus at Halicarnassus, and paid troops of sculptured angels to mourn for ever and ever amen. A Crimean warrior crossed sabres on his tomb. A defunct pianist left behind a grand piano of stone among the weeds, its propped-up lid like the boards of a coffin prised open. This was where Dante Gabriel Rossetti exhumed his muse Lizzie, when he repented of having buried his poems with her. Marble nymphs and obsequious dogs pined in a dripping jungle of nettles and ferns. Doors of the vaults had fallen open, exhaling mould; tree roots nudged skeletons towards the surface, kicked crucifixes askew and snaked into sight, fattened by the decay they had tunnelled through; creepers at once wrapped tourniquets around these limbs of wood. An animal scratched and rustled somewhere. A bird let loose a shrill single note which the sodden air stifled.

The rusted gate, temptingly ajar, led into another dimension. Beyond it, the past itself was an unsealed crypt, or a catacomb walled with remembrance. I had strolled out of my own life into someone else's death – or into this compendious death, which allowed human beings to evaporate and left only their out-of-commission sabres and carved mastiffs to fend off a self-seeding nature. What did Rossetti think his poems would have learned from their closeness to Lizzie's decay? Did imagination make you a secret necrophile? The anxiety to be outside yourself was a desire for rebirth on your own terms; it entailed first arranging your own demise.

After half an hour I forgot about Marx, bursting irrelevantly back into life through his block of masonry and ordering us to change the world rather than acquiescently describing it. To describe it, after all, *was* to change it. Not, certainly, in the way Marx meant, but in the only way which would ever work – subjectively, by seeing it differently. And yet what kind of hostages were these which we handed over to hungry time, to the prickles and the prolific sycamores? That unplayable, funereal, tone-deaf piano.

I left the cemetery and trailed back down the hill, stumbling into a maze of dingy streets named after people in Shakespeare: Miranda, Cressida, Parolles. The experiment had gone no further. Perhaps someone had discovered that Cressida was a faithless hoyden, and Parolles a cowardly liar. Still, for me during that first winter in London, there was no detail of desecration which couldn't – in an emergency – be made romantic: the warm cosy stench of fuel from the Euston line, over the wall of the dusty garden back in Highbury; the morning light like thin gruel, the blear-eyed sunsets in early afternoon; the blur of yellow sodium vapour pitched over the city every night; the oily rainbows which shook in the surface of the river when I took a boat through the docks down to Greenwich.

At least one Londoner was irritated by my insistence on liking his city, weather and all. I caught a train to Richmond from Waterloo in the fog, and as it slid through the muddy brick and wet slates of Clapham, with everything befuddled by the thick furry air, I pulled down the streaked and spotted window to see it better, and let in a blast of cold. The old man sharing the compartment with me (I have supplied him, after the event, with a handlebar moustache to splutter behind) snarled, and changed to another carriage at the next station. How could he have known my delight at finding myself on the loose inside my fantasy – or inside one of them?

This London, dim, stained, mitigated by mist, was my refuge from the bright blandness at the other end of the world. Reality here was warped by atmosphere. The gas tanks behind King's Cross were black rusted coronets; through the murk and drizzle glowed the blue entry to a tube station which had the audacity to call itself ANGEL.

New York had its own romance. The young provincial travels to the city in quest of sin (to look at, if not to commit). The Tasmanian painter I had come to visit walked me, on my first night, up the avenue in the direction of the neon big bang. 'I'm going to take you,' Tony said, 'to the wickedest place on earth.' But though body rubs were advertised for twenty-five cents just off Times Square, we opted for a milk shake in Howard Johnson's and watched the flushed crowds through the window. Later, in the Chelsea Hotel, an elevator disgorged Janis Joplin, who veered across the lobby, slobbering, to a limousine. I was agog.

What I expected from New York was the full inventory of vices my own first small, timid world had not yet imagined, the full range of human splendours and vicissitudes which the society I had come from, middlingly contented, had not had room for. I was not disappointed. The seditious thrill of being made to surrender any bag you carried when you went into a bookstore: they assumed you had crime in mind. The bracing difficulty, like some existential game, of life in a place where no one would do you a favour and where nothing was for free: no change for the pay-phone without a purchase, no browsing, no toilet except for customers, no tourist information given, no entry to shops whose doors were operated by a buzzer unless you looked as if you might have a credit rating,

nowhere to sit since if seats were provided they'd only be monopol-
ised by vagrants, no eye contact on public transport except with
sexual intention because you might look into the gaze of a
crazy, and no reading of the newspaper over a fellow passenger's
shoulder because that counted as invasion of a paper-thin
privacy . . .

The city was an obstacle course of invisible, unforeseeable taboos
and trip wires. Those who had learned how to read it could function
in it, could buy and sell it. I spent my time looking at them do so,
through clear barriers of bullet-proof plate glass, like the one which
showed off but also debarred a solemn, silent vault door in the
lobby of a bank on Fifth Avenue. Money slumbered in its sarco-
phagus; unlike the open graves of the past at Highgate, there was no
way in.

After a week I left the city to drive in a lackadaisical loop across
the continent and back. With my friend the painter I sat in the back
seat of a rust-nibbled, shuddering car bought for the purpose. In the
front were a Welsh conceptual artist on a fellowship (he did stripes)
and his crabby wife. They looked on the journey as 'our trip of a
lifetime', and when we arrived at the ocean on the other side of the
continent they filled an orange juice bottle with Pacific water,
intending to take it home to show their relatives. On the way back
east, I emptied the bottle after a tiff with them, and refilled it from a
rusty tap behind a gas station. For tonal authenticity I added a squirt
of soap suds and a gobbet of spit. I often imagine that bottle in pride
of place on their Welsh dresser. It is only very recently that I have
begun to feel guilty about the substitution.

Through the tunnel under the river, America was a larger, realer,
ruder world than any of us had counted on, profuse in unwelcome
adventures.

In Chicago the car disappeared. We left it on a vacant lot, in
company with a few other vehicles. These were decoys; the lot was
owned by a consortium of pirates, who posted a tiny notice in a
corner saying NO PARKING and waited across the street for the
bait to be swallowed by out-of-towners. We tracked the car to a
pound on the South Side, behind barbed wire and a cordon of
prowling dogs. The pirates, who had Sioux features, demanded
fifty dollars ransom for it. The Welsh girl righteously threatened
them with the law, at which one of them ambled into the street and

waved down a squad car. The cop told us to pay. 'They towed away the FBI last week,' he chuckled, unable to conceal his admiration for such buccaneering free enterprise.

In Richland Center, Wisconsin, we were confronted by a deputation consisting of the police chief and the preacher, who advised us in unison to leave town. A posse of little old ladies behind lace curtains had reported an invasion force of long-hairs slouching down Main Street; we were escorted as far as the interstate highway.

Somewhere in Idaho – my memory has spared me the details – the pup tent I slept in was washed away by a sudden downpour. Still zipped in my sleeping bag, I floundered in a slough of mud. (Later, in Louisiana, the same tent was dismantled, with me inside it, by a traffic cop who found it cowering under a bridge. He dismantled it with his boot.)

In San Francisco, on Market Street, I made the mistake of going to a down-at-heel picture palace which advertised three films for two dollars. I genuinely wanted to see the films, but soon discovered that I was the only patron with this quaint idea. And yet I was determined to sit my ground: I had invested two dollars, and was relying on it to keep me off the streets for half the day. Within an hour I was back on the bruising, blistering asphalt. I had to stay on the go until I felt sleepy, since it didn't do to face our hotel on Geary Street while conscious. A double room there cost a dollar a day. The door had no lock. When I mentioned this, the slattern who pocketed the daily dollar said, 'Honey, the folks we have here don't own nothing that needs locking', and looked me quizzically up and down, wondering what my problem was and why I thought myself so valuable.

In Los Angeles, I almost died of fright at Disneyland, in the black spiralling underworld of the Space Mountain, which those with heart conditions were warned to avoid. I was strapped into a two-seater bucket for the ride through lurching intestinal inner space with the uniformed conscript – on leave from or en route to Vietnam? – who had been in front of me in the queue. As the car soared, plummeted, veered backwards or free-fell, with nothing to see and only your jolting innards to narrate the experience to you, the soldier boy flung himself, gibbering in terror, into my arms. Back on the surface of the earth, with its friendly rodents, its cross-sectioned Matterhorn and its smell of frying, his face re-set in stoical cement and we went our separate ways.

I also almost died in Death Valley, when a happy-go-lucky girl pushed me fully clothed into a thermal pool where I enjoyed a brief replay of my life so far before I was hauled out to heave and hyperventilate on the gritty edge, and again at the Grand Canyon where – unable to afford the hire of a mule – I walked down into the layered geological sunset and, with the heat droning in my ears and drumming in my temples, fainted from dehydration. America, it appeared, had an ultimate experience in store for me somewhere or other.

In El Paso, I walked briefly out of the United States, across the bridge to Juarez in Mexico. My first drink of tequila axed me, and the immigration officials on the Texan side took an hour or two to decide whether I was worth re-admitting.

In Kentucky, at a booth below the mountains which gave out maps for tourists, I opened one of these on the counter and asked the man in charge if he could point out the Mason-Dixon line to me. His red neck grew redder, his jowels quivered, and he smote the counter with a fist the size of a ham. 'Sonny,' he said, 'I bin up and down this here land from Alaska to Mexico, and I ain't *never* met anyone could tell me that. I reckon it only exists in the heads of critters so iggerant they don't know the South won the Civil War. Now git.' I got.

I had caught up, in those two months on the road, on a lifetime's worth of destitution, alienation, hunger pangs and distraught insomnia. America was a great place for disabusing you of your dreams.

England had compliantly confirmed most of my illusions. Its literature at least promised me assimilation: I could walk into that reserved past as into the populous cemetery on the hill in north London. But on this continent there was nothing for me to belong to, and no reason at all why I should exist. As we drove north-east towards New York and the circle began to close, I looked back on a road unreeling for thousands of miles like celluloid on a spool, every frame of which seemed to contain the flapping pennants of a used-car salesman or a mobile home being mobilised on the back of a truck or the cheery orange chalet of a Ho Jo's or a motel boasting in neon of mirrored rooms and hourly rates. Occasionally a sign would announce a comfort station. That meant a lavatory. There was no other comfort available out there.

Once we had ducked through the tunnel beneath the Hudson – I began to think – I would be safe; it would be over; home needn't be where they took you in, it was merely the place you returned to. So when we crossed the dank marshes and flaming refineries of New Jersey and curved at last down the concrete slide towards the Lincoln Tunnel, I almost yelped to see the line-up of elderly technology on the other bank, with the Empire State Building still poking into the sky a spire which indicated no world upstairs but jabbed the clouds in sheer hubris. Though I may not have been home, I was at least back.

I was also, as I realised later that night after crossing under the river, broke. The Tasmanian painter, his fellowship at its end, returned to the place he could still call home; I had three weeks left in the city before my charter flight to England. In Oxford at least they would have to take me in: the Rhodes Trust after all had paid my fees. Meanwhile, I counted out my last few dollars, calculated how many words they would buy, and sent a telegram to my parents asking for a loan. Western Union took the cash, but omitted to deliver the message. The postal workers got to know me quite well at the General Delivery grille on Eighth Avenue, where twice a day I presented myself to collect a reply which never came.

I was indigent, for the first and only time (so far) in my life. Here was the ultimate experience America had been saving up for me. This – I thought one day as I slunk back down the pompous steps of the post office, resolving that this would be the last time I'd make my naively hopeful enquiry – was reality. A world where when I announced myself I was told twice daily, 'We have nothing in that name'. A world which couldn't care less, and defied you to continue bothering to exist. I had landed myself here by choice, by my desire for independence. It was another version of birth, though less auspicious than that on Waterloo Bridge a year before. Eighth Avenue looked like an orphanage to me. Off I trudged to start from scratch.

I became the innocuous Robinson Crusoe of 23rd Street, scavenging the makings of my life from the flotsam which the street provided. I was able to occupy a gutted room in a tenement on the corner of Seventh Avenue reserved for one more optimistic out-of-town artist who hadn't arrived yet; I slept on a mattress someone had thoughtfully abandoned on the stoop, and didn't speculate about its history of smirches and apparent stab-wounds, through which it shed its innards of fleece.

The room possessed a wash-basin to piddle in. For anything more elaborate, I had to sneak into the YMCA along the block. My two windows had been occultly painted black and jammed shut. I could see the avenue – or rather a sign on a brick wall above it, advertising a funeral service for the Chelsea seniors who tottered through the miasmal heat with their walking frames – by courtesy of a scratched rift in the paint.

Getting out there, however, was yet another adventure. The building was open to the street, so its halls and stairways harboured a nightly crew of derelicts. The landlord refused to replace light-bulbs (and in less than a year an arsonist obliged him by burning the place down: a sleek apartment building has now replaced it, with balconies cantilevered over the hubbub below). Having opened my door – at which there were often scrapings in the small hours, and investigative fumblings with the lock – I had to risk a corridor, turn right, penetrate another length of unlit passage, and hope that I hadn't in the meantime tripped over a sleeper. Then I was at the stairs, with 23rd Street attainable two floors below through the acid scent of urine.

I prepared myself for these exits as I would have done for a parachute jump. Behind the door, I would draw the bolt and count to ten. Sometimes twenty. On one occasion to thirty. Once I had ejected myself, it took an interval of fidgeting anguish to lock the door in the dark. That done, I was away. The right-angled corridor reminded me of the black bottomless shafts inside the mountain at Disneyland: it was my few seconds of free fall, and I often kept my courage up in the murk through which I tumbled by shouts and screams, to announce to anyone skulking there that I was deranged myself, and shouldn't be messed with.

Having got to the stairs, I had the earth in sight. Day leaked up from below; my parachute had blossomed. By the time I bumped and glided down to 23rd Street, I could manage a strolling nonchalance.

Not (as I soon learned) that arrival on ground level made me safe. One night I was sitting on the stoop, recovering from the aerial thrills of the journey down. A black youth loped past, paused, studied me for a while to savour my unease, then stepped forward and punched me in the face. I was more mystified than hurt. 'What was that *for*?' I called after him. He didn't answer; I would still like to know. People are odd, I remember thinking in anaesthetised amazement. Then I noticed the blood on my shirt.

Up in the room, my diet consisted of brown rice, which gave me a fancied solidarity with the peasants of Vietnam. This was 1969, an abstinently principled time: under-nourishment, I told myself, fine-tuned the senses. Which did not stop me from wistfully salivating outside the coffee-shops where – on glass shelves in revolving cabinets – inaccessible, unaffordable cakes twirled like ballerinas, all bright yellow foam rubber with an icy stratum of vanilla concrete on top. I spent the day in the Public Library on 42nd Street, at a table with tramps dozing over their newspapers. I read my way through Shakespeare, remembered the owl-like scholar on the ladder in the Bodleian roosting among the books, and was grateful for the life-saving properties of literature and its atlas of alternative worlds.

It was the summer of the moon landing, the Manson gang and *Midnight Cowboy*. I had been at Yellowstone when the man from Ohio took his small step, and remembered a pot-bellied citizen watching television outside his parked trailer say, 'Now ain't that something?' as the puppet dressed in puffy silver paper bobbed through a set of weightless papier-mâché rocks. Yes, it was something, but quite what I couldn't say. Back on earth, the acolytes of Charles Manson – who was soon to be acclaimed by an Oxford colleague of mine as Zoroaster reborn – crawled down from their shacks in the hills to Bel Air and hacked the life out of Sharon Tate. I was in Los Angeles when they did so, and heard about it on a car radio driving down the Ventura freeway. Every time we drove under a bridge, the radio coughed and swallowed a gory detail or two. I saw *Midnight Cowboy* in New Orleans, and by the time I got back to New York the film had defined the city for me. I believed in Schlesinger's nasty census: the streets jostled with randy harridans, repressed conventioneers wearing dentures, acne-pocked hustlers and frothy-mouthed evangelists baptising their flocks in privies. I had changed from one of *Midnight Cowboy*'s two characters to the other: from open-mouthed, inane Joe Buck to street-smart, case-hardened Ratso Rizzo. I never was big or brash or blond enough to be Jon Voight, but I could feel myself shrinking into Dustin Hoffman as the pavements wore me down.

When the library closed, discharging me and my fellow readers into the night, I would wander along 42nd Street on the way back to Chelsea and scout for monsters in Times Square. There were fewer in reality than in Schlesinger's film. The man on the cigarette billboard compulsively puffed out smoke rings, like a fire-breathing dragon with ruined lungs; the imploded plastic ladies in the sex-shops awaited the customer who could inflate them. The crossroads of wickedness seemed dreary after a week. Nothing remained but to dawdle down Seventh Avenue, stand on the corner looking at my blacked-out windows, run on the spot for a while to stoke up energy for the assault, then charge into the building, key ready in my hand, clutched in preparation for the moment when I reached – if I ever did – the door of my flimsy fortress.

I returned to England in October. By contrast with my spell of destitution, it qualified as a homecoming. When I heard a few months later that the warren I camped in on my bruised, punctured mattress had been burned down, I was startled by how happy and relieved I felt. In retrospect, I wondered at (and was grateful for) my naivety. I had actually enjoyed the city's devastations, since I'd never before had the experience of falling through the floor. But while permitting you to recreate yourself, New York didn't mind if you were destroyed in the process. Its cheap hotels, announcing TRANSIENT RATES on faded placards, declared its disbelief in continuity and fixity. I was glad to find that the dotty brainworms of Oxford still tramped the meadow in circles of self-pursuit; I took up residence in my books once more. It was a long time before I had the courage to face New York again.

The addition of Lisbon happened at Easter the following year. I went there to visit a Portuguese friend I had made in Oxford, and to stay with his family. My friend Jorge was a scientist, and kept all-night vigils in the chemistry labs, watching arcane encounters between liquids. He explained the second law of thermodynamics to me, deplored the entropic messiness of heat, and added that all his experiments were at low temperatures. Frost grew on his meccano cities of tubes and phials. He was also, when not dabbling in the lab, better read than me, although he had done the reading in his spare time. Most impressive of all, he knew how to live. He could cook, drank what the English admiringly referred to as 'real coffee', and once wore a pair of yellow socks, which to me seemed supremely stylish; after trips home he would return to Oxford with ancient bottles of brandy and cakes called angels' breasts (made from gooey egg yolks and an avalanche of sugar) or pieces of fruit which had been crystallised into edible sculptures. He apologised tactfully for the regime, as if it were his personal fault.

Apart from the sweets and Salazar, I had no advance ideas. I told my Oxford tutor before I set off that I was excited to be going to Lisbon because I'd never seen the Mediterranean; the howler enjoyed a rapid circulation. London and New York I memorised before I arrived there. Actuality was pre-empted by images. My experience of the northern hemisphere's notion of the south was confined to Las Palmas, where the boat on which I sailed to England made a last, procrastinating stop. I didn't know where or what Las Palmas was. Impatient for England and its fabled fogs, I wasn't at all curious. I dragged myself around the island – which is what I took Las Palmas to be – for a few hours, and remember now only flies, frying-oil, contingents of operetta cops and the lazy slapping of plastic strips hung in doorways on account of the aforementioned flies. I hoped Lisbon would not be like that.

Nor was it. The road through the city from the airport bobbed nautically over hills which were coral reefs of sunned plaster and shining tiles, pink, orange and ceramic blue, with baroque church domes baked from the egg whites left over after whipping up a batch of angels' breasts; emerged into a ravine over which an aqueduct gigantically strutted on stony stilts, a shanty town clinging by its fingertips to the cliff beneath; looped and twisted through a forest of eucalypts; over the last hill glimpsed the ocean, a plate of shining metal, then veered into a suburb where the streets were powdered with mimosa and jacaranda blossoms; pulled up at a gate, a hedge, a house, another life.

Almost as soon as I was inside the door, Jorge's father – who had phonetically mugged up a welcoming speech in English – produced an atlas and pointed out the bereft speck of Tasmania, so remote that even the navigators who left from the chapel on the bluff nearby had omitted to discover it. Mine was one of the worlds they hadn't given to the world: this hospitality made reparation. I found myself adopted.

Later in the afternoon we went along to the chapel, and stood on the steps looking over the red bridge suspended like a cobweb across the river, the all-embracing Christ with arms spread on the southern bank, the flotilla of monuments to the discoveries, and the cape which was Europe's last western lookout, from where it peered in the direction of America, its other, altered ego. As the view was explained, I had the feeling that it was being offered to me; I accepted.

It was my future I was surveying from this grassy hilltop. Or, to be precise, a quarter of my future. I may not have known it, but I already had my four bases – I refer to the ball-game, not to military imperialism – and I have spent the twenty years since then running between them. The analogy with the ball-park only falters when I have to decide which of them is home base.

At the bottom of the hill on which the chapel kept watch for other continents, the worlds the Portuguese set out to find had been brought back and reconstructed in facsimile. An exhibition mapping the *Mundo Português* was built on the fields between the monastery and the river in 1940. The American, African, Asian colonial societies were housed in a caravanserai of white, ephemeral pavilions, mostly long since demolished. But traces remained, and as I got to know the area I began to piece them together again in my head. The political motive of the show didn't bother me; it was to me a matter of space rearranged and ordained by imagination, of insignificant terrain staked out and ruled into the lineaments of myth.

It reminded me again of baseball, of the way we would demarcate the streets where I grew up in preparation for a game, defying cars to drive through what we insisted on seeing as an arena, a zone where all moves were ritualised, a zodiac whose sky of symbols had been scratched with chalk-ends brought home from a school blackboard on to the concrete pavement and bitumen road.

A tropical garden across from the monastery contained stray mementoes of the sample villages which sprouted there in 1940. Exotically plumed ducks waddled among the headless or limbless classical statuary; while Greek figures aimed the discus on a lawn or a matron dispensed Roman charity, on gate-posts in the shrubbery were propped the carved heads of African girls with braided hair and rope necklets, turbanned Indians and Chinese with eyes incised by knives. A brick arch with an oriental peak was labelled MACAU. Once it framed an extradited Chinese street, strung with lanterns and swarming with merchants in fancy dress. Now it bestrode a compost heap. If I closed my eyes, the perspective re-opened.

Subjective worlds overlapped, imprints of different imaginations which squabbled to redeem space by gathering it into meaning or else chose to leave it infidel, outlawed, a mere patch of clods and pebbles. On one side of a wall was the encampment of vanished colonies – African bush huts, a Chinese market, a Brazilian square; an archipelago of brave, improbable fictions in this suburb which had baptised itself Bethlehem. Over the wall was anathema, earth cut off from human association, sterilised by a curse. I was led up an alley to see a pillar standing on a plinth, ringed along its length by five thick bands like garrotting collars. The pillar recalls the plot of some regicides in 1758; each band numbers an executed plotter. The palace of the conspirators which stood here was razed, and the ground sown with salt so that nothing would grow from its ruins. In this place of infamy, the inscription on the column commands that no one shall ever build. A desert had been laid out – as meticulously as if it were a garden – in the centre of the city.

But a curse couldn't deter human efforts to claim this earth as a foundation. Dwellings encroached, crouching so low that the politicians forgave them for trespassing on the waste. Inch by inch the community extended, until now the prohibition on the base of the pillar booms unheeded in a warren of squat doors, restaurant chimneys belching sardine smells, and jocose lines of baggy, jitter-bugging underclothes. The blood-stained, saline-poisoned nowhere was a home again.

Beyond the railway line, on the river bank where one of the surviving exhibition halls had been taken over as a boat shed, I found another emblem of embargo, of worlds and their outer limits, beyond which reality ends (or imagination begins). Medieval map-makers warned of dragons just across the border of tribal knowledge. Inside the pavilion, a dim mural shows a bearded kraken rearing from the ocean to frighten trespassers in his unmapped domain. This is Adamastor, who terrorises Vasco da

Gama's fleet in *Os Lusíadas*. Vasco is on his way to India; Adamastor appears at the southern tip of Africa, warns that woe betides anyone who tries to sail round the Cape of Storms, and foretells the drowning of another Portuguese voyager, Bartolomeu Dias. In fact it is his phantom which addresses Vasco. Adamastor himself is the embodied Cape, gnarled, perilous and impassable. He signifies the dangers the mariners actually did encounter on their way to the east, and also stands for the vanishing point of the western world, the gate leading either to death or to vision, like the pillars of Hercules in the ancient fable.

I recognised Adamastor's prohibition, because I had come upon it from the other side. For Vasco, he debarred the east; for me, he policed the dividing-line between hemispheres, and thundered about the risks of my journey west. I had rounded his Cape in the liner two years before, and could still recall the nausea of the ocean, heaving and lurching at this place of transit between worlds. Once we were past the Cape, the weather relented. We were in the Atlantic, and looking upwards: the goal was distantly in view. The ferocious Adamastor, converted by a new name, was the Cape of Good Hope. But hopes have a necessary quotient of fear. As the ship droned up the second ocean – reversing seasons as we crossed another notional line written on water and advanced into a half-world which was to me the real one, though only real because I had fed myself on fictions about it – I wasn't sure that I would survive this small, self-willed reincarnation.

In Lisbon, however, I had strayed into acceptance. I enjoyed belonging to a family, so long as it was someone else's. This one came complete with a grandmother in a black shawl who addressed me at length and refused to understand that I didn't understand the language, and a shaggy mountain dog who by the third day no longer barked at me (except when a haircut made me briefly illegible) and by the end of the week had taken to tugging me round the block on nocturnal missions while I panted at the end of his chain and experimentally asked him in Portuguese not to pull.

I felt, unexpectedly, at home. The emotion meant for me then not much more than being looked after. The baby squawls, and its wants are attended to; I pressed a bell beside my bed when I woke and a maid called Olga brought me – some time later, and with a scowl – a cup of coffee. Through the shuttered window the garden buzzed, the ocean gleamed. The mattress with its forensic stains and stiletto holes and my diet of brown rice seemed a long way off. I enjoyed again the child's sensation of being able to relax into a ready-made world. Since affection treats its object as a miniature, small and therefore vulnerable, Jorge's mother invented a diminutive form of my name, unembarrassed by the fact that it didn't end on a vowel so she had to splice consonants together: I was rebaptised Peterzinho. Nothing seemed to be demanded in return for so much nurturing care; no test of worthiness impended, as at Oxford. The house was an extension of my feathery bed. It was also a condition of glut, food being the form that love and communion take. I regularly over-ate.

Once, aware that I didn't deserve it, I asked Jorge why his parents were so good to me. 'Because they're Portuguese,' he said. The smile at the corners of his mouth gave notice of a complicated statement: a shrug, a joke, or a truth whose reasons I would have to deduce for myself? In one sense, he was literally right. Charity in this country entailed the donation of surplus – coins, or affection – to those who needed it. Kindness was the instinctive policy of humankind. They had taken me in, and not because they had to.

In London I was a pilgrim, fervently trusting that the shrine I had come to venerate was not empty. In Oxford I was a candidate, awaiting classification. In New York I had been a vagrant, expecting rejection or exclusion. In Lisbon there were no such insecurities. The place I knew least about, which had not figured on the conjectural map of my future, was the one where I felt safest. Here, in the intervals between being an adult in Oxford and elsewhere, I could catch up on the childhood I hadn't yet had time for, and fill in some of the years before my second nativity on Waterloo Bridge.

3
Moving Day

PERHAPS, JORGE'S MOTHER SAID TO ME ONCE, YOU WERE
meant to fall to earth here. I was happy to believe in the mistake.
The world must have turned before I could be delivered to the
pre-assigned spot – there could have been low clouds, poor visibility, a fault in the radar – and I landed in Tasmania instead.
Somehow, by accident or chemical scent, I had wandered back to
the place where I should have been all along.

Still, the notion worried me. The ponderously rotating globe,
with lives landing on it as arbitrarily as aerial wreckage. Each of us
spends a lifetime asking over again the questions which our first
articulate ancestor must have uttered: why me? why here? why me
here? Despite the thousands of intervening years, we are no closer
to an answer. Indeed, now that we can see the plurality of places and
possible worlds from above – so beautiful, so uninhabitable, so
indifferent to habitation: multiple Americas of ocean, desert,
mountain, prairie, like pages not yet inscribed – we are further away
from answering. Air travel gives us lessons in unreality, and in the
brave improbability of home.

Once, in January, I flew over Chicago. The pilot pointed it out,
through the chilling rarefied air thirty-nine thousand feet below. Or
could it have been thirty-nine inches? For it wasn't a city at all, but a
ridge of twigs on an icy lake (or pond, or puddle, or drop of glazed
water); a patternless plot of matchsticks stuck in a white, alien
planet. Meanwhile, at our alleged height of thirty-nine thousand
feet, middle America behaved as if on solid ground and dispensed
good cheer. 'Will you have our scrumptious beef or our delightful

chicken today?' the stewardess insisted on knowing. She almost bit her varnished lip in suspense as I thought it over.

I set foot in Chicago a few weeks later, to change planes for a trip back to Australia. I wasn't convinced this time either that the place existed. Its towers had vaporised in a bluey, brownish smog of early spring. A highway purported to lead downtown; all I saw was a plantation of glinting tarmac.

The same doubts about place and our pretence of belonging wherever we find ourselves overtook me in Dallas some months after I saw that Chicago of snapped twigs. Along the crimson sky in the afternoon, the granite, glass and marble spars arranged themselves, bevelled or whittled, terminating in spikes or in whirls like cream on pastry. They too, like the earth, mocked the notion of habitability. On one of them, a scarlet flying horse cantered on clouds. Coming in on the highway, I passed a building calling itself Colony Parke. The supernumerary 'e' pined for a past which was only ever a matter of spelling. Ahead, a sign announced that the nearest Polynesian restaurant – unless you doubled back to the one you had just shot by – was 3784 miles away. Would the highway go on that far, unstoppably? The sudden invocation of distance made me panic. Where is this? Above, the metaphors of pink marble and blue glass; beneath, wet empty concrete fields for the repose of cars.

Next morning there was no Dallas. Demolished to be rebuilt once more, conjured by abracadabra not the piling up of stones? The damp condensing air drifted between the skyscrapers and dissolved them. Even the sign locating us 3784 miles from somewhere else was erased. The cars whined on the highway in both directions, to and fro, hedging their bets.

It all happens so abruptly. One moment you are an earthling, held in place by the ball and chain of gravity and by earnest sentiment. Then the plane tilts upwards, and you are ejected from life, hovering over a world you once thought you belonged in. The cord has frayed, loosened, broken within minutes. Leaving London for India at dusk, the pilot strained to keep alive our sense of connection: 'That's the M25 down there in the northern suburbs; you can watch all those Londoners enjoying their drive home from work.' But it was already too late to think like that, to accredit local habitations and names. The city where I once perhaps lived was an orange dust speckling blackness.

Re-entry counts as the shock of birth: the same geographical disconcertment, and groggy, indistinct memories of a previous or an alternative life. Occasionally we are let down in a world englobed, visible briefly as a whole. Flying into New York from the south, you have the city fitted inside your double-strength porthole. It is made small, thus safe, thus portable; it can be taken away like a souvenir. The principle is the same as that of the infantile diminutive: Peter squeezed into Peterzinho. Liberty, the unsmiling Amazon, is a statuette of herself, the Brooklyn Bridge a cat's cradle, Central Park a tuft of moss. The island is the train-set you always dreamed of owning, whose switches you could control, whose gadabout avenues and perilous junctions you personally oversaw. Is it possible that people live in this toy-town, and that I am one of them? If so, where is the infinitesimal dot I occupy?

A life is the making of a microcosm. When you take a photograph of the city, its rowdy unfinished immensity curves and contracts into a pin-hole; its brassy light narrows to a sliver and takes refuge in darkness; the vanishing act occurs in the fractional second that the lens winks open. New York, for all its sins and its material grossness, slips through the needle's eye. So it is with my windows, and the space behind them. The obscured box absorbs the glare outside it; one little room tries to contain or comprehend an everywhere.

I always return to New York with a question fluttering in my stomach. Has my one-room microcosm survived my absence? Will I have to start again from the indigence of twenty years ago? I acquired the apartment as an expensive whim. Picked out from the columns of *The New York Times*, it seemed a good idea; it was the only one I looked at; I unloaded my savings into a long L-shaped room. Now what was I to do in it? I would have to divide Oxford vacations – Christmas, Easter and summer – between Lisbon and New York. Since the apartment served as an exit from the reality of my life in England, it remained slightly unreal, more impalpable than realty ought to be. Returning, I am genuinely amazed to find that it is still there.

Out of the subway, things are as they were before on Sixth Avenue: the quirky gables of the old court-house, and Crazy

Eddie's emporium of unhinged electronics. Along Christopher Street, the clothes in the shops are slightly freakier than the last time (which only means that I am older), with built-in muscles for the shoulders and belts whose buckles spell out BUTCH or SEXY. Around the corner, the part-time barbers – who drop in between auditions, or when suffering writer's block – are still designing hair not cutting it, and slapping gelatinations of mousse on scalps. Further up, a laundry deodorises the street with draughts of hot clean steam, preaching the American cult of renovation. Across the streets, macaws and toucans imported from another jungle preen and scratch or clack their leathery comma-shaped tongues in the pet shop. It is all the same as it always was, except that I can't locate myself in it.

Now I am at the park I must cross to get to my building. Already – before having sidled through the population of can-collectors, child-minders, dog-trainers, python-handlers and roller-skating dare-devils who occupy the park, along with a few stewed, innocent derelicts dozing at the tables marked with checker-boards – I have isolated the correct keys in my pocket, and got them into the proper sequence. There are five of them. This is the moment of greatest trepidation, the cliff-edge. Perhaps the building is no longer there. And even if it is, they could have changed the locks . . .

A deep breath is required before I can turn the corner. The building *is* there. I mean that so far it always has been. And by counting zig-zags on the fire-escape and tracking sideways I can identify the two windows which are mine. Did I really (a last rush of terror) leave the blinds open?

After two more hurdles – streets to be crossed, and by this stage I am too unnerved to wait for the traffic lights – our doorman greets me. He knows my name; ergo I must exist. Though he would not be above macabrely pretending that I existed in order to play some sinister joke on me. He is Transylvanian, proud of his vampirish heritage, with a menacing lipless grin. If I ask him how he is, expecting in return some polite English formula, he is likely to reply, 'Oh, I am dying, thank you. But it is no matter. Nostradamus says the world will end in 1992.' Welcome to New York.

The mail-box bulges with bills to pay, and personalised requests for charitable contributions signed with an automatic pen by the likes of Charlton Heston and Elizabeth Taylor: yes, it seems I *do* exist. But upstairs, with the last three locks undone and the chain removed, the question recurs as I look at the room with its months of bottled heat and its epidermis of dust, twining round stray hairs under the tables like lengths of lightweight tumbleweed. Who lived here? Can this tomb be encouraged back to life?

After a while, its vital signs are restored. The gas licks up from the stove, the refrigerator grumbles, the first gush of rusty water flushes down the pipes, the television set (after an initial rasping cough as its tubes are startled awake) reports on the emergencies of the afternoon. I throw away the roach traps, with their infirmaries of pinioned victims and litters of still-born eggs. I set the clock on the video recorder and start up time again in this crypt. The blinking digits begin the countdown to my departure.

These acts of resuscitation, however, allow another worry to advance in the queue. I am never able to resist the temptation to telephone my London number, and listen to it comfortingly, inconclusively ring in that emptied space – at least until the operator determines that there is no one home, and advises me in her electronic sing-song to please try later.

In London, the uncertainties of arrival are acuter still. The street denies all knowledge of my house, ergo of me. A terrace of stucco, all its windows lidded, won't let on what lies behind it. It has the special sanctimonious look of the English when they don't want to oblige, citing the rules while giving you to understand in the studied pleasure of their refusal that it is personal whim not official edict which they are serving. If I look for my house, for the evidence that I have a life, for a safety-pin to hold that life together, I can hear the street primly answer, 'I really can't say, I'm sure.' It does so in the tone of shop assistants who aren't authorised – as they put it – to give you change for the phone or a parking meter; of the woman who sells the evening paper a mile away in Bond Street, and who has posted a notice beside her hutch warning tourists not to bother asking her for directions. When my hard-faced street with its stucco complexion gives me that stare, I have to force myself to stand my ground and repeat the question. Because I do, after all, live here. Don't I?

This weekly, sometimes daily anxiety begins at Marble Arch,

where I get off the bus from Oxford. Here, for a couple of minutes, is London at its most self-caricaturing: cockney spivs dressed like the beefeaters on gin bottles, with extra rosettes on their lace-up bovver boots, entice new arrivals onto a tour bus with an upper deck open to the rain. Also London at its most characterless, a displaced excerpt from the modern world: Arab banks, a kiosk of foreign newspapers with jabbering type, a Kentucky frying franchise and a croissant outlet, a hotel lobby (through which I have found a diagonal short-cut, in one door and out the other) with American flight crews chewing gum and awaiting dispersal. Then I am in the back streets, where London resumes. A brick mews houses stockbrokers in erstwhile stables. Next there is a square I must skirt, since its trees are private and can be visited only by key-holders, though they drip onto me all summer and I kick my way through their piled leaves in the autumn. Then comes a church, whose clock is my street's punctilious time-keeper. It divides the day into quarter-hours but omits the idle night. The chimes are turned off at midnight so the elderly gentlefolk in their mansion block can sleep.

The snooty street, keeping up appearances at all costs, disowns my house and even feigns indifference to the FOR SALE signs which come and go like seasonal blooms on its iron railings. To find the recess I live in I have to burrow: downstairs into a basement, along a passage under the house above, out through another door into a courtyard. Every so often I make the process more complicated for myself, adding extra locks, interposing another door. This is as much to ritualise the underground adventure as to secure what's inside. Narrative requires postponement, suspension, the deferring of arrival: my fears are necessary to the nervous business of induction into the city. Each trip to London repeats that first apprehensive crossing of Waterloo Bridge. But now, instead of the golden sooty gateway between cliffs of masonry where the bridge ran out, my second last subterranean door squeaks open – I hope – on a screen of wet leaves, tickling fronds and dangling tendrils, with a startled flutter of wings as the sparrows fan themselves up to the safety of a television antenna. Behind the green film is the last door of all, behind that the leavings of this particular life.

I can't help it if the journey casts shadows of significance as I tick off the keys and graduate through the separate stages of entry. The door in the wall; light at the tunnel's end; the secret garden. To clamber down the steps from the street is to re-enact a fantasy we all know by heart. The city is a treasure-hunt. Somewhere, along a serpentine chain of coincidence, are lurking the bell that will one day have your name printed next to it, the long-sought-for book you know will explain everything, the record with that unidentified snatch of music you've never heard again but which orchestrates your happiness, the person you realise you have to love. The city promises that we will stumble on all these prizes if we seek them tirelessly enough. Every walk round the block instigates or continues a quest. I never leave home without pocketing my current want-list. London: universal junk-shop of dreams. My search, for the present, pauses here.

The house is a shed which grew – UNIQUE COTTAGE, according to the estate agent's sign-board – without waiting for permission. Among my deeds and titles to its freehold is a wearily resigned letter from a council officer deciding, in order to terminate what must have been a correspondence of attrition, that he would take no further action in the matter of the aforesaid illicit one-family dwelling. I could not resist the idea of inhabiting a two-storey coop in this sunken yard, like a hermit in his grotto; it pleased me to learn that the building was the despair of bureaucracy, allowed to persist outside the law. Here is my child's cabin, my fugitive's unlicensed hide-out, my observer's oblique periscope, with its view of a blank wall and its mirrored relay of messages from the sky.

I arrived in Oxford twenty years ago with a suitcase of clothes and a trunk of books. I unpacked them in a minimal, monastic cell looking out on the medieval city wall, and on a horse-chestnut tree which I studied through the long months of my first northern winter for some inkling of spring. The starkness of my room pleased me, being the antithesis of home with its cosy kitsch and its mantelpiece of sentimental trophies. An electric kettle was provided; I invested in a single mug. If someone came to see me and I remembered to boil the kettle, we shared the mug and agreed in advance who would drink from which side.

For the first year I hung nothing on the walls. I had nothing to hang on them in any case, and I despised the notion of decor. The more astringent my denials, the fiercer I thought my concentration would be. It was the same gawky puritanism with which I tried to reconcile myself to the bowls of brown rice in New York. The white room, scrubbed bare of associations, was a cubicle for reading and writing in. It satisfied me because I had no desires beyond those two activities, though once a week I would look out at the chestnut tree and wonder if there would ever be buds.

After the fancy-dress exams, I moved round the corner to All Souls. All I owned I trundled down the street in a garden barrow on loan from the New College porters, stacking my books on the grass clippings. This time I unpacked in an attic, with some dental stumps of battlement outside the window and a truncated, crockety tower. The books were assigned to new shelves in the old order. My iconoclastic cleanliness had weakened a little: slightly ashamed, I tacked some prints from Italian museums on the wall.

Domestically, I faced a setback. All Souls supplied no plug-in kettle. I guessed that solitary tea- or coffee-making was discouraged, since all meals were supposed to be communal. I wasn't equal to egg-headed breakfasts with my colleagues; on the sly I acquired a coffee pot, an electric ring to stand it on and a carcinogenic square of asbestos to stand that on. The shaky apparatus operated on a corner of my bedroom floor. When my scout came to make the bed, I packed it shiftily away in the wardrobe.

Yet as I opened the wardrobe, another inadequacy assailed me. Fixed inside the door was a valet's memo, for use by gentlemen togging up for country house weekends: a two-columned list of items to be packed, which you could mark off one by one with crayon as you proceeded; once your bag was complete, you rubbed out the marks and were ready for the next invitation. Tails? the list inquired. Morning suit? (There might always be a wedding at the village church.) Shooting stick? Field glasses? Collars, cufflinks, shirt studs? The answer in my case was: None of the above. Nor, adding insult to injury, did I need them, since I never received a summons to a country house weekend.

After three years spent enduring the humiliation of that list as I fished out my lightweight Australian suits and peg-legged pants, I packed up for the next move. The books were piled in cartons cadged from the college wine cellar. This time a van was hired; I ruled out the All Souls garden barrow, not because of my exalted status but because I was going to Christ Church, which entailed crossing the High Street. There were no traffic lights then, and I didn't fancy steering an unwieldy rumbling chariot of books between the city buses.

Five years after disembarking from the boat train and stowing my suitcase and trunk as left luggage at Waterloo, I unpacked again in six rooms straggling along the west side of the Christ Church quadrangle. When all my chattels were unloaded, they made no more than a modest pile in the middle of one hungry room. And there were five more, not to mention a lobby. However would I fill them up? It was not possessions I lacked, but personality. I had no clue about where to put things, or how to assign functions to the rooms (which meant devising roles for myself), or what should replace the remnants of clerical taste: autumnally flowery curtains, and lamp-shades the colour of nicotine. I holed up initially in a back bedroom, with only sporadic forays into the other, uncolonised areas.

I must have grown into the space, like a thickening waist which gradually finds use for all those supernumerary notches on a belt. The shrinking timidity with which I asked myself how I would ever fill it up has been replaced by a different perplexity. Now, plodding up the stairs to open the door with my name above it after a month or more away, I look around and think, whatever shall I do with all this *stuff*? It is like being my own fatigued executor. However did I accumulate all this lumber? The stuffed owl with the moulting belly, the Zen alignment of smoothed stones. The wall-clock in the shape of a giant's Mickey Mouse watch, with a yard of trailing black plastic for its wrist-band: the mouse's hands are twisted at a paraplegic angle. The candle made of honeycomb, rolled tightly into a flute and never lit; the opera singer in the photograph with open mouth and closed eyes, her face stretched taut in voluptuous anguish – devotional objects? Above the bath, the sign requesting PLEASE DON'T PEE IN OUR POOL, WE DON'T SWIM IN YOUR TOILET. (This, I know, was bought in a New Jersey shopping mall.)

Possessions are a means of weighting ourselves, adhering to earth. But all this hybrid clutter hadn't made its owner solid, or rooted him to the spot. It merely testified to the casual, messy mixing which comprises a person. Who could it be who coveted both Piranesi prints of mouldering Roman viaducts and a poster of James Dean lolling in a jalopy, cowboy boots poking the air, outside a Gothic farmhouse on a dry Texan plain? Those meditative stones and a wind-up plastic bumble-bee which, activated, waddles round a table buzzing drowsily? They all have stories to tell, but their small, individual chronicles don't add up, any more than the people occupying separate partitions of an apartment building make a community.

My reaction, to squirm out from beneath the muddled pyre of obtuse, useless things, is to reduce my life to the contents of a bag small enough to fit under an aeroplane seat and go somewhere else. Camped for the first few weeks in the unfurnished New York apartment, I used to lie on the floor at night and watch the lights from cars on Hudson Street drive striated banks of shadow through the blinds across the ceiling and down the white, imageless walls. I was back to the cerebral cell I first occupied in Oxford: the room was an erased tablet, a cleaned state. The shadows raked the ceiling and skidded down the walls, then were wiped away. Nothing had happened here yet. The place had no memories, no impedimenta, and no sadness.

Soon these walls – once the playground of passing shadows – were opaque with images. A picture is a window, an opening into elsewhere. But there are now so many windows that there's no wall left for them to open in.

I registered at a hotel in Los Angeles once, during a week of spring floods. There were mud slides in Santa Monica. Soaked hills turned to lapping bogs, and slurped over the highway onto the beach. Cantilevered houses went along for the ride. One of the evacuees was also checking into the hotel. 'I came back from work,' she said to no one in particular, 'and there was my home, floating out into the ocean.' Her voice soared on the excitement of it. I have seldom seen anyone so happy.

When I telephone the house in Lisbon, someone always answers. I can ring the bell and know the door will be opened. I don't even need a key.

The route there is clear of trepidations for me: it is a countdown to reunion. The taxi avoids the city, which careens towards the river from its jumbled hilltops on the other side of the forest – a confection of blue tiles, orange roofs and bleached chimneys, of iron wrought into curlicues, crazily swirling mosaic pavements, fountains which carve water into arcs and feathers, columns imitating palm trees or rope ladders or prehensile ivy, every square or circle of its jumbled geometry equipped with a bewigged lawgiving marquis who enlightens some lions and oxen from his plinth or an equestrian general rearing in bronze or a poet who declaims to the traffic from an open book of verses or a novelist in a bourgeois frockcoat rapturously hugging his flagrant marble Art Nouveau muse.

All that, however, has to be imagined. On its circumlocutory outer circle, the taxi drives across a churned wreckage of farms whose fields now grow concrete pillars with sprouts of steel, past a stadium with a screeching metallic eagle above the gate, down a lane of shanties with children larking in the gutter and gypsies selling rugs in a defunct garage among drying waist-high grass, their horses tethered to olive trees; then into the avenue named after the discoveries where the girls who look as if they are dressed as whores for a school play haggle with truckers, round by the horned moon of the Turkish embassy which some kamikaze terrorists bombed a few years ago, and through the suburb with its violet dust of jacaranda and its backyard orange groves, its pensioned-off watchdogs slumped in reminiscence on the footpath and its swallows discharged like a quiver of arrows into the evening. The last stage of this particular ritual is telling the taxi driver to pull up at the third lamp-post on the right.

The house, like much else conceived in the 1950s, has the shape of a television set. Through a gate in the hedge, the front door opens in the back of the box, where the wires fit into the sockets and the knobs can be twiddled with. Inside all is dark, shuttered against the western sun. But if you walk through the house and raise the shutters, you're at the front of the tube and a picture lights up: the garden of pines and cedars, the clump of cacti with striped yellow leaves like a twined nest of cobras pretending not to move, the lemons fluorescently bright, bees and butterflies cross-hatching the air, a lizard which flicks on a ledge; down the hill, the river with its cargo of tankers, ferries, yachts and white swanning liners. From the top balcony, you can see along the scalloped coast to its end, where the sun goes down, where Europe runs out, and where they detonate fireworks from the casino to signify a fresh start at midnight on New Year's Eve.

In London or New York, the only voices in the rooms – even after they have been electrically coaxed back to life – are those from inside appliances, which interpret the world outside for me: the gloomy British weatherman sticking a squadron of cut-out clouds on the map, or the clowning American newscasters with their digests of disaster. In Lisbon, I am surrounded by people. When I first came to visit, there were four generations of two different families living in the house.

The father who made his prepared speech at the front door with an almost mayoral floridity on the day I arrived had a seigneurial, ceremonious manner, assisted by waistcoats, fob watches, and shoes which Olga the maid knelt at his feet to shine before he left the house after lunch to meet old friends in a café for a session of whispered slander against the decrepit regime. He had been a mathematician, and was commemorated in action by an oil painting in the sitting room, poised with a digit of chalk before some abstruse equation on a blackboard and smiling sympathetically at our puzzlement: the wise paterfamilias.

Now, retired, he busied himself with collecting stamps and coins and piecing together the history of the country from them. The stamps led him only a certain way back; the coins, some of them hoarily ancient despite their gold sheen, took him the rest of the distance. He didn't trust bank vaults, and in any case liked to handle the coins and polish them, so they were stashed round the house in false drawers, under floorboards or behind loose panels. The filing system was clandestine, and when he died suddenly a few years ago it died with him. The treasure remains buried in the house, but no one searches for it: its presence there is an almost pharaonic provision for the after-life, a hostage left by him when he was carried away in a suit with a waistcoat and a pair of shining shoes but no fob watch.

The further the monarchical coins receded into the past, the more they roused him to shaming comparisons with the present. The Portuguese are obsessed and tormented by their history, and by that dream of universality rigged up in the pavilions for that imperial exhibition at the bottom of the hill. The fascists with their doomed colonial wars kept the dream alive beyond its time, sending out armies to shoot at reality. But their stubbornness and their bewilderment expressed the national quandary. The Portuguese navigators discovered a world, and thereby discovered Portugal's physical insignificance within it. For a while during the nineteenth century, Portugal itself was governed from Brazil. While cherishing the illusion of empire, the country had dwindled to a colony of richer northern Europe. All it had to sell was its sun. History seemed to rebuke it, like a stern elder whose hopes had been disappointed.

Jorge's father was fond of quoting Byron on the subject. He would often promenade on the balcony, looking sadly at the garden, the dazzling river, the silhouette of mountains carved and crenellated into the shape of a Moorish palace at Sintra. Byron had sent Childe Harold there in 1809, and allowed him to be sententious about the gap between pristine landscape and political disgrace:

> Poor, paltry slaves! Yet born 'midst noblest scenes –
> Why, Nature, waste thy wonders on such men?

Jorge's father paraphrased the Childe, never taking offence at his presumption. 'Nature was prodigal to these savages,' he would say, and shake his head at the unmerited bounty of the scene. Yet though he accepted the self-important Harold's judgement, he couldn't help delighting in the garden with the gurgling nightingale and the river and the purple ridges of Sintra. The mixture of shy satisfaction and vague guilt, of blithe sunlight and disinterested depression, was a very Portuguese mood. Having come from a lucky country, which dealt with its own brief history by conveniently forgetting it, I found this melancholy hard to understand.

While he frowned at the brightness on the balcony, indoors Jorge's mother practised the domestic arts, positioning flowers in vases, consulting the index of cookery books in quest of dishes I had not sampled yet, teaching Olga and the housekeeper Rosalina – who both had thick, un-nimble fingers – how to sew. She was fair-haired and blue-eyed, the remote legatee of a visit from the seafaring Celts centuries ago; the maid and the housekeeper, dark-haired with wary, deep-set eyes, derived their features from the

Moorish invaders. Their sewing-circle in the evening looked like a little painted allegory of the technically canny north trying to enlighten the swarthy, clumsy south, which was forever dropping stitches.

A chair was provided in the corner of every room for Jorge's grandmother, a Biblical matriarch called Nazaré who nodded me into the number of her progeny. Stolid and grumpy, she occupied one or another of the chairs with official intentness, as if presiding over a meeting or supervising a life which others now were living in obedience to her instructions. On summer afternoons she transferred to a seat outside the front door. The garden would have been cooler, but she chose the front door because she felt an obligation to keep an eye on the street. She reported at dinner on the loiterings of local maids with policemen; on the identities of dogs which squatted outside the gate and – knowing her well – grimaced at her imprecations while they strained to emit a steamy sausage; on the cheekiness of the boys who cycled past blowing cadences on pan pipes which announced them as knife- and scissor-sharpeners or cat- and rabbit-castrators or sellers of birch brooms. In winter, if the light was good, she stitched woollen rugs on which lambs gambolled, birds preened and cows vegetated: the scenery of everyone's childhood, remembered by her on our behalf whether we experienced it or not.

She gruffly, balefully enjoyed ill health, which she looked upon as one of the prerogatives of age. At meals, she waved the serving dish away, citing her delicate stomach, as if affronted by the insensitivity of the offer. Then she would steal half a helping from someone else's plate, and look aggrieved by the neglect which had driven her to it.

She had a weakness for the chocolates I brought from England, despite the gastric damage they did her. Usually they were kept out of sight. Nearing ninety, she sometimes couldn't think what name to put to the particular thing she craved. If I came into whichever room she was invigilating and there was no one else around to countermand the order, she'd often ask me to bring her one of these obscure, forbidden objects which – resorting in confusion to a metaphor – she called 'black fingers'. For a while I could pretend not to understand; eventually she learned to stare me down into complicity, and when I handed over the chocolate she would suck it

68

with such carnivorous relish that it seemed to have become the black, meaty extremity she imagined. There would always be an emergency in the bathroom a while later.

When raiding the plates of others, she most often burgled that of Jorge's elder brother, who had meningitis in childhood and since then had suffered through a long sequence of physical distortions and mental dislocations, triggered inside him as the years passed like a set of noiseless, cataclysmic explosions. His spine bent in a curve which would have been elegant and elastic if only it had been voluntary; his frame quaked and contracted like a spasmodic engine, so his hands could never rest but were always being forced to fiddle, clutch or tear; the body worked overtime while doing nothing, so the flesh wasted from him. Yet he remained indomitably jolly, and even tolerated the robberies from his plate (which were anyway soon made good by a second helping).

He adapted to each unfolding stage of the illness, as it set him new functional problems to solve every year or so, with a skill which reminded me how heroically improbable our evolution was – except that in his case the gradient was irresistibly downward, and he could only adjust to lowering inevitability. The parabola of the spine threw him off balance; he compensated by walking with one arm extended like a tiller. Since his head jutted out at an angle, it was at risk when he went through a door; he did so sideways, and when he swivelled into position his thin sapling of a body briefly disappeared. Eventually he could no longer support himself upright to get dressed; he devised a system for taking off and putting on his clothes while lying flat on his back on the bed.

As the rest of him wilted or kinked or tangled in useless knots, his eyes seemed to grow larger, and burned in mute reproach or, like wounds, exposed the trepidation and terror within as he waited to learn which outpost of the organism would betray him next. Still, I never heard him complain, or pity himself for having been allocated a life sentence inside this prison of twitching bones and self-willed, defiant reflexes. On the contrary, he took a grateful pleasure in everything. Highlight of the month was the arrival of the niggardly cheque for his disability pension. He couldn't spend the money, and anyway it would have bought very little, but it qualified as a salary, or perhaps an honorarium. It conferred status and recognition on him; at the very least, it imprinted his name on an envelope once a month.

His name, which was José Manuel, mattered to him. One of his pastimes consisted of writing it, on the pages of an unused diary for a used-up year. The exercise was meant to prove that he could still manage the manual feat, and that he still possessed the identity it attested to. Every time the effort became more difficult, and the existential proof harder to accomplish. The hand wouldn't stay in control long enough. The loops made by the pencil bounced out across the page like springs; he'd get one letter right and then find that his hand was repeating it, as if some diligent machine were printing its way to infinity; his aim faltering, the strokes would scratch and dip up and down the paper with the agitated rhythm of a cardiograph, trailing out in a terminal blip when he signed off.

It took hours and sometimes days, but he always managed to produce a fair copy, with both of his forenames and his three surnames. On my second visit he presented me with one of these, embellished at the bottom of the dog-eared page with the numbers 1 to 9 (jumbled up, admittedly) for grace notes. I have the paper in my wallet: I understood the value of the bequest.

Rosalina had a supplementary brood of her own. She was bringing up a grandson, sent to school nearby to save him from the slums. It was he who told me about the worlds which began just past the lighthouse in the river. Her whiskered ancient mother came to stay, and stumbled – she had cataracts – around the kitchen propped on an apple bough which one of her sons had chopped down for her as a cane, crankily muttering *Ai Jesus* or *Ai meu Deus* as she went: whether she was shaking her fist at these gents or appealing for their intercession I couldn't be sure. Jorge's grandmother declined to make common cause with her. Apart from the social niceties, they couldn't even be considered contemporaries: Jorge's grandmother lived in the nineteenth century, Rosalina's mother in the twelfth.

In the summer there were courtesy calls from Rosalina's cousin, who had made good as a stevedore in New Jersey. He swaggered about with a reeking cigar, his emblem of emigrant affluence: visiting another relative in a shanty-town, he had stubbed out one of these on a cardboard wall and scorched a hole in it. Her sister trudged down from the mountains in the autumn with extracts from a pig slaughtered on her farm and bottles of fizzy crimson wine, still fermenting in chemical dyspepsia.

After dinner Jorge's mother instructed the maid and the house-keeper in the intricacies of crochet. All three bent over their hooked needles under a lamp. Rosalina did some violence to a thumb protectively hardened by a childhood of labour in the fields. Olga sat on an infantile chair whose cane bottom reached only a few inches above the floor. It was, I was told, the chair that grand-mother Nazaré had to carry with her every day to the village school when she was a child in the 1890s. (I assume the school provided desks.) Nazaré herself played cards at the dining table. Crapeau was her favourite game, and she prided herself on never having lost: she had a fiendishly accurate recall of every card dealt to an opponent. Balked of victims, she would sometimes have to content herself with the dull QED of patience. She played it impatiently, annoyed that there was no chance to outsmart the cards. Jorge's father attended to his collections, either easing stamps into albums with a pair of tweezers or varnishing his coins, some of them impressed on gold worn as thin as foil. José Manuel played virtuoso doodles on the harmonica next door, or listened to his *fado* records. As the rancid voices chanted their muezzins of despair, he chuckled in amusement. Families, I perceived, could be happy – with the proviso, of course, that they were someone else's.

Like the views organised in my windows, this one left out a certain amount. The grandmother fell ill, and on my later visits she would occasionally roam the corridors in her night-dress, quietly moaning in dismay. She wandered into my bedroom once, and stood over me like a flannelled spectre. I think she demanded a black finger. The parents were tormented all their lives by their elder son's illness, which they couldn't help suspecting was a judgement on them; they loved him inordinately to atone for what they saw as their fault. His dozy good humour, I found, owed everything to a diet of Valium.

Even Olga, daintily plying her needle and fond of asserting that she would have become a nun if she hadn't diverged into domestic service, went to the bad. Already there was a war of nerves with Rosalina, on whose morals and personal hygiene she cast doubts. One night we were woken by her screams of virginal outrage. A man, she claimed, had been trying to climb into her room. All the windows were promptly fitted with bars; but she turned out to be the one with the habit of climbing in, after having climbed out, and the bars were an impediment to her. She enjoyed a clandestine love-life with a succession of local tradesmen under the pine trees at the bottom of the garden. After the revolution in 1974, she exchanged her religion for communism, in which the suburb's radicalised butcher was her mentor. She withdrew her labour while still living on the premises, and threatened legal redress when sacked. She is living in a shanty now, her establishment founded – according to informants in Rosalina's family – on pilferings from the house. The crochet lessons were all in vain.

She is nevertheless remembered in the house with a nickname, and a nightly extermination drive during the summer. Olga has become osga, which is the name of the gecko, a white lizard which infests the creepers around the front door. It is a fabled pest: it will invade the house through open windows; if it attaches itself to your flesh, it has to be burned off. So at night in July and August there are osga hunts, using brooms wrapped in wet cloth. Once spotted, they are thwacked from the wall. As they drop, they cast off their tails, which continue writhing for hours. Rosalina takes a post-dated pleasure in thumping the white heads, and watching the tiny dinosaur jaws open and shut in a silent shriek. Olga comes back to life in order to be killed: we have our sessions of sacrificial magic in the driveway before going to bed.

One by one, the members of the group split off from it. First Nazaré, having routed all comers or lost patience with the slow-witted cards, laboured up the stairs to bed. Rosalina followed, to help her undress. When Jorge's mother packed away the kit of needles and lacey thread, Olga trooped docilely to her own room (and out of its window, in the era before the frustrating grille). Jorge's father, having made the coins glow like oiled flesh, took them off to their burial place up a chimney or behind a tile or under a rug.

José Manuel's preparations for departure were the most elaborate and punctilious, because he had a baggage-train of possessions which he carried back and forth between floors every morning and evening. This luggage was his portable world, his personal history, arranged in a makeshift parade of containers – a battered brief-case, a small wicker picnic-hamper, a nautical shoulder bag donated by the stevedore from New Jersey, and a more informal series of plastic hold-alls from foreign shops. You could imagine a battalion of pages unloading them all from a limousine outside a grand hotel.

The bags and cases contained his archive, and indexed his memories: children's picture-books from four decades ago; a ring with keys which corresponded to no locks; the mouth-organ; the diary for writing his name in; a watch which had retired from telling time; a prudishly antique and prickly swimming-costume of woolly fabric with a belt attached to it which he had worn to the beach and now took trustingly out to the garden on summer afternoons, wrapped in a towel with a pair of winged 1960s sunglasses someone else had become embarrassed by. The filing system had a dumbfounding recessive logic. Inside a lacquered box was a leather purse with a broken latch, holding non-exchangeable coins brought back from countries he would never see; inside that he had put a miniature handbag made of gilt filigree which was one of the favours interred in the dough of a Christmas cake. It was only because this handbag didn't open and was too tiny to hold anything that the diminishing perspective stopped there.

When the luggage was at its most expansive, Rosalina and Olga helped to ferry it upstairs in stages. Olga slyly protested by periodically dropping some of the bags and strewing the prized worthless knick-knacks over the floor. In one of those unspontaneous accidents, she smashed a plaster dwarf, bought at the Lisbon opening of Walt Disney's *Snow White*; her grief was a picture. After an incident like this, José Manuel would be convinced of the need for simplification, repacking, de-acquisitioning.

Upstairs, the equipment was sorted out for the night, ranged around his bed in concentric circles which were degrees of sentimental value. The things he was fondest of shared his pillow: a wallet with family snapshots and some English pound notes which were no longer legal tender; the diary, in case he should need to remind himself of his identity. On a table and chair beside the bed were the semi-precious items: the nursery books, the beach gear. On the floor he left the rest, which had to be transported between rooms but didn't merit unpacking. With his world arranged for inspection, his past all present and correct, he could go to sleep. When he awoke, there would be another day exactly repeating the previous one – unless his body chose to make it different, and therefore worse.

Those first evenings are almost two decades distant. Now when I think about them, see the figures getting up to quit the warm halo of the lamp-light, hear their footsteps dispersing through the house – the grandmother heavily huffing and puffing; the mother following with a light, delicate, graceful dancer's walk; the father bustling in a darkened room somewhere, accompanied by the odd mysterious creak of a prised panel; the brother with his ill-distributed weight treading lumpily on one foot and banging the wall with the bags he held in his other, outstretched, balancing hand – they seem to be trooping in a slow procession upstairs to die. I am left below with a vacant aura of light; instead of presences, I have only descriptions.

Upstairs, another family loved and suffered in a corner cabinet. The grandmother's bedroom had a gilded cupboard in a niche, curtained off from view. Its doors parted on a hierarchical heaven of shelves, with bleeding Christs, agonised maternal Marys clasping their hearts in their hands, putti who must spend their time in paradise gorging on marshmallows, and (on a post-card obsequiously supplied by Olga) a shrivelled, browning cadaver in a wedding-dress, venerated by some northern villagers because its flesh had dried but not decayed. A candle with a low-voltage electric filament glared in perpetuity. A tin box for pills manufactured in Wiesbaden doubled as a reliquary: it held a chip of yellow bone, the fragment perhaps of some saint's toothpick-like tibia. Santa Luzia, venerated by the village which adopted her as the protector of sight, gripped a plate of rolling eyes. One of the Marys wore her baroque crown at a rakish angle. Trying to straighten it, I found it was fastened by a nail driven directly into her skull – as was the pentecostal dove with stretched wings on a nimbus of flame which she wore behind it, like a Spanish matron's mantilla. Among the beatified company was a secular stray: a porcelain schoolboy in a top-hat, dressed in knickerbockers with a satchel over his shoulder. But no, he was a further manifestation of baby Jesus (not to be mistaken for the three adult Christs with their abdominal wounds), dressed up as little Lord Fauntleroy by his adherents in one more pious village.

A prie-dieu stood ready before the cupboard of icons, its kneeling cushion worn threadbare – by moths, I deduced, not prayers. The doors of the oratory stayed mostly closed, the curtain drawn. Still, this was a home, and these were the bruised, cherished gods of its hearth.

At Christmas, boxes of figurines separately wrapped in twists of paper were brought out from a trunk, and we assembled a crib beside the fireplace. Around the straw-roofed manger which sheltered the original nuclear family, this midget population was arranged in clusters.

It had accumulated for decades, and was increased by one or two new characters each December. Biblical camel-drivers and goatherds consorted with Portuguese artisans: a shoemaker whose pants were patched with leather, a boy from Sintra with punnets of strawberries, a man from the northern mountains wearing a coat of straw. A stone stream ran – or pretended to run – through hillocks of green crêpe paper; a washerwoman scrubbed her sheets beside the immobile, concrete-coloured water. The more devout cattle genuflected in adoration. Others got on with their grazing. Boys shooed a flock of flustered ducks, and rounded up silly sheep. Pigs figured prominently at the profaner outer limits of the scene. A peasant lad took one for a walk with a leash attached to a rear trotter; another boy had climbed aboard his pig for a squeaky ride. Two gloating adults had up-ended their animal and were sawing open its belly. Its blood congealed as quickly as the grey, pebbly stream in the field of paper. Here and there in the throng of farmhands, fishermen and pumpkin-sellers stood the odd information-gathering angel.

Just off the crinkly floor, the magi bumped along on their camels. Each day they were nudged forward an inch or so, down the green slopes and through the mob, until they arrived at the elected barn on Twelfth Night. When that happened, the whole heterogeneous, like-minded community broke up. Next day its members were swaddled in paper and interred once more in the trunk.

Reconstructing this small feudal world, where the spheres moved in orchestral unison and every figurine knew its place, took the best part of a dark afternoon on Christmas Eve. I was still too full of adolescent rectitude to want anything to do with the triangular group beneath the rustic roof. But I finickily positioned the livestock in the middle distance, and made myself responsible for the half-believers, the resident aliens, the estranged skulkers on the edge of the crowd, who doubted their desire or perhaps their fitness for inclusion: the lookers-on.

4

The Worlds

M Y STREET IN LONDON HAS A SHORT LIFE: ONE BLOCK only. There is no reason to notice it; no one in a car can ever find it. Workmen with appointments to repair the roof or unclog the drains park, frustrated, a hundred yards away and demand on their mobile phones, 'Where *are* you?' At one end, traffic coasts down a slope, then creeps, throbbing, along the Marylebone Road: this passes the exit from my street, but there is no way in. The area has no name for itself. The station, near me, is Marylebone, though its High Street is half a mile away. I seem to remember buying and selling something in Marylebone – perhaps the dishonoured station, with its ceremonious booking hall where the Irish winos cluster – on the Monopoly board during my childhood in Tasmania. Even so, that has not made me proprietorial about it. I have never been quite sure how to pronounce the word: there is a tricky elision somewhere in the middle which I am afraid of. It hardly matters, because the name connotes nothing to me.

Four main roads box the precinct in, each with its own incompatible character. Marylebone Road processes traffic to and from the west, except when it is blocked from time to time by ecstatic androgynes with purple mascara and coolie pigtails awaiting Boy George's arrival at my local court for a drug hearing, or (further along) by Michael Jackson lookalikes watching Michael Jackson arrive to look at Madame Tussaud's likeness of him; down Baker Street, impostors sweating in tweedy capes and buttoned beagling caps (but without the meditative pipe) usher American tourists into the Sherlock Holmes Hotel; along Oxford Street, Selfridges depart-mentalises our desires and promises to satisfy them all, while a fanatically abstemious old man with a sandwich board patrols the pavement outside counselling LESS PROTEIN LESS PASSION and distributes copies of a pamphlet which tells you how to overcome the carnivore's unwholesome lusts; up Edgware Road, the Arab wives with their black-beaked masks and veils made of swarming wasps potter wearily, and African diplomatic personnel shop for safari suits. Inside this polyglot, polymorphous square, my block is resolutely characterless, performing in none of London's historical pageants or ethnic charades.

The street is nondescript – until you begin to describe it. For the rule of the home-made microcosm is this: a sampled square inch of earth is abundant, all-sufficient, no matter how paltry its contents; wherever you are is the centre of a world. Looked at carefully, my street turns out to comprise everything.

Its first oddity is that its two sides do not match. One is a plastered row of houses, whose front doors open onto the footpath (except mine, down stairs, through the tunnel, across the yard). The other is empty, unbuilt – a bomb site? These gaps obtrude everywhere in the centre of teeming London, where land is so precious and contested. Yet the city has not filled them in. Like the famously bad teeth of the English, they advertise the nation's doleful stoicism and its adoption of the depressingly long view: why bother to patch things up when in time they'll decay again? Meanwhile some rudimentary containers have been unloaded on the site and declared a school. The blitzed area, under tarmac and behind a wire fence, constitutes a playground.

At mid-morning, when the young are uncaged to hop, skip, jump, pull one another's hair and covet one another's sandwiches, the sound leapfrogs over the row of houses and dives into my yard: a twittering of manic starlings. There are souvenirs of childhood in the basement at the front of the house: a jetsam of sweet wrappings, crisp packets and juice cartons, dropped from the street above.

At first I was surprised by the patience with which I swept up these daily donations. Never once have I tried to administer a civics lesson to the juvenile litter-bugs. Then I remembered the reason for my forbearance. When I was a child I used to covet these wrappers, and hoard them when I had the chance (not often). They symbolised surfeit and luxury, but more than that they were beautiful in themselves. The foil which chocolate came in, for instance: it was the activity of hours to smooth out this veined, wrinkled silver paper, like beating gold. But no matter how long I spent on it and how many weights I crushed it under, the foil would never shed all its resistant creases. It seemed to have the textured, tactile intricacy of skin. Perhaps to get rid of those imperfections was to expunge identity, like burning off your finger-prints. My rubbing and ironing and desperate pulling strained the thin surface. More than once I felt that I was close to removing the last kinks when the paper, unable to tolerate any more punishment, ripped in half. Then there were tears. These are the tragedies of childhood: science knows no way of soldering together two torn scraps of foil. We do sometimes find the remnants of our ancient, infant selves in the gutter; the crumpled wind-blown discards from the street were gifts of a kind.

Diagonally across from the school, at the bottom end of the street in the cellar of a red-brick Victorian mansion block, a later age of man has its headquarters. From the street you can see down into the kitchen of a day-care centre for the elders of Westminster. On a sink there are bottles of Lucozade and HP sauce, boxes of tea bags and tins of biscuits; on a wall a poster which warns against hypothermia and a censorious placard asking 'Have you paid your quarterly sub?' The subscribers arrive each morning in a van like a cheery green ambulance. They can't cope with stairs, so a ramp has been lowered on a gentle gradient into the basement for them. Its slope is as gradual and remorseless as the body's decline. They totter down it inside their walking-frames or on the arm of their minders, and pass the day in drinking tea and reminiscing. At Christmas there are singalongs; a church opposite discreetly lays on occasional funerals.

I pass the halting procession down the ramp most mornings on my way to buy the newspaper, and am always startled by its mood of smiling anticipation, quieter than the shrill hilarity from the school playground but no less gleeful. Are the old so easily pleased, or is age a role which requires geniality and makes do with treats like those in wait in the cellar? Does their relief at no longer having to function – at being driven about in a clubbable van and shepherded along the street like a troop of obedient hand-holding schoolchildren – correspond to the joy of the young who have not been made to function yet? Though the sides of the street don't rhyme, the beginning and the end, juxtaposed across it, apparently do.

The basement advertises a Hearing Aid Clinic every month for those who are gradually reducing the volume of their lives. At the top of the street, the distresses of another organ are catered to. A dismal eye hospital, its own windows bleary with soot, squints onto Marylebone Road; the emergency entrance is round the corner in my street. It has few customers, but the odd patient is discharged from the side door, head a bulging onion of bandages. Again there is a false discordant rhyme, since the entry for casualties faces the front door of a pub on the other side of the street. The pavement here briefly mediterraneanises itself. Behind a hedge of wine casks and beer kegs an optimistic open-air café is arranged, with tables and chairs of white wrought iron. Luckily they are rain-proof; they are also prudently chained to the spot at closing time.

Despite its belief that my street is a boulevard, the pub is named after a castle which it pictures – shaggy and forbidding – on its sign. At night it does secretly castellate itself. Once the publican goes through the motions of ringing the bell and calling time, he chains up the outdoor chairs and tables, then locks the door and dims the lights with his coterie of regulars still inside. I can vaguely see them through the mottled glass on my way home to bed, roistering around the bar into the small hours. Like most other things in London – the inaccessible square I pass on my way to and from Marble Arch, for instance – the pub would rather be private than public. Those late-night sessions with their lowered chuckling voices and their conspiratorial orange glow are its boast of exclusiveness. How many years will I have to live in the street to qualify for inclusion?

By day the pub serves food to the office workers of the area. A blackboard outside advertises its menu, chalked in every morning by the same aproned barmaid who – after having listed the game pies and pork sausages and apple crumbles and spotted dicks on offer – pulls out the coloured crayons from a pocket in her apron and begins to decorate the sign. First she adds a frilly border like a pastry crust; capital letters grow fat outer layers as if they had been stuffed with the food they are naming, or they ignite as ruddily as radiators; the spotted dick gets freckled with extra spots. It's like watching a medieval illustrator sketching dragon-infested tendrils and herbaceous twiddles in the margin of a manuscript.

Then comes her final touch, squeezed as deliciously as a dollop of cream from a muslin confectionery funnel: she chalks the apostrophe into the headline word, which is LUNCHE'S or (in the afternoon) MEAL'S. That air-borne comma, gaily attributing possessiveness to something which can possess nothing, receives her most careful treatment. Its head is rounded like a quivery dew-drop, its tail refined into a tadpole's wiggling rear-end. When I see her at it, my pedantic soul lets out a shriek of silent distress. I've often thought of remonstrating with her, or of sneaking back when she has gone and rubbing out that otiose, exultant apostrophe. Of course I have never done so. On reflection, it may be the single truly vainglorious art-work in all the humdrum street's short length.

Or do I underestimate my inglorious block? One morning, traipsing out to the shops, I discovered that the street was about to arrive on the map.

Police blocked the bottom end, and grandly debarred the occasional van. A street-sweeper paused on his broom to speculate. Lessons had been cancelled in the school; the children were marshalled along the pavement towards the corner. A gaggle of women with handbags chattered. On the scrubbed steps of the mansion block, a jittery delegation waited: council dignitaries with emblems of office, pensioners in their burial suits. No photographers though, and no hysterical androgynes – less of a turn-out than Boy George could expect for his court appearances a block away. There was a false alarm when the driver of a car which the police waved away with their semaphore blew his horn and teased the crowd with a royal wave, hand pivoting back and forth as if suspended from a snapped wrist, the arm paralytically still. Some muffled tutting ensued on the kerb.

As the church clock began to strike eleven, it all started to happen; on the eleventh stroke, it was punctually over. A sleek black feline car slunk round the corner. The children chirped and squeaked, the ladies with the handbags waved with the whole of their other arms, the police stiffened, and on the steps a pair of elderly ankles perilously curtsied. From the car a hat like a posy alighted, bobbed up the steps, received the homage of those fragile ankles, and breezed away into the building. The hat was shorthand for the

Queen Mother, who had come and gone. Now how were we to occupy the rest of our lives?

She was visiting the cellar where her contemporaries drank tea and sang along. But she could hardly be expected to suffer the doddering indignity of the ramp, so she entered the building around the corner, by the front door. I expect a wall was knocked down to let her into the basement. At any rate, I hope she brought her own Earl Grey, and escaped the clay-coloured swill they brewed down there from their tea bags.

With the traffic halted and the world arrested on the stroke of eleven, it was an absurdly touching scene. What power a symbol has! This old lady, sister under the skin to the tea-drinkers she visited, had been singled out more or less at random to spend her life as an image, a personification not a person. She had versatilely signified most things in the course of her life – maternity, empire, embattled resistance during the Blitz (might she once have come to see our bomb site, to hearten my predecessors in the street?), dowagerish granniehood – and changed her meaning as the age or her own age directed. She never, at least in public, performed an act or registered an expression which was not a ritual, or uttered a phrase which had not been scripted for her; and this enabled her to confer significance on whatever she encountered. My ordinary, ungraced street, for instance.

Except that I realised afterwards she had not been in my street at all. Using the front stairs not the ramp at the side of the building, she had stepped to earth in the street round the corner, which goes by a different name. We did not rate a mention in the court circular.

The street is still waiting for its consecration. Who knows, perhaps someone living in it will one day commit an especially grisly murder, with heads boiling on the stove and blood bucketing down the drains? In the interim – knocking holes in my hope that the street might mean something, and be part of an eternal city – they are demolishing an office building at the top end.

On Friday its six floors did business as usual; over the weekend the furniture was carted off; on Monday morning the wreckers arrived, set up their crane and began to swing a ball which banged its blunt head remorselessly against the brick outer walls. Soon a staircase was exposed, reeling at a woozy angle into the empty air to vomit clods of masonry and shards of glass. As the siege continued, with the window panes which were still in place veined like leaves with splintering cracks, punctured gullets of pipe stuck out, and streamers of twisted metal. From the roof a red scarf seemed to dangle, flapping. It was a jagged, throttled drainpipe, not soft fabric but a knife-edge of rusty metal. The floors capsized into blobs of amoeboid cement held together by bent steel cables: a dying parody of molecular structure. The basement gave off the chill clammy graveyard stench of plaster pulverised, dust to dust.

The sight of temporariness and the smell of mortality dismayed me so much that I began taking detours round the block to avoid the operation. The street, it suggested, was only a husk. A few hours' butting from the dense round bullet-headed missile would undo it. Reminders like this are best not remembered. Soon there will be a brash new cost-effective box on the corner of Marylebone Road, and I will have forgotten that things were ever any different.

In Oxford there is no need to make a microcosm. It is ready-made for me in the form of Christ Church, the largest college in the university and the most imposing, a city or a little England in itself. A macrocosm, I ought to call it.

It is a world I am still, after fifteen years, startled to find myself in. As a student at New College (which according to the local double-speak is one of the oldest), I scarcely ever ventured across the High Street and into Christ Church. I remember just one sortie, to hear W. H. Auden preach in the college chapel. This doubles, with typical swank, as Oxford's cathedral. Auden, I recall, struggled to make his false teeth enunciate some moral about the money-lenders in the temple, and declaimed a poem using American vowels. I made haste home, crossing the High Street as if gratefully returning to the wrong side of the tracks. Christ Church was the rumoured headquarters, in those days, of public-school rowdyism, where outsiders were rumoured to suffer dunkings in the fountain.

The quadrangle, like a New York elevator, seemed to expect grand gestures on entry. When I first lived in it, the lordliest toffs and 'vicecounts' as the scouts called them affected metal cleats on the toes of their shoes so they could clack across the flagstones (having already banged shut the wooden gate under the bell-tower and made the foundations shudder) when they came back late at night from some aristocratic riot. Later still, there would be rugger grunts of 'Uggy, uggy, uggy' converging from the four corners, or tree-top ululations from a titled Tarzan; then the inevitable splash as someone was hurled into the pool. Most weekends would feature a *Kristallnacht* of smashed, tinkling beer glasses. But the secretest, most masonic revels were reserved for the quad around the corner, which had the year's rowing score chalked on its sandy stone walls. Here, if Christ Church emerged as head of the river after the week of races in the spring, the victors (fresh from food-fights with blob-shaped missiles of chocolate mousse in the hall) burned their boats like hallooing Vikings; more recently another ancient custom was invented, and a rain dance followed some annual club dinner, with whooping braves stamping naked through the mud. At New College we were less aboriginal, and stumbled demurely along the top of the medieval city wall when drunk, generally slipping off into the shrubbery.

Christ Church had its own rules and rites. The most solemn of these was its declaration every evening of self-enclosure. At five past nine, the bell in the tower above me begins to clang out a hundred strokes: its warning to the hundred original members that the gate was about to be bolted for the night, and that they should leave their breviaries or their assignations on top of haystacks and hurry back. The gate of course no longer closes at this hour, but the hundred dull, leaden gongs still have to be sounded. During my first few weeks underneath the tower, I thought the bell would drive me mad. It was like having your head pummelled exactly a hundred times by a giant iron boxing glove. Now I no longer hear it, even if I make myself listen out for it. The trump of doom could be rung up there and I would be no wiser. When the Queen dies, it will toll for an hour without respite. Will I notice that, I wonder?

So self-sufficient is Christ Church, with all its fortified gates slammed shut and its hundred old members accounted for, that it even, like the globe, has its own time-zones. There is a difference of five minutes between one side of the quadrangle and the other. Tom time is deemed to be five minutes ahead of cathedral time, which is why the nocturnal summons is belted out at 9.05 and why Christ Church says its Latin grace and tucks into its dinner five minutes later than all other Oxford colleges, at 7.20. The proviso is a quirky

84

result of the meridians into which the globe is ruled. The observatory at Greenwich declares itself the world's starting-point: it is situated at O. But Christ Church is not, strictly speaking, on that meridian. Academics like hair-splitting distinctions, and therefore calculate that Christ Church lies five minutes to the west (just as New York lies five longitudinal hours from London). So when we ring the bell and say grace, we take care to be out of step with everyone else. What better evidence could there be of England's anachronistic quaintness?

Once Christ Church has begun – down a hill from four-faced Carfax which is the centre of Oxford, allowing room for only four other squeezed colleges on its south side of the High Street – it goes on for as long as there is land to occupy: outside the walls is its meadow, with a population of long-horn steers, foxes and prolific rabbits, and that is only curtailed by a meeting of two rivers. One is the Thames (which in order to run through Oxford calls itself the Thamesis and is abbreviated to Isis, suggesting the Nile and cults of fertility), the other its tributary the Cherwell (known as the Char).

If Christ Church time has its anachronisms, like the invisible seam down the middle of the quad or the sundial on a wall which in the absence of sun declares this a timeless zone, Christ Church space bewilders the compass. The meadow distends on one side until it almost touches the village of Iffley, in the eastern suburbs. It is visible through the trees, across the rivulet of the Char. But the stream cannot be crossed. A barge lies beached on the other side, attached to a pulley which should haul it over to you. Tug as you might, it won't move. You can only go west by following the meadow back to where it begins and tramping the long way down the road.

Within Christ Church there are folds of puckered space which, levered open, disclose small pockets of forgotten time, like Lewis Carroll's rabbit-holes digging into the fourth dimension. A door in the quadrangle opposite my window hides a sunken garden beside the cathedral; around a corner it straggles into a field of uncut grass and an overgrown orchard. In the meadow, a barn built for farm machinery is a jumbled grave of donnish knick-knacks: sofas where mice nest, mildewed screens, overbearing armies of oak chairs with aquiline claws for feet and cardinals' hats carved in lumpy relief on the head-rests; my stuffed, balding owl will one day feel at home here.

Inside the walls, all times concur, all ages overlap. It's a world compressed, like the old Hollywood backlots where a row of chocolatey New York brownstones ran into a thatched English village, and a dusty Western town with its makeshift shingles backed up against the convivial pavements of the Quartier Latin. You can walk through the centuries, if you know the route. Christ Church manages to fit in Gothic gloom, baroque floridity, copy-book neoclassicism, and some modern brutishness in concrete. The quadrangle where the boats are torched and the savages do their rain dance is a homage to senatorial Rome; the wall of buildings which shuts out the meadow is Ruskin's vision of Venice, its arched balconies (used as open-air refrigerators for bottles of milk in winter) looking out on a lagoon of sodden grass, its raked, peaked roofs afloat above the fog which slithers up from the river. Renaissance cherubs disport themselves on a bastion, and pallid Victorian saints pine on a stained-glass window by Burne-Jones in the cathedral.

Once in America I opened a magazine on a photograph of the college library. The Augustan expanse of varnished wood, frilly stucco and polished bindings spread over two pages. I recognised the readers at the desks. But there, on the floor of this upper room, accessible only by way of a coiling stair with a guard of periwigged worthies, was the latest Fiat or Audi or BMW, having glided through the windows to halt inside the advertisement. It didn't seem unlikely, or even especially incongruous.

Christ Church is most itself when rearranged for a summer ball. These are famously expensive occasions, and those unable to afford tickets are said to swim sewers in wet-suits in order to gatecrash. Other stories tell of tunnels under the wall, like those which plucky POWs scratched away at in war films. Burly paratroopers are hired to swagger round the perimeter with sniffer dogs. The college becomes for an evening a paradise of giddy pleasures, regainable by anyone who can pay the price (or else ford the drains). Dodgem cars bump and butt each other in the quad, and girls shriek down slippery slides beneath the joyless sundial. A platform was built under my window one year for a pop band; the cathedral spire, usually lit by a dull mustardy flood-lamp, was atomised by a blizzard of lasers, as if invaders from space were besieging this staid English citadel. It all ends at dawn with a round-up of wrecked, tousled, glutted youth beside the fountain. There a photographer takes the picture which will be the only evidence that the night has happened, and by breakfast the lorries have shunted in to pack away the dented dodgems and merry-go-rounds and to knock down the marquee. For twelve hours, the academic factory is a fun-fair, which is how everyone wants to remember it.

Socially too, the place is a compact cosmos. If I am wearing a tie and am looking more than usually care-worn, a man at the gate in a black bowler hat will probably – well, will perhaps – take it off when I come from the street. I am allowed to walk on the grass in the quadrangle, from which tourists are shooed away by the same bowler-hatted watch-dogs. There is a strict league of seniority, which sometimes now I am aghast to find myself at the top of: if that happens at dinner, I have to mutter a Latin grace which I can never get right.

Around the dining hall, our tribal ancestors look down from their frames or pedestals : prime ministers, viceroys, rubicund clerics, one sage (Locke) and one poet (Auden of course, with a hangdog expression which beautifully contradicts the severity or smugness of everyone else). Privilege is enforced gastronomically. On our raised table, we wade through lashings of artery-obstructing cream; down below, the students search for meat in their stew – but they always seem to be enjoying themselves more. Once, to upstage us, they invited Princess Margaret to dinner. She came, and caused a minor stir by producing her cigarette-holder and lighting up between courses. At Oxford dinners, no one smokes until after the loyal toast to her sister (who was present, from the neck up, on a ledge above our table: I wish I could say that the Princess blew dainty smoke rings in that direction).

The whole edifice of reverence and rank is sustained, supposedly, by cheery servility below. A wall plaque in the cloister cites an exemplar :

In memory of *William Pound*,
many years one of the Porters of this College,
Who, by an exemplary Life and Behaviour,
and an honest attention

to the Duties of his Station,
deferved and obtained
the approbation and efteem
of the whole Society.
1787

With its sonorous line-ends and its stanzaic lay-out, the tablet is almost a poem; I especially love the patrician lisp of those effs. Beside it there is an honorary mention for a verger and library clerk who died in 1940 aged ninety-eight, having served the college for seventy of his years.

The college's employees nowadays treat their employers with a deference which only just conceals their bemusement at us. The carpenter Cyril, a hearty soul who resembled Father Christmas, once arrived at my door to measure me for some bookshelves and slowly took in my play-pen of musty birds, Zen stones and James Dean pin-ups. 'My word, sir, you've got a few oddments here,' he said. And added, with a private smirk, 'If you don't mind me saying so'. He collected stamps, and when he got to know me better browbeat me for Australian specimens. I never had many, because my parents used air-letters; he did not believe the excuse, and clearly thought I had been abandoned. He died unfussily on the job one day, killed by a cancer he had never bothered to see a doctor about.

The plumber Percy, now retired, did a sly impersonation of an Oxfordshire yokel, with the requisite cud-chewing drawl. He had no teeth, and sucked his gums as if they were sculpted from toffee. He always wore one of those woolly caps which murderers and sex offenders in Identikit portraits seem to favour, and carried with him everywhere a piece of paper on which was scrawled his all-purpose alibi. I would chase him across the quad to plead for replacement of my immersion heater, or for a house call to inspect a regurgitating toilet, only to have the paper waved at me. 'I've got a crisis on in the Deanery, sir,' he would say; 'I'll be round to you just as soon as I can.' He lived in a cellar beside the back gate of the college, but there was no tracking him into this burrow. A piece of paper akin to the one he brandished as his work-sheet was tacked on the door, and like a mastiff growled PRIVATE.

He did an electrical favour for me once, rewiring an old lamp I was fond of. I wanted to thank him somehow, and tried to find out what he would like. A bottle? He didn't drink. A box of chocolates? He never touched them. A book? I asked in desperation. He got his from the library, he said, and hadn't ever read one he wanted to own. Then *what* would he accept? 'I can't help you sir, I'm sorry,' he said, with much degustation of gums. 'I don't have no pleasures.' One of his workmates, listening in, told me later that Percy took such pride in being miserable that he had kept his black and white television set, and refused to recognise the existence of colour.

His successor, Dave, extends the ripe royal line of eccentricity. He wears a piratical earring, has a hillbilly's thicket of beard reaching over the bib of his overalls, keeps bloodhounds in a corral off the meadow and is rearing cattle from two progenitors he has named Archimedes and Alice. He intends to proceed through the entire alphabet, and when Alice bore Archimedes their first calf he named her Buttercup. He apologised to me with a grin for such an unscholarly choice, 'but you can't have a herd,' as he put it, 'without a cow called Buttercup. Now can you?' I had to agree.

The little old lady who dishes out our lunch is just as much of a traditionalist. One day as I extended my plate to her, she removed the lid of the serving dish and found she had been sent up a tray of pasta. She recoiled, refused to believe that it wasn't a mistake, disappeared behind a serving door to check, then returned to announce with a grimace that this indeed was it. She was un-impressed by my confession that I liked the stuff. 'I wouldn't touch it myself,' she said, pursing her lips as she ladled some out to me. 'If you ask me, it's like biting into rubber. Give me the good old English ways. Some of the dons would turn in their graves if they knew what we were dishing up now.' I crept to the table with my foreign helping, shamed by the voice of history.

Below stairs, Christ Church has its crypts and catacombs: a brick vault, smelling of damp and sticky with cobwebs, to house the wine; in the library's basement a box marked SKELETON which contains exactly that.

Other worlds are tucked in upstairs, under the eaves. For my first few months in the place, I was mystified by nocturnal rustlings and rumblings above my ceiling. So far as I knew, I was on the top floor; the staircase stopped at my front door. Rats? Bats? But neither of these creatures listened to disco music, which also throbbed remorselessly up there. One night, when the gremlins were still scampering and thumping at two o'clock, I set out to investigate. From the staircase next to mine, climbing beside the bell-tower, you could reach an extra floor which had been inserted recently beneath the roof: a corridor, like stuffy steerage on a migrant ship, ran the length of the quad above my rooms. Here was where the disco-dancing weevils lived. Every year there would be one in particular who tormented me: an American who exercised at midnight, jogging on the spot for an hour or so directly above my bed; further along, a drummer who rehearsed on a kit of resonant skins and excruciating brass in his room; another sallow youth who lived in a den of sickly, suspicious fumes and heavy metal. At three in the morning I toiled up to remonstrate with this one. He didn't answer my knock on the door, or even my banging. But the door was open. I pushed it: he was in the midst of a musical and narcotic paroxysm, mouthing the words to a Twisted Sister song. His face slowly fell, from ecstasy to nausea more or less, when he saw me.

'Who the fuck are you?' he said.

I have never been very good at pulling rank. 'I'm a tutor here,' I murmured, 'actually.' It must have sounded as if I had dropped in at three in the morning, with clothes thrown on over my pyjamas, to critique his essays.

'Well, you don't fucking tutor me,' he replied, and pushed me out into the corridor. They rusticated him for a fortnight. Slight bodily harm to a so-called senior member doesn't really count as damaging college property. Soon afterwards, the college began to admit women, and all has been sweetness and quiet ever since.

Along this corridor, freshly mopped with disinfectant and – since there are no windows – buzzing in the glare of neon tubes, the linoleum perspective continues until another staircase lets you down into the north-west corner of the quad. Where the linoleum runs out, one of Christ Church's small, alternative, imaginary worlds used to be tucked away. Lewis Carroll, when a half-hearted cleric and mathematics tutor in the college, had his spooky sanctum here, with the use of two turrets, a cubby-hole where he developed his photographs of sulky nymphets and fuddy-duddy dons, and (eventually) a studio on the roof which he called the glass-house, for the same purpose.

Above me, once, was the magician's hidey-hole. In a space now stripped and reconstructed, Carroll used to stare into a fireplace tiled with ogres, dodos, gryphons and eaglets, make his battery of music-boxes play their tunes backwards like occult reversals of the Lord's Prayer, and activate his automata: Bob the Bat, for example, with a body of wire, wings of gauze and a heart of twisted elastic, would circle the room in a frenzy for thirty seconds, and on one occasion escaped through the window to land in a bowl of salad a scout was carrying, which crashed to the ground with the fright he got. I think of Bob with a shiver whenever in the summer one of those fuzzy insects blunders in through a window and does a few demoniac circuits of my bedroom.

But the glass-house on the roof, between loquacious Tom and the flag-pole, is what intrigues me most: an alchemical cabin where he made images like revenants materialise on a plate coated with egg whites. Black and white were the opposing fates of photography, reversible (like the music-boxes playing backwards) on the negative. They were also the uniforms of the two worlds Carroll inhabited. His Alice, the Dean's daughter, remembered that he always wore clergyman's black in Oxford, but whenever he took her on picnic expeditions down the river in the direction of wonderland he changed to white flannels and replaced his shiny top-hat with a white straw boater. She regretted that he lived too early to have worn tennis shoes, and had to keep his institutional black boots when changing for the trip into fantasy.

After Lewis Carroll, the next fantastication of Christ Church was by Evelyn Waugh. In *Brideshead Revisited* the college constitutes a lost Eden, and Oxford – no longer Carroll's dual creation of black and white – is 'a city of aquatint'. The diluted resin of the aquatint was swamped, when they made the television film of the novel, in gold. I remember the October night when they showed the first episode. On the screen, the stone flanks of the college seemed to be sealed in treacle. I glanced out of my window to check on the original: the same scene was a murk of icy drizzle. Unlike my London street, Christ Church needs no consecrating. The problem is to keep the alluring myths at bay. We wouldn't let the cameras in, not wanting to perpetuate the notion that our undergraduates swished about ephebically with teddy bears under their arms; all the same, Anthony Andrews and Jeremy Irons sneaked through the gate and had their photograph taken with Aloysius, his pelt as golden as the Cotswold stone behind them, underneath my window.

For Auden too, Christ Church comprised a free-standing world, as autonomous as Manhattan. He spent his middle age coping with the aggravations of New York, then came home with the intention of dying in a cottage provided by his alma mater. If the American city meant anxious modernity, the English college symbolised a snuggling, forgiving past, a nursery of maternal comforts. After the angularity of New York, Christ Church – with its ogee cap and stolid towers and rose window and its pillars which fan across the ceiling outside the hall like swirling surf – was baroque, the style which (according to Auden) 'reveals, perhaps unintentionally, the essential "camp" of all worldly greatness'. It was therefore the aptest place for a great man of the world to decay. Who was Wolsey, after all? His palaces hadn't saved him from disgrace. And who did Queen Anne, histrionically shaking her fist above the gate, imagine herself to be? Baroque, with the cheating sweetness of all art, indulged their desire for pomp while hinting at its fatuity.

In the same spirit, Auden composed a brace of flattering couplets for a canon of the cathedral who had his eightieth birthday in 1957. All the college's warring cliques and hierarchical estates, 'the tribes who study and the sporting clan', raise voices in enthusiastic unison; the fish in Mercury's pond 'from well-fed tummies belch a birthday wish'. When Canon Jenkins is promoted to the sky, Auden imagines that heaven will be a continuation of Christ Church: scholastic discussion with Augustine and Dorigen fuelled by fixes of immortal snuff, while 'Baroquish Cherubim' keep up the anthems of praise. The poem is a marvel of honorific camp.

Auden longed to believe his own fond myth of the place, yet felt obliged also – since he knew about its baroque vanity – to prove it false. He spent a sad last year living out his mistake. There were no more evenings of talk and decanter-passing in the common room, and precious few seraphim to hand. Morose and disillusioned, he died in Vienna in 1973 on his way back to the cottage he had furnished with a formation of black leather chairs, some harsh interrogating desk lamps, and a layer of papers like volcanic ash. The dream of home was precious to him; reality would not co-operate. The error was to think that it might have done.

My own favourite myth about Christ Church, by contrast,

uproots and breezily transplants it. Michael Cimino manages the feat at the beginning of his Western, *Heaven's Gate*. The title cards, white on black, mount up like bereavement notices. Then the first image glimmers out of the dark: a winter dawn, with dull orange embers in the sky; a screen of bony, unresuscitated branches; through them, the vane on Tom Tower, as stiff as death. The camera droops like a tired, rheumy, elderly eye to look in through the opened gate. The ponderous door, swung back on its hinges, frames the quadrangle, where the dim flare from the sky now gathers. The long perspective is a telescope which penetrates the past, kindled into life again there in the brightening kiln of stone. But it is not a past to be yearningly revisited, like the submerged youthful Oxford of Evelyn Waugh's characters. On the contrary, it is ejecting someone; or he is fleeing from it in panic and guilt. A figure is running towards us (it turns out to be Kris Kristofferson, who is merely late for his graduation ceremony).

Then, as he sprints through the gate, out of that rude morning into the cold street where his feet begin to echo, a final title tells us where we are, and when:

HARVARD COLLEGE

CAMBRIDGE, MASSACHUSETTS

1870

In New York, I start with another problem of orientation. My apartment is on Bank Street. (The preposition denotes a difference: Londoners live *in* streets, New Yorkers *on* them. The London life is interior, while New Yorkers colonise the sidewalk with its rank garbage and its snoring bums as their stage, like Fred Astaire twinkling along 42nd Street in *The Band Wagon*. The true New Yorker is on the street, and is of it as well.) The building I live in is called The Left Bank. An awning says so, and the name is incorporated so we can make out cheques to it. But the left bank of what? Rivers surround Manhattan, rather than bifurcating it as in Paris; if the Hudson, just down the street, is taken to be our ersatz Seine, then the status of being on its radical far-left wing, over where the Maxwell House cup weeps its unstaunchable, ruby tear, belongs to New Jersey.

However, the bank after which the street is named is not a

riverside at all. It was a financial institution. When yellow fever raged in New York in 1822, the city moved its money from the Battery to a healthier climate far north. A lane down which cattle had plodded became Wall Street in exile when all the downtown banks established temporary quarters there. Bank Street today has a carpenter, a theatre, a supermarket, half a dozen restaurants which change nationality as gastronomic fashion directs, a plaque at one end remembering Willa Cather who lived here and a sagging, rotted pier at the other, but no bank. Still, this is Greenwich Village, a would-be Quartier Latin, where apartment buildings commemorate painters who are imagined – I suppose – to be bohemian French Impressionists: one near mine is called The Van Gogh. The Village is always on the left bank of everything and everywhere.

In London, I must make do with that glorious, gratuitous apostrophe in the word LUNCHE'S. The Village by contrast is indefatigably aesthetic. Downtown, money is made; uptown, it is spent. The economy of Wall Street begets the society of Fifth Avenue. The Village officially disdains both. Its business is art. At the end of my street, a rearing whitewashed block sums up its creed. This used to be the Bell Telephone laboratories, boxily utilitarian, thrown up between an elevated railway track which is overgrown with weeds and an elevated highway which was dismantled. Beside it a parking lot for trucks has been fenced off because the squelching, oily alleys between the vehicles were a catacomb of sexual adventure. When science moved out of the building, art moved in. The glum factory became Westbeth, where tenants had to qualify as 'serious artists' in the judgement of their fellow-tenants, and to possess, in 1969, an income *below* $12,700 a year. From the street, you can see into some of the ground-floor studios: sculptors torment substance into form with sand-blasters, to the sound of percussive rock. Actors sometimes declaim or primally scream in the courtyard.

Villagers who aren't making art are probably transforming themselves into art-works. The artist used to be a mortal man with the usual mental worries and physical afflictions, who overcame the annoyances of life by producing a thing of beauty. It existed outside experience, coolly imperturbable like a Grecian urn. Perhaps its immuneness to mortality, its selfish perfection, mocked him. Anyway, the Village has abolished the punishing division between limited, painful life and immaculate art; and as well, with a native democratic generosity, it has recognised that art shouldn't be confined to the artists. Here the self is the supreme fiction, and the body is everyone's home-grown thing of beauty.

The body can be acquired at the Village's gyms and tanning salons; the self is available from its hair-cutters and clothes shops. The image is no longer marble or crystal or fragile porcelain. It has been made flesh, and exhibits itself on Village streets in strategically torn T-shirts and fancifully distressed jeans. One of my Village friends, dissatisfied with the allowance nature had made him, built himself a new body. Jake began as a gangling skeleton; within two years he was an armoured vehicle, fuelled by protein shakes and raw beef. At first his head was something of an embarrassment, because it could not be pumped up in proportion to his neck and shoulders and chest and arms. It surmounted the ridges and pillars and buttresses of his trunk like a humble pimple. Perhaps, like a Greek statue, he might have preferred decapitation. He had been a bookish youth, and the shy, withdrawn face glanced down in awe and fear at the bronze tank he had engineered. But a few months later a new head was willed into being; angular, invulnerable, burnished, ready to emit the cry – a grunt terminating in a roar – with which he dramatised his straining under the weights. He now had a robotic walk, legs pushed apart and arms swinging a few inches from a body whose build-up of muscles had forbidden them to touch it.

It was a strange spectacle to one who, like me, regarded the body as at best a convenience (the thing the head is attached to, which keeps it off the ground), at worst an inconvenience (its untimely appetites; its incorrigible habit of getting dirty; yes, its tendency to sicken and die). 'But you don't understand,' Jake said. 'You think it's a sport, but it's not. This,' he added, flexing, 'is performance art.' He thought up a routine which matched his poses to a musical soundtrack. He would clench his fist, set his jaw, grit his teeth, and thrust whole mountain ranges of sinew into profile from under the skin; Strauss's Zarathustra spoke (or rather roared) from his stereo. Sculpture was another analogy he used: 'It's like being Michelangelo and the model – both at once.' Michelangelo chiselled into the stone to free those tense, writhing forms imprisoned in there. Jake, locked inside the Nautilus or bent like Samson under a pediment of iron, had worked from the inside out, adding not subtracting, transforming spongy flesh into a megalith. The thing he was proudest of was its uselessness. This bombastic organism was not made for fighting wars, like Rambo's. All its work was play. Like the Grecian urn, it signified nothing but itself.

Eventually he took it off to California. In New York it had to hibernate for half the year. 'Let's face it,' he said to me, 'here you really can't wear a ripped T-shirt in February.' He now trains Bel Air millionaires for a living, charging them a hundred dollars for an hour of physical and verbal abuse.

Back in the Village, the next stop for the processed body is the tanning salon. The gym turns hard labour into a leisure-time activity. Adding the tan requires inertia not exertion, but the rhetoric of vigour persists. As Cher sneers in a commercial for a health spa, sweating in enthralment to the Nautilus, 'if it was *easy* to get a good body, everyone would have one'. The shop with the ultra-violet machines on Greenwich Avenue used to advertise itself as 'New York's passive exercise center'. Passive exercise: a nice paradox, like the designed body it supplements. The athletes of immobility sit there all day, their heads inside boxes, their arms and hands glowing chemically blue. You might be spying through the front window on some arcane factory where the final sheen of pigmentation is applied to a new race of androids.

Around the corner, the hardest test awaits: the haircut. Will they even consent to snip the semblance of a self for you? Off Seventh Avenue, a barber of unforgivingly high standards has posted a warning in his window. 'Our prices are reasonable,' it says, 'but don't expect to be chosen. We screen out the spiritually ugly.' He is very popular; people think it worth the risk to have their spiritual beauty confirmed. But what happens during the screening? I paused outside one day, wondering whether my curiosity would make up for my lack of courage. The barber, idling over a scalp which didn't look especially spiritual, noticed me there, and in slow motion fastidiously blinked. That was all it took: those eyelids had drawn down the blinds. I was screened out. I now walk past, by preference, on the other side of the street.

But for all its rigour, the Village has not managed to debar the ugly. It can't seal itself off from the city, or from the poor, tired masses who at first stocked America. They wander its streets sullenly pan-handling, and bed down in the three triangular parks carved out by the sudden whim of Hudson Street which, under my window, confuses the grid by deciding to change its name and direction in mid-career and gallivants off at a forty-five degree angle, to be known from then on as Eighth Avenue. The parks once made a robust effort to mean something and remember some hero: an infantryman waves a verdigris banner in one of them. They also have the fond notion that they might be places of recreation, with sandpits, monkey-bars and fountains. Instead they are dormitories, every bench reserved by a sleeper.

Here the microcosm contracts to a scavenged, portable world you can wrap around you. One resident in the park below me makes a bed for himself each afternoon. For a bottom sheet, draped over the hard ribs of the bench, he has a wad of newspaper; the top sheet is the real thing, in pink flannel. He is particular about changing the bottom sheet every day: he won't sleep in stale news. His last act of the day, before extending himself along the planks at dusk, is to take off his sneakers and place them under his head as a bolster (and for safekeeping). I often pass him at mid-morning, still blessedly unconscious. Much of the afternoon is spent selecting the day's fresh linen from the litter bins next to the bench. A neighbour takes his cue from Cleopatra when she had herself delivered to Caesar's barge, and snuggles inside a tubular length of carpet. It might have been made to measure: only a greying twist of hair protrudes from the top end of the pipe. Two others have commandeered a portion of Abingdon Square where a line-up of swings in a wire enclosure is restricted, according to a sign, to children and their guardians. They sprawl on the asphalt, somehow protected by the sign – I have never seen a legitimate user there – as if claiming the privileges of childhood. And in this attitudinising, image-obsessed city, they do look as guileless as infants.

It is terrifying to see someone asleep in a public place, especially when (as here) they are surrounded by all their unguarded belongings, in a knotted bundle or a tattered bag from Saks. Sleep is a state of total vulnerability and of complete self-exposure, which is why it is best indulged in with the lights off and the doors locked, in the company only of the beloved. These men have abandoned all disguises, and that makes them look – despite the tangled hair, the crusts of dirt, and a stench which stops your breath even here in the open air – like babies in their cots. One of them actually clenches his fists on his chest in the most infantile gesture of all, as if shadow-boxing with his dreams. The other has his arms crossed in front of him self-defensively. Glancing over the fence, I saw one red swollen eye staring back at me, and at the same time taking the full glare of the sun: it sizzled like a coal; he couldn't close it. Asleep or dead? You must walk carefully through these irregular triangles which are all called squares; you can tread on corpses, or trample on dreams.

The street is not only a catwalk for the fashionable. It also prides itself on its meanness. Between the parks, our neighbourhood private eye has his consulting room. On the window he has stuck a yellow shield like the old Warner Bros logo, with the promise of service round the clock all year long and the boast of polygraph facilities – for mistrusted spouses? The cramped lobby behind the window has a chair, a table and a dog-eared magazine; on the wall is the silver panel of a two-way mirror. Is the eye which never blinks (unlike the choosy barber's) observing me even now from the inner office, tallying the troops of spiritually ugly passers-by?

Down the street, other sages keep watch on the pavement from similar cubicles. The Village has a tribe of adulterated gypsies who tell fortunes, chart the stars and read what their signs call the Torat cards. Have they cross-bred the ghoulish emblems of the Tarot pack with the mosaic injunctions of the Torah? You can choose your counsellor – the invisible sleuth on the other side of the mirror or the flabby prophetess with the bangles and carmined mouth who browses in a scandal-sheet between bouts of inspiration. The unseen or the far-seeing eye, Sam Spade or Madame Sosostris? The redress of previous wrongs, or a sneak preview of the future? Vindication or divination? And if the gumshoe and the soothsayer are not enough, another amateur wizard sits on a stool at selected corners along Seventh Avenue: a thin unsmiling youth with matted curly hair and a Columbia University knapsack, who on a hand-lettered cardboard sign offers FREE ADVICE to the distressed, the thwarted and the heartbroken. While he waits for clients (or patients), he searches through a tattered dictionary for words to offer as panaceas. Through long winter weekends, he shivers on his stool like an oracle on a shaky tripod, with only a mothy sweater to keep out the gales which keen down the avenue; I have never seen anyone consult him.

The street is four-dimensional: a hard-bitten tunnel boring into the past if you slog along after the private eye; a magic carpet to puff you over the roof-tops if you listen to the gypsies. You don't so much walk down the pavement as allow it to take you somewhere, everywhere. All destinations in time and space are available.

The antique shops sell hairless teddy bears with newly-implanted eyes and stitched-up ears – the childhood of someone else, available at a premium – or mementos of the 1939 World's Fair, which everyone imagines having attended because it was the last time the world was hopeful and wholesome. The clothes shops recall a different decade to life each autumn, and also decide what country of fantasy they will despatch to you. On Bleecker Street, the Marquis de Suède zips and trusses you up for a dungeon on the waterfront, Constantine & Knight for duck-hunting on Long Island, L'Uomo for a stroll on the Via Veneto, Banana Republic for safaris in a jungle of the urban variety. Ring the buzzer, and every door admits you to a fiction.

Behind this row of scenic flats, around the corner from my building, the Village keeps its dirty work out of sight. Here other transformations occur. Along gutters puddled with blood and fragrant with lanolin, where flies converse by day over scraps of gristle and fires spark at night in braziers, animals are hauled on hooks into cool surgeries to emerge again as franks, salamis, bolognas, knockwurst, skirt steaks and corned bottom rounds. 'Meat is murder' protests a vegetarian graffito, but the packing plants seem unembarrassed by the carnage that goes on inside. One specialises in hot-house baby lambs, suckling pigs and kid goats; another calls itself the Veal Boning Corporation. No section of the carcase is allowed to be useless or inedible: Flavor-Rite Deli Products advertises Fresh Navels. I have always been baffled by the sign which announces that Complete Lamb Fabrication happens within. Underneath is an image of a cuddly, smiling sheep. Has it been fabricated here, and if so, of what? Soya beans?

Perhaps the meat-packers too have taken up the Village's cult of art, and its competition with biology. Nothing can hold out for long here against being made an object of aesthetic appraisal and thus of erotic fascination. The area with its squashy offal and sweet rank smell used to be chic. After dark, the butchers were replaced by motorcyclists arriving by taxi to play-act butchery and brutality in underground sex clubs.

Everywhere imagination mitigates, augments, extends the real. One such extension happens at the end of my street. The Village's illusion gives up after a few blocks, disproved by warehouses, regiments of parked trucks, the highway along the river and the unlovely façade of New Jersey across the water. Bank Street had a brief continuation as a pier, where ferries connected with the railways on the other shore.

The pier has long outlived its function. Its planks, splintered or charred by fire open sudden sucking exits to the river beneath; at its edges, where the metal piles have foundered, the boards buckle as if they had melted. But decay suits the pier. It has changed from a metropolitan landing-stage to a rickety rural jetty. Weeds and brambles and irrepressible bushes sprout from seed-beds in the wet, crumbled wood. Gulls perch on the lichened, shell-studded stumps, treating them as a submerged forest. Instead of dwindling into the water because there is nowhere else to go, the street enjoys an epilogue as a park of festering timber, or a would-be beach. A few years ago, before it too was prohibited by a fence and a concrete buttress, it used to be clogged on summer weekends with bodies stripped down to their gold chains and basted with coconut oil. Entrepreneurs even circulated selling splits of Perrier. It was a Coney Island of the mind.

I still go down there to watch the sun set, which triggers the coffee cup to drip and switches on the torch of the Statue of Liberty, a statuette down in the bay. Five hours before, it was quenched by the ocean west of Lisbon; now it subsides again, lunging into New Jersey. The sun spends all its life setting, and does so differently everywhere. In Lisbon it stains the water grey, then blackens it. The horizon becomes, for as long as the night lasts, a forbidding terminus, an end to speculation. Here, to suit New York, the sun sets more flamboyantly, in an apocalypse of crimson or burnt orange which ought to be neon. It sometimes earns cheers and wolf-whistles on the pier, as if it were happening inside Radio City Music Hall.

A straight line drawn across the river arrives at the arches of the old ferry. Painted green, it looks like a stranded, emptied conservatory. It has been disused so long that it has almost forgotten its name, but ERIE LACKAWANNA can still be puzzled out above the berth. The two words have always been a spell for me, summoning up the worlds behind that ridge. It was here, through the green cave of the Erie Lackawanna railway, that I considered America to begin. Landscapes were stacked on the other side like cards in a file: first the stagnant marshes around Newark, then thickening woods, valleys of steel and smoke, cornfields and dairy farms, a barrier of fractured rock, a saline lake and an acid desert, the greenery of a new coast and its demise in another ocean. Imagination supplies what reality has omitted. The Village fancies itself a universe; why shouldn't my street go on indefinitely?

Since my Lisbon life was a perpetuation of childhood, it existed outside time, prior to history. Then one morning I woke up to be told there had been a revolution during the night. My first reaction, even before I asked what kind of revolution, was annoyance. It was the end of a university vacation; I was due to return to Oxford that day, and the airport was closed for the duration. How dare the national destiny interfere with my travel plans?

We learned about the revolution from the radio, which made clipped announcements of the fact every once in a while, requested calm, then played some jaunty, ideologically ambiguous marches. In the suburban street, nothing happened. This was not a revolt made by mobs and accompanied by shouting. A few battalions had moved out from a barracks in the city after midnight; the coded message of a protest song was heard on the radio; the regime quietly capsized.

In the afternoon, we saw our first and only evidence of convulsion. An old man in the house across the street was ushered sternly to a car, with him a sharp-featured wife in a fur-collared coat and a shrewish spinster daughter. The parents looked bewildered; the daughter was in a foul temper. The President and his family, neighbours of my friends, were being taken away. To be shot? we wondered. No, to exile in Brazil – which seemed more a bonus than an infliction. That night, a cavalcade of cars staged a drive-past in the street below, blowing horns at the empty house.

Fascism in Portugal was already enfeebled by 1974: a joke, though a nasty one. The President, a numbskulled naval man prized by Salazar for his obtuseness, was known to all as pumpkin-head or (by reason of his insipidity) boiled chicken. He lived, just beyond the vegetable garden, in a style of valiantly wishful ostentation.

Brigades of outriders escorted him to the opera; policemen smoked and gossiped at his front gate all night long. His deranged poodle Bow-Bow bit the tradesmen with impunity. The daughter, whose scowl could curdle milk, returned most afternoons in her limousine from shopping binges and screeched from the gate for maids to carry in her beribboned booty: 'Fatima! Conceicão! Bernardina! Maria José!' The girls hauled into the house the bags and boxes with whose aid the President's daughter laboured to make herself beautiful. I hope they looted her wardrobe that evening. The chapel on the bluff where the navigators prayed in contemplation of those waiting worlds had been opened every Sunday for the President's exclusive use; now it was locked, and its priest reassigned.

The revolutionaries punished the suburb where the President lived by re-routing the bus line. The rich, it was claimed, had no need of public transport. But the rich had already decamped to Brazil, disposing of their gaudy villas to Third World governments.

The house above was a tycoon's Xanadu, a flaky pastry which unfurled down the hill in decks and ledges of pastel icing. The roof over the top balcony had been inlaid with a marzipan heaven: from star-shaped recesses, pink and peppermint and daffodil bulbs lit up at dusk. It is occupied now by the Zaire embassy, and the self-made man's private constellation no longer works. The national pennant billows underneath: on a field of green, a yellow disc inside which a black hand grips a torch. The real sun, glaring back every afternoon on its way into the ocean, has bleached the sun of cloth and extinguished the torch as if it were the moon. In the Ambassador's reception room, where the curtains sag listlessly off their rods, Constable's 'Hay Wain' hangs larger than life on the wall. Every so often someone comes to turn off the water at the mains, or unplug the house from the electric grid; small diplomatic incidents occur on the pavement.

Down the road, the Turkish embassy – blown up by the Portuguese security forces a few years ago, to flush out some terrorists who had already taken the precaution of killing themselves inside – glowers behind a palisade of steel topped with spikes shaped like twisted, lacerating flames, and hoops of wire threaded through razor-blades. Nations with a grievance complain to the unheeding street. Libya has a glass show-case on the footpath, with

Colonel Gadaffi spruce in white cotton, gold braid and dark glasses next to a cartoon (unexplained) of a firing squad; Iran displays the blotched, flayed victims of Iraqi chemical warfare, and a tableau vouching for agricultural progress: benign village elders hold sheaves of wheat and bales of wool like clip-on beards. The Iranian placards look out on a dry slope of olive trees and spiny-finned cacti, with cicadas shrilling through the air. I'm surely the only person who has ever paused to read them, and my response is hardly the intended one.

The rich who have stayed keep out burglars and beggars with the help of starved Alsatians and German Shepherds. Next door I have befriended a cowardly Dobermann, which licks my face without lifting any of its four paws from the ground. Otherwise I avoid the footpaths and walk down the middle of the street to keep clear of the sudden lunge of drooling teeth through the hedges. Though I make sure the lines of fence are equidistant, the dogs still smell meat ambling seductively past. I always have the feeling that I am inside a canine mouth: on either side, there is the gleam of enamel being sharpened like cutlasses.

Up on the hill, paranoia has its spikes, wolves, banshee alarms and unblinking closed-circuit cameras. Down in the valley, where the suburb runs out and Lisbon itself ends among a chaos of carved-up farms on a beach of blackened, greasy sand, the poor have other devices for guarding their property. In their shanty-town, roofs made of scavenged tin or planks wrapped in plastic are held in place by tyres, boulders, wine barrels and even an upturned porcelain kitchen sink (useless inside the gimcrack huts because they have no water supply). Above the choppy sea of tin with its reefs of wilting flowers planted in sawn-off detergent containers, a mast flaunts the colours of the local football team.

The shanty-town had tempted me for years. It was my Casbah, my thieves' kitchen, my forbidden city. And yet why should a city, which exists to compound and commingle all the lives which are possible, forbid any part of itself? From the balcony on the hill, I could see the edge of the squeezed settlement, beneath a building on whose side a painted credit card had long ago been invalidated by the sun.

Closer up, I had wandered round it, between the market – disgorging fish-wives with their pudgy arms, capacious aprons and zip-up ankle boots – and the circle of scabby earth which used to be the bull-ring, all russet onion domes and scimitar-shaped moons. On one side, the shanties were open to view. Here in a clearing the concrete washtubs stood, around a dribbling fountain where the settlers filled their buckets, bottles, pans and mouths with water. There was also a gutted automatic washer tipped on its side, someone's tribute to the impossible dream of plumbing. Everywhere else, the ways in were slits between the lean-tos. People ducked under drying sheets or rounded abrupt twists in the alleys and were gone. I studied all the entries, longing to follow. But I had been assured I would have my throat cut in there, and clung timidly to the other side of the street.

It appealed to me as a hand-made world, fabricated in haste from the ground up and fastened together with twine, glue, rusty nails and locks stolen from other people's doors. It recited (I was sure) our first years on an unfriendly earth, where we struggle to convince ourselves that we belong. On the border of the city, disconnected from society (its water-mains did not extend this far, though there was electricity so the settlers could watch Brazilian soap operas on television), the people who occupied this desert of rubble and rubbish had built for themselves a little, labyrinthine city. They were mostly migrants from the one-time Portuguese colonies in Africa: strangers here, whose every ingenuity with wood and tin and plastic made palpable the notion and the necessity of home.

At the rim of their warren, just behind the bulldozed bull-ring, was one structure which made my heart ache as few other works of architecture – if this could be called that – have ever done. It was a box made habitable. The walls were the leaf-thin, shaved pine of tea-chests, still oily and reeking of newness, carried back from the docks nearby. Destination and shipping details were stamped on the outside, as if the house itself might soon be sent off to another arbitrary spot in space; there were also inky prints of unfurled umbrellas, to show which way up the chest should be handled in passage. The fanged wire which once held the crates together had been used too, as a barbed defence along the top of the garden wall. I call it a garden because the box was assembled around a mutilated palm tree, already there, now enclosed by the proprietor. He had painted a blue heart on one of the walls, with the legend AMOR splashed underneath it. Every house, I guess, requires a blessing. I remembered the niche of interceding Madonnas in the bedroom up the hill, or the plaintive request of my sign that visitors shouldn't pee in the pool.

It had to happen, I told myself. Sooner or later I would have to find out what it was like in there. No one was keen to chaperone me, so one day I took care not to have a bath, removed my watch, then walked down the hill, hoping I had left my affairs in order. I avoided the clearing with the washtubs, where a scrawny dog was worrying a bone. I chose an entry round the corner, a crevice between the toppling shacks. The alley was a paved hillside of concrete steps, inlaid pebbles and chipped tiles: it had been a quarry once, before this primeval city grew on it. At first, I saw not the houses but the eyes looking out of them at me. Their gazes, however, were not hostile, merely curious, wondering how I had blundered in off the street.

I thought it best to declare an interest. With an effort at the avuncular, I asked a muddy child what his name was. He was called nothing, he said (though he later, after much cajoling, owned up to being Victor). I asked a young woman sitting in an open door and vaguely twitching to some African music from inside what the name of the street was. It didn't have one, she said. And the name of the settlement? It had not occurred to her that it might have one either.

By then her husband had emerged from a back room to investigate the intrusion. He was dressed for the world outside: pleated pants with a belt of purple snake-skin, a handbag under his arm, dark glasses. The woman assured him in their African language that I was a harmless loon, and he answered my question, with some recognition of its oddity and its importance. The cramped town with its walls of printers' typographic plates and its roofs of scrap from dismembered cars was called Ferro Velho: old iron. It was a cemetery of corroding metal and buckled wood; a junkyard. A girl came out of the next door and squirmed between us with a bucket. On top, a layer of pimply chicken skin; underneath, a bedding of glossy paper from a magazine; below that, I deduced, the household dung.

I asked the man how long he had lived here.

'Ten years,' he said.

And what was it like?

'Can't you see?' he asked. There were infestations of fleas and rats, diseases, and fires which couldn't be put out because there was no water. In Guiné-Bissau where they came from, his wife said, only animals lived in huts like this. And she laughed as she said it – not an ironic chuckle but an explosion of incredulous mirth. The husband (who meanwhile had dispensed a Band-aid to a Muslim friend in a buttonless shift of tarnished white) seemed ashamed of her laughter, with its confession of despair and of the exhilaration which follows the last surrender of hope. He adjusted the bag under his arm and gave his wrist-watch a perfunctory wind.

'We may have to live here,' he said, 'but we still try to preserve a certain civilisation.'

His last word startled me as much as his wife's glee had done. Those who speak Latin languages are always springing these lexical surprises, using words you wouldn't expect from their Anglo-Saxon counterparts. (I had once overheard a woman in a Lisbon street compliment a friend whose little boy, sulkily tagging along, had put on weight: he used to be quasi-skeletal, she said.) But there was more to it than that. What shocked me was my sudden glimpse of a truth about the shanty-town. It *was* a civilisation. Indeed it told, with terrible candour, the story of all civilisations, in its constructive artifice, its fiction of permanence, and its wistful homage to a theoretical home which – not willed into reality here – is shifted by the imagination somewhere else.

The couple from Guiné, lacking water, lived surrounded by the trophies of bourgeois comfort. She sat at a formica kitchen table, and a stout pair of stereo speakers pumped out her music. On the wall were two identical calendars, from a shop selling African foods in Paris. The calendar had been designed for multi-cultural use: though in this case it advertised African delicacies, a Chinese model preened on it, and under the shop's address was the red announcement of the nearest metro station, Stalingrad. Through other doors I saw cocktail cabinets, varnished dressers with vinyl-bound volumes of abbreviations from the *Reader's Digest*, flights of domestic angels.

The huddle survives only so long as the council pretends it doesn't exist. It is on land neither owned nor leased; there are no deeds or papers of entitlement; sometimes shanty-towns are knocked down overnight, after a peremptory order to evacuate. Yet a value has been created, even though there is nothing to guarantee it. The shelters change hands for huge sums, are fiercely coveted, and maintained with immaculate domestic pride. The temporariness of our tenure can never be admitted (or only as a joke, in the laughter of the woman from Guiné). We have to operate on the assumption of eternity.

And if we have only one life, and it is *this* one? That too is something not to be tolerated. If we are not at home in our life, we envisage – or remember – another one for ourselves.

While I was talking to the couple from Guiné, a friend of theirs from Cabo Verde, also on the west African coast, advanced down the alley to see if I was giving them any trouble. He probably thought I was a debt-collector. Once he was appeased, we all began reminiscing about forfeited homelands, their defects repaired by fantasy. Guiné is marshy, drenched, malarial, a humid incubator for insects. But here, where water had to be lugged twice a day from the fountain, the man and woman burbled lyrically about it. 'Everywhere you go there are mineral springs. It's not like the desert in the north. And it's a beautiful water, a sweet water.' They teased their friend from Cabo Verde because his country was so dry, perpetually drought-stricken. But though he laughed with them, his own imagination belied the charge. When he found out where I came from, he said, 'Australia is like Africa, isn't it? A brown country?' Scorched barrenness had been replaced by vistas of coppery earth and polished skies. Our dreams looked different, but they were the same dream. He didn't ask how I came to be there: a fellow-refugee, he probably assumed.

Both inside and out, the Guinéans had painted their house in one of the dream's dazzling primary colours. Everything was blue. Not the blue of sea or sky, not watery or merely reflected, the shimmer of some optical trick. It was a blue dug from the earth, like gems – turquoise, or opal which they grub from the Australian desert. It wasn't liquid or airy but hard, like those gems: a substance itself, not an attribute. A blue best guarded in the bedrock, as turquoise or opal or cobalt are, because above ground its fire would dim, like blue eyes turning grey as the years pass. The blue of an attainable, not illusory horizon. Like a flame of gas, it made the house and alley hot with brilliance.

107

Along the street between the shanty-town and the beach, where the trams run clanging into Lisbon, there are other definitions of beauty. A novelty shop owned by white settlers forced back from the colonies after the revolution sells coconut monkey faces, busts of Salazar, models in wax of a Nordic warrior-god with a strapped-on harness, a horned helmet and a slashing sword or of David's Napoleon, rearing on the horse which he is pointing across the Alps: souvenirs of dispersed empire, holy relics of dictatorship.

In the gutters between the tram-stops, gypsies (ethnically more *echt* than those of Greenwich Village) sit with their baskets of Benetton tracksuits and Lacoste shirts. They're not supposed to sell without licences, and during winter the police pass the time by chasing them inconclusively round the corner. Today, since it's summer, the local policeman is tired and sweaty. The gypsies, when they see him coming, languidly pull shawls over the baskets and set to picking their teeth or combing their children's hair. The policeman in his turn studies an object in mid-air. As he strolls by, shawls slide off baskets one by one and the business of society resumes. On the corner, someone's great-grandmother has been parked to beg. She brings her own stool, or has it brought for her: mouth agape, eyes unfocussed, hand out-stretched in the shape of a tremulous cup, she is deposited there in the morning by her dependents and collected (I hope) at the end of the day.

The beach beyond the railway-line is used only by people from the shanty-town, who can't afford a fare to go anywhere better. The sand cakes drying dog shit and an old boot; once from the breakwater I saw a distended condom in the river, elasticised by the tides to fabulous lengths.

A family has come to live for the season against the wire fence of the fish factory. Their house is made from two canvas blinds and a rug of jute tied together with string; a rod of bamboo is their tent pole. A rabble of babies wails inside. For simultaneous wardrobe and larder, there is a supermarket trolley. It contains, at present, a pile of nappies, a bucket and spade, two pine cones (free food, if you batter the wooden pellets to release the seeds) and a bag of browning apples.

Did the journey through this microcosm, which began among the bullet-proofed embassies and finished a mile away at this see-through dwelling on the beach, comprise two worlds or only one? One, I thought: the difference was merely in the degree of reinforcement. Motives up on the hill and down in the valley were the same. The villas and the shanties were both engaged in conceiving, sanctifying and armour-plating the idea of home. But engineering and concrete and electric cables can't save the idea from its own ideal, tantalising flimsiness.

The water, seen from this close, is brown. The sky in the afternoon haze looks livid. Blue is confined to the walls of that lane through the slum, where it cheats reality by representing nothing.

5
Passwords

SOCIETY HAS ALWAYS SEEMED TO ME AN IDEA DREAMED UP by conspirators. The tribe adheres thanks to shared understandings, which never need to be voiced; it celebrates its uniqueness by the exchange of private jokes, by perfecting a dialect of signals. I used to be amazed, before I could understand the language, by the sight of a whole world which conversed in Portuguese. Everything was unintelligible: I couldn't even read the gestures, and because of their vehemence – having come from the land of laconicism, where only madmen or migrants talked with their hands – I used to assume that people were quarrelling when they were only being exuberant.

These days I know what they are saying, but that's no consolation, since all societies are like foreign languages. You can learn the words and perhaps even manage the grammar, but will never be able to colour vowels as the natives do, or achieve some tiny glottal or lingual effect which defines the difference. I was amazed, when struggling with Portuguese, at the inability of my tongue to roll an r, or to sibillate – as the natives were so properly doing – without a spray of spit. I cheered myself up by remembering that I had the same difficulties with English. I would never (though I admit it was not one of my ambitions) be able to say 'Thank you *so* much' in the precise way Oxford colleagues did when a dinner plate was set down before them or taken away, inflecting the adverb with an emphatic squeeze in exactly inverse proportion to the amount of gratitude they were feeling; but equally I could not bring myself to forgo the formalities as New Yorkers did and demand things with an undertone not of threat but of harried urgency, anxious to move on to the next item in an over-scheduled existence – 'Give me a regular coffee/a cheese Danish/a transfer/two tickets in the mezzanine' – so I wasted everyone's time with pretty pleases and apologies for the bother, the necessary sweeteners to secure a favour in England but here fatal evidence of feebleness or mental bewilderment. Every group has its idiolect, unintelligible – or liable to grievous misinterpretation – once you reach the border.

It is a world of small worlds with words as their disputed frontiers. You move in and out of shambolic, accidental places which, like the leaky boxes in the shanty-town, are a home to someone. Every speck or spot on the globe is a centre to whichever group speaks its language and knows the stories about it. Since everywhere is convinced of its own centrality, there is no real centre anywhere. But this is a truth, like that of our homelessness, which we would sooner die than recognise. So we reorganise geography and make the map radiate out from wherever we happen to find ourselves.

Oxford euphemistically cancels its rival Cambridge by referring to it as 'the other place'. I suppose Cambridge does the same to Oxford. London, messily endless, imagines itself confined within a series of concentric rings which all dilate from the same mid-point: the underground Circle Line, the outer girdle of trucks chugging round the Circular Road, then the sacrosanct Green Belt. Manhattan secedes from the other boroughs and from America with the aid of its rivers, fathomless as the English Channel. Those who come across bridges or through tunnels are the crass and polyester-clad, the infidel and unspeakable.

Once I heard the super in my building – a strict and haughty man, forever bewailing the squalor of those he had to clean up after, who explained his temper by reference to his Italian blood and Latin American birth – reprimand some new arrivals whom he had caught throwing rubbish from a window. 'Where you think this is?' I heard him ask. 'The Bronze? Brookline?' It was the ultimate insult, and carried with it the threat of banishment to those benighted boroughs. After that, I doubt that they dared to open the window, let alone drop anything from it.

Portugal, as the view down the river from Lisbon suggests, has its own fond myth of universality. It turns its back on Spain and scans the ocean for those dispersed worlds, in Africa, South America and Asia, which were imperial extensions of itself.

The mind is its own cartographer. The maids in Lisbon divide the world into three regions: *terra*, *Lisboa*, and *lá fora*. *Terra*, the terra firma of home, is where they are not. It is the village in the mountains they have had to leave, to which they return every summer for religious processions. *Lisboa* is where they have come to work and where they spend their adult lives, but it is never allowed to be home. *Lá fora* is everywhere else, and is of no consequence; it means, dismissively, 'out there'. The housekeeper Rosalina once asked me what countries Britain had on its frontier. She was merely expressing a polite interest, and I could see was not expecting much from the answer. But when I told her it had no other country on its borders, she gaped. She assumed that somewhere or other it must abut on Spain.

Whenever she notices some extraneous event on the television news – a war or a flood or an earthquake or a royal wedding – she asks 'Is that out there?' As soon as we tell her it is, she is pacified: out there, it is beyond needing to be thought about. We conserve our patch of reality by deeming all the rest unreal.

How do you earn the right to graduate from out there to in here? Usually there are gruesome initiations. The cost of tribal membership is scars.

When I was first in Oxford, I was amazed to find how differently they did things. I seemed always to be encountering embargoes: I became conscious of the rules only after a pause of discomfort or a frosted glance told me I had broken one of them.

Invited out to tea while a student, I made the mistake of praising my hostess's scones. I did so in all the guileless, gluttonous enthusiasm of youth, and anyway I knew a bit about scones, which my aunties specialised in (though I made no comparisons). The lady of the house treated the compliment as a slur, but was gracious enough to ignore it. I worried over the incident for ages, and eventually worked out what I had done wrong. To praise the food was illbred because it implied she had prepared it (which she had), not some unseen menial. And anyway, only an oaf would expect the scones to be other than perfect. Added to which, eating was a bodily function.

More puzzling still were the protocols of avoidance. On a brief walk through Oxford, you are bound to pass most of the people you know on the exiguous pavements. Some diplomatic agreement is essential, otherwise you'd never get wherever it is you are going. So an elaborate routine has been devised, a sequence of oblique recognitions comprehensible to those on the inside but wounding for those from out there. When your target is sighted a few yards off, you begin to reorganise your face. The eyes turn opaque, or swivel round to contemplate something inside the head: the slightly loony look of self-absorption indicates that thinking is in progress, not to be disturbed.

It is the ocular equivalent to sporting your oak, closing the outer door of your room to semaphore that visits are unwelcome. While the eyes go somewhere else, a smile can be left on the mouth to confirm that someone *is* at home – though it has to be a quizzical, gently threatening one, like the watch-dog's before it barks and bites. Those with long practice can bring off marvels of co-ordination, as if simultaneously rubbing their tummies clockwise and patting the top of their heads. The eyes fix on a putative object in mid-air, or a shop window on the other side of the street; but a tiny inclination of the head happens just at the instant when you pass the person you're so ostentatiously not looking at.

Since it was my chirpy instinct to say a full frontal 'Hi' to anyone I knew, it was years before I mastered these mandarin tactics. To save myself embarrassment, I'd more often make an impromptu dash across the street to escape an advancing colleague who would give me this treatment. I generally risked my life between the lurching buses and armoured Securicor vans only to find another social peril advancing on the opposite pavement. That limp was the gait of my confused inadequacy.

If the street was dangerous, the platform at the railway station was a possible disaster area. You couldn't, as on the street, pretend to be late for a lecture, or to be headed in another direction. Everyone caught the down train (i.e. the one to London), and since it was mostly late, there were intervals of unguarded waiting, followed by the hour-long jeopardy of the journey itself, in those stuffy compartments with their sliding doors where six people who very often knew each other well sat on two dusty upholstered benches facing each other, their knees probably touching. Here extreme precautions had to be taken. Absolute invisibility therefore prevailed.

Having bought your ticket and walked onto the platform you vapourised, and only returned to the occupation of your body as the train passed through Ealing Broadway, a few minutes from the London terminus. Once a corpulent don at whose house I had eaten the previous weekend – an expert on Victorian complacency – scrambled aboard the train as it was leaving, and took the only seat left in the carriage, wedging himself into the space in front of me. I grinned and said hello. I had forgotten my invisibility: he couldn't see me, and ignored the greeting.

I spent the next hour in squirming humiliation, wondering whether to bolt for the buffet. I did stay my ground, and since I had no book to hide in studied the film unrolling outside the window, which I already knew by heart – allotments with their crops of cabbages, the stormy funnels of the power station, a weedy tow-path beside the canal, the field of half-constructed houses where London that week began.

Then, punctually as the train lunged under the bridge at Ealing Broadway, my companion and acquaintance opposite came to. He huffed, puffed, shook himself as if recovering from anaesthesia, and blinked with amazement at the sight of me. 'How *are* you, dear chap?' he asked; he seemed to be intensely concerned about the answer. All was cordiality until we slowed into Paddington three minutes later. By the time the train stopped, we had etherised again, and drifted off like separate wisps of smoke into uncaring, mercifully anonymous London.

Another of the austere Oxford forms I learned about in guest nights during my time at All Souls. After dinner, the company was stirred up, made to rotate round the common room. People floated into groups they hadn't joined before, and seemed to know just when to float away again. Much rearranging of chairs was called for, and I noticed the odd habit of a colleague, a somewhat prissy anthropologist. Whenever someone left his little circle, he'd carry off the leather-bottomed chair which had been vacated, replace it against the wall, and substitute a fresh chair from the long line-up. The circle was then ready for any new drop-in. It was as scrupulous as changing the sheets in a guest bedroom: he disliked the idea that anyone should have to occupy the concave impress of another's buttocks, or feel with a shudder some stored-up warmth. Propriety enjoined a cool chair. It had not occurred to me to worry about this before, but he was an anthropologist and therefore had to be trusted. Chair-bottoms should be served raw, not half-cooked.

All Souls was one of my initiations. Two years after emerging from the bush onto Waterloo Bridge, I found myself seated at a college meeting between the Lord Chancellor of the realm who, while our agricultural rents and clerical livings were discussed, worked through the contents of his scuffed red despatch-box, and the historian A. L. Rowse, who spent the time tearing open cheques and tabulating the day's gains, with many a well-earned chuckle. He was in the process of definitively identifying Shakespeare's Dark Lady, and once or twice canvassed my support against the 'filthy third-rate fools' who dared to doubt him; it was my policy to agree with everyone.

At All Souls, in my early twenties, I had the experience of an English public-school education which geography had earlier spared me. A refined variety of fagging was in operation, to induct the two new boys elected to fellowships every autumn into the gerontocracy. The junior fellow was used like a sheepdog before dinner, to round up stragglers and yap the diners into formation. The butler, whose name (I swear) was Quelch, would hand me a list of those dining; I then had to wriggle in and out of the gossiping clusters and do quick additions in my head to make sure all were present and correct. When they were, I would obsequiously inform the Warden or whoever was presiding, and dinner could begin.

After dinner we trooped down a corridor to another room for dessert. There the junior fellow had to change from sheepdog to pot-boy. In this incarnation, he was known as Mr Screw. Whenever one of the decanters which slid round the table dispensing port or syrupy Sauternes ran dry, the drinker who had been cheated would bellow or (if it was the saturnine, sinister Warden) hiss 'Mr Screw!' Then meek Mr Screw would get up and press a bell on the panelled wall to summon Mr Quelch, who took the decanter away to refill it and, on returning, awarded Mr Screw a free glass of whatever it contained as his tip. While being screwed, you could at least get drunk cheaply. Then after a year there was someone more junior than me, onto whom these chores devolved. I began to perceive the advantage of getting older.

Soon after my election, a colleague invited me for a drink before dinner. He was, it seemed, an authority on French statecraft in one or another century. All I knew was what I saw: he looked like a pudding, and had a stammer from which he rescued himself by a whinnying snort; that disentangled his tongue, and launched him – sometimes leaving a gap you'd have to fill in for yourself – onto the next word. His rooms, he insisted, were in a famously inaccessible turret, and I would never be able to get there unaided. There turned out to be a procedure for finding them. You went to the second landing on a particular staircase, then he came to fetch you. But how to attract his attention? 'You give me a shout. You call out h-h-h-hoi!' The 'hoi' burst from him, propelled by the stammer, with the note of a huntsman's bugle. 'Mind you, it has to be h-hoi!'

I could see there was going to be a problem.

'Why's that?' I asked. 'How about if I just said hello? There isn't a bell, or a door-knocker?'

'Nothing like that, no,' he said. 'H-hoi will do the trick.'

I thought I'd best check whether the stammer was part of the deal.

'Just hoi?' Already I winced as I heard myself squeak, without his clear, brassy, tootling note. Had he chosen it because it was the first word of hoi polloi? Perhaps it was the cue for some nasty rite to trounce young vulgarians.

'That's it, h-h-hoi,' he said, 'that'll do,' giving it the benefit of a double-jerk emission, like an engine stuttering into life on a cold morning.

I brooded on the matter all afternoon, and rehearsed the braying syllable once or twice in the bathroom. It never sounded right: a strangled quack not a call to arms; sometimes a pathetic whimper. Ah well, I thought, it will be all right on the night.

That evening I left for the ominous staircase five minutes ahead of time, walking very slowly. Even so, I arrived four minutes early, since it was only a couple of hundred yards away. I decided to take in a few steadying laps of the quad, while I waited for the chime. The turret where my host had his eyrie shivered in the black sky. Could that be his light, up there at the top? At last the bell, as Macbeth euphemistically put it, invited me. In I limped.

The landing where I had to give voice was as dim and ambiguous as the crossroads in an allegory. A selection of unmarked doors, another flight going up, a passage sideways. I had the feeling that, rather than climbing the stairs, I was about to jump off them. The landing reminded me of the diving-board above a swimming pool, which bounced expectantly as you walked its plank. At the end, if you peep over, is the winking, dimpling oblong of water, a long way below. No, perhaps you should go back and start again . . . I had always given myself the final push by reflecting that, once you *did* the thing you were frightened of, the fear at least ceased (though in the case of the pool, concussion or death by drowning might very well replace it). I tried calling the man's name. I even thought I might creep up from behind on the awful word by trying 'Helloo'. Nothing worked. I would have to take the vocal plunge.

My mouth creaked open, like a cobwebbed Gothic portal with rusty hinges. It readied itself to form the sound above the tonsils, amplify it in the echo chamber behind the face, and filter it (with the hint of an oink) through the nose. But the syllable died within me. Amen stuck in my throat. After two more false starts, I began to worry that someone might come and find me straining ineffectually to produce a honk on the staircase. I ran back to my room, telephoned my host to say I was ill and would not be coming. Hours later – after the college gates had been locked for the night – I slunk out to a van parked down the High Street to buy an indigestible kebab for my supper.

'Hoi!', I realised, was the password, the universal open sesame. And I just could not bring myself to utter it.

In New York, the border between out there and in here is sternly guarded. All visitors, as the signs in the apartment lobbies warn, must be announced; and the doorman – a Haitian, a deracinated Russian from Coney Island, or a Puerto Rican – will probably garble your name unintelligibly in doing so, and turn you back into a stranger. Even those with spiritually beautiful haircuts are not guaranteed admission.

At odd spots on the lawless streets, stoically hopeful queues form, trying to qualify for entry to some precious interior. On Ellis Island, people had to squeeze through a strait gate and a narrow way in order to gain the free continental emptiness of America. Perhaps, on their way through the turnstile, they were assigned a new identity, if the name they brought from Europe was too unspellable for the immigration clerks. The rite of passage is still in progress. Coming home late at night down the cratered, paper-strewn waste of 14th Street, I used to notice a line of applicants spilling from the pavement into the gutter, stomping and shuddering in the cold. Their goal was a brown door in an iron wall, one slice in a shabby, raucous façade of liquor stores, donut shops, fortune-tellers and undertakers.

The door disclosed nothing of what lay behind it. Of course it didn't need to: everyone has their door in a wall. Charles Ryder sought his throughout Oxford in *Brideshead Revisited*, and people there are forever disappearing inside such doors or emerging from them, stepping into or out of some garden of evergreen, overgrown fantasy. Lionel in H. G. Wells's story *The Door in the Wall* finds his, painted green and twined with a crimson Virginia creeper, down an innocuous West Kensington byway; it opens onto happiness, a flowery expanse of 'translucent unreality'. I had my own door fitted into the wall at the end of my London tunnel, less for security than for the pleasure of being able, every time I reached the city, to unlock it. When we were ejected from paradise or childhood, a door slammed shut, a key grated, a bolt slid into place and rusted there. The wall thickened, loomed taller, cast longer shadows. The way back was barred. Yet who ever walks down a city street without wondering whether this door – with its apparatus of buzzers and chains and its choosy camera eye which watches you squirm on the step – might not be the one?

The postulants on 14th Street had found theirs: the gate to grace. It opened a few teasing inches every few minutes, and a uniformed porter took stock of the crowd. Figures which had been quaking with cold, hopping from foot to foot on the icy concrete and digging fingers into their armpits like clients at a soup kitchen, made haste to preen, flaunt and say cheese through chattering teeth. A few were beckoned forward, though never from the front of the queue : the last here were capriciously promoted to first. They wriggled into the bright, loud warmth; the door clanged behind them; one or two of the rejects, let down by their loafers or their acid-washed jeans, slouched off down the street, in quest of doors in less forbidding walls.

What lay inside, inches from the pavement with its ridges of soiled snow and its crushed cartons? This month's definition of centrality, social arrival, spiritual pulchritude: the city's newest and most whimsically exclusive night-club. Since then, the aura has moved on to another door in some other wall.

Up on Sixth Avenue, a few blocks to the north, crowds jostle after midnight at a portico which glares a sullen, smouldering red. It opens into a side-aisle of a church, but the congregation outside is waiting for no Mass, not even for a vacant confessional. The church of blackened russet bricks, stranded on the avenue in the aftermath of Christianity, has been reconsecrated to another religion: energy, frenzy, the athletic mania of the dance; it is now a disco. A black satellite dish on the roof receives a stream of images which are not transmitted from heaven.

Inside, the conversion has a pointed, profaning wit. The baptismal font is a bar, the altar a stage for the band, the chapels are lounges for reconnoitering in between dances. In the rafters, laser beams slash and puncture the air, like a dog-fight of intersecting purple crucifixes. The night I went, Nona Hendrix sashayed out to sing in a nun's habit; after some snide benedictions, she ripped her outfit open along a seam of Velcro and stepped forth in fish-net stockings and a skimpy leopard skin, like a raunchy convertite who had unfrocked herself. (I was with the photographer who had been commissioned to do her next album cover; we were waved forward by the bouncer, wafted out of the demoralised queue by a gust of social power.)

On the floor where the pews once were, squads of men in skins of glistening sweat mimed ecstasy: shadow-boxing fists, pelvic pistons, eyes dazed by the concussion of noise, dancing at their partners rather than with them. Apt, I thought, the appropriation of a church. The dancer is a throbbing, gyrating dervish; but enclosed – like wild-eyed visionaries, and like all New Yorkers – in a private, incommunicable dream. This was dancing as a soliloquy, not a contact sport. It reminded me of the Oxford railway carriage, with the passengers erecting walls of newspaper or simply resorting to invisibility. My friend the photographer, who professionally sees life through a pane of ground glass and studies light from within a shuttered darkness, looked wistfully down at the floor of flesh from what was once the organ loft. 'You know,' he said (this was in 1984), 'it's some consolation to think that all those humpy bodies can't make love to each other.' As we were leaving, it occurred to him that his parents had been married here, in the age of another faith.

Despite the church's preparedness for an orgy, the dance was as austere and ascetic as prayer, or weight-lifting. The crowd on the sidewalk shared a common aim. Singled out for admission, its members reverted to solitude. Everyone pounded fists and bumped hips against the narrow sides of a transparent cubicle. Then at four in the morning the blitzkrieg of lightning in the rafters switched off, the music was unplugged, the doors banged shut, and the communicants who had not communicated dispersed to their separate niches in the city. Home was where you went to sleep for a while, before resuming the search.

In Lisbon, alienation was easier, because I expected to stay behind my transparent, impassible window, out there looking in. Unfamiliarity estranges everything. The Portuguese call a foreigner *estrangeiro*: a stranger, the bemused *étranger* of Albert Camus, outside a reality he can gape at but never be part of. Ignorance of the language made me a spectator, baffled by an orchestra of unaccustomed sounds – miaowing vowels, splashy consonants – and by the bombardment of unreadable signs: the patterning of chain-mail or dizzy turbulent waves made by the square stones inlaid on the pavement; the riddling bone system of a fish, served up with its tail gripped in its razory teeth and needing to be picked apart; the gilt carriages, like glassed-in play-pens on wheels, which were eyed so dolefully in the streets (children's hearses, I discovered).

To me, the Portuguese were the strange ones. A woman on a bus yawned cavernously, then sketched a crucifix with her thumb in front of her mouth before closing it. It was a precaution, I gathered later, to ensure that the devil did not seize the chance of a gaping aperture to wriggle in. I had always been told it was rude to yawn in public unless you covered your mouth with your hand; here you risked more than social disapproval – you imperilled your soul. Daily life involved constant skirmishes with demons, or frisky spirits of whatever denomination. Whenever you dropped a plate or a glass, I discovered, you transferred the blame to the slippery object by explaining that it got away from you – likewise, if you wanted to sneeze but couldn't, you could say that it too had escaped you. But if you managed to expel it, you could count on someone declaring *Santinho!* to bless you, because you had ejected a spirit. In Oxford the body was a gimcrack casing for the brain. In New York it was your own walking work of art, to be pumped up, jogged, tanned, kept young and lean at all costs. Here it belonged to others, and they battled invisibly for control of it: the saints who protected its organs – Luzia, for instance, with her platter of eyes – and the devils who awaited their moment to burgle and defile it. You had it on loan, and were due sooner or later to return it to its owner or maker, who might piece it back together, clad with other flesh. In Evora, south of the river, I was taken to a chapel walled with bones, which announced in an inscription that they were waiting for you to donate them yours. It sounded even grislier in Portuguese, with its sinister whistling sibillants like wind in a crypt: *Nós os ossos que aqui estamos/Pelos Vossos esperamos.* The words even looked funereal, made up of neutering multiplied zeros. Still, no-one shivered but me. Death here was no embarrassment. Coffins were opened a last time at the graveside, and the lace coverlets unwrapped from the cold face for a final kiss. Then the diggers poured buckets of lime on top of the body, still in its Sunday best, to speed up decomposition: the bones were impatient to be extricated.

The national emotion, the clue to this morbidity, was *saudades* – a yearning which covered all losses from homesickness to unrequited love to mourning. This was one of the first words I learned, after I had heard it strung out and tormentingly vibrated like a taut, aching nerve by a *fado* singer. It was the sound of a universal grief: the dog in the garden next door made the same cry wordlessly at night. What did it mean? Its wild, untuned wail lay outside the range of well-tempered Europe, to whose far western shore the narrow country clung. Perhaps it was an Arab sound, left behind by the Moors along with all the buzzing 'z's in the language and those dazzling whitewashed walls? Or could it be Celtic melancholy, displaced from the north by another race of wanderers? The fish-wives and fruit-sellers who sang the *fado* in back-street clubs produced the cry from some unreachable recess in the past. They fastened their black shawls around them, stiffened their faces to tragic masks, and began to keen. When the song was over they removed the shawl, let the anguished muscles relax, and went back to joking and gossiping with their friends. The cry did not originate inside them; it passed through them, reverberating down a tunnel of time.

Whenever I saw Rosalina trudging upstairs with a tray of ironed clothes balanced on her head, hands on jutting hips to anchor the load, or heard her muttering in time to the *Avés* which crackled from her kitchen radio in the afternoon as she sorted and sifted the rice, checking each grain before she cooked it as critically as if these seeds were souls on which she was passing judgement, she seemed to have arrived from this remote, tantalising distance.

She came down out of the hills in early middle age, having raised three children while working in the fields when her shiftless husband deserted her. She wore a pigtail, twined and wreathed around the crown of her head. She had never cut it, and later donated it, greying, to the saint who oversaw affairs back in her village. Her neck and wrists were looped with holy medallions, so she moved round the house inside a jingling cordon of sanctity. She brought with her, in the absence of any other luggage, an entire mental world of customs, sayings and stories which lived on in her long after the pigtail was sacrificed and she learned to operate the blender, the coffee-grinder, the vacuum-cleaner and the washer, storing most of the lucky charms in a camphor-scented drawer because they ran the risk of being caught in the machines. Soon after arriving, she accidentally blew up the pressure cooker, and blamed the devil. He also allegedly stole one of the frying-pans, but was foiled when she knotted a towel and hung it in a corner of the kitchen: this tied his tail, thus impeding his mischief. And the pan did turn up, a week later, in a corner of the garden where she had absent-mindedly left it while scraping out left-overs. If Jorge's parents had guests in the afternoon who overstayed their welcome and caused the dinner to burn, she up-ended a stool and placed a broom inside it. The devil, summoned back by this contrivance, invisibly frog-marched the visitors out of the house.

Rosalina was a handsome woman: I don't say beautiful because it suggests perishability, and the bones in her face were a bulwark, set beneath the skin into a resistant plate which kept storms out and emotions in. Her refrain, as she hoisted up those burdens onto her head or settled down to scrutinise the rice, was that you had to fight against life. She hardly ever laughed – she didn't have the mental leisure for it – but when she did, it was like a deluge. She shook with hilarity, amazed at her freedom now the fight against life was suspended. Later she looked ashamed, as if an interval of happiness might have broken the rules, or cheated the God who dealt our fates. Her eyes remained wary, expecting a blow.

If only she would talk to me, I thought, I could learn from her the history of the human race. The past of others is our past too, and when she caught the bus down from the hills that day to wander from door to door looking for a job as a maid, she had traversed several centuries in a couple of hours. Her reminiscences kept the ancestral ways alive, in a tense which was always present. When I discovered how to cue her, the stories were delivered over and over again, always the same like memorised poetry: they were rituals, and the telling was a ritual too.

The first time was the trickiest. She could not imagine why this vagabond from out there should be so curious about doings in her *terra*. (Home doesn't properly translate that sacred word: in English it's a notion belonging to the indoors, and too much of a genteel euphemism for house; the adjective nice always seems to be lurking nearby. *Terra* connotes earth. The idea has soil clinging to it. And it names our final resting-place.) I allayed her suspicions by barter, trading memories of my own – apple-picking on the Tasmanian farm, hanging my dead grandfather's suit in a cherry tree to flap at the crows. Paltry though they were, she accepted them; she took me a little more seriously when I said I had once milked a cow. In exchange for these meagre, half-invented anecdotes, I got a saga. Every tale generated others, like a family's proliferation. Even when I had heard a particular episode a dozen times and merely alluded to it, it was recapitulated with all its details, and every scrap of dialogue. Summary or synopsis were disrespectful to the dead, frustrating their return to life. In between bouts of housework, she was a bard.

One of my favourite incidents had to do with milking: the case of the dry nanny-goat. The goat in question, grazing industriously all day, never yielded a drop in the evening. There was consternation in the family. Could a snake be suckling her on the sly? (It was believed that the wily local snakes had ways of ingratiating.) Then Rosalina's father stumbled on the solution one afternoon. He found the goat contentedly browsing in the grass while, prone beneath it, his two youngest sons took turns to drink from her. They admitted, as he unbuckled his belt, that they made a habit of it, on their way home from school.

The first time I heard the story, all my pasteurised puritanism reacted in disgust. I could see from her face – which didn't sympathise with my grimace – that it was the wrong response. To her, there was nothing unsavoury about it. The only moral was that they should not have diverted a supply which belonged to the whole family. But despite her prosaic matter-of-factness, the more I thought about it, and the more often I heard the tale, the more fabulous it seemed: a fable indeed, ancient and archetypal; a pastoral idyll about our kinship with other creatures and our fostering by maternal nature, less bellicose (since it concerned a distracted undiscriminating goat not a she-wolf) than the rearing of Romulus and Remus. It had the daring truth of myth, beyond credibility. Could it really have happened?

I also misinterpreted another story, which happened on the midsummer holiday celebrating the Assumption. A cousin who had studied for the priesthood was to say his first Mass in the village; Rosalina and her brood of sisters were treated to new white dresses for the occasion. Her father was late coming home, to brush up for the four-mile hike to the settlement. One of the goat-nurtured brothers went off to look for him, and found him stretched dead in a field: a heart attack presumably, though there was no way of determining, and – since the ordaining of his death mattered more than its momentary cause inside the body – no point in doing so. The girls took off the white dresses, in which they had imagined themselves angels. That afternoon they dipped them in a cauldron of black dye and hung them on the bushes outside the house. Next day they wore them to the funeral.

It seemed to me a cruel abbreviation of childhood, and of life itself: white blackened to mourning overnight, as if the dresses were bodies stained and shadowed by mortality. Again I got it wrong. She couldn't share my sadness, which was anyway just a reflex of self-pity. Her father, she said, had chosen a beautiful day to die on – a church festival, and the date of his nephew's first Mass. Regret, especially for yourself, was irrelevant. Each anniversary she revives the story, and admires the symmetry of it all over again.

Along with the braid of hair and the lucky charms and the rope of beads for enumerating prayers, she brought down to the city her own pharmacopoeia. She still looks at my hoards of pills with disbelief: how can these sugar-coated chemical pellets have any power over my itches, anxieties and insomnia? Where is the virtue, the goodness in them? She doctors the body with remedies collected from the vegetable garden. For a headache, an onion inside a wet rag clamped onto the skull; for corns on the feet, a prescription involving a cactus – you take one of its pronged fronds, slice away the thorns, peel off the rubbery top layer of skin but not the bottom, then lay the bared side on the callous; tie it with string, put on your bed socks, and by next morning the horny skin is white, puffy, and can be eased off. Another cactus cured whooping-cough in the village. It is an evil plant with spiked ears, called hell's fig tree. But even the devil could be made to part with a healing sweetness. You cut a leaf in half, nail it to the wall, cake the split with sugar. The succulents inside guzzle the sugar, then drip a syrupy juice; you collect that and take it by the spoonful. Only one man in her village, very rich by local standards, had this bush, and mothers with children in danger from the cough used to plead for a leaf.

Deprived of the right cacti in Lisbon, she still had her cartons of purgative tea. There were teas for gastric disorders, for the heart, lungs and kidneys, for cramps and nervous tension, teas to fortify the blood and to thin it out, teas which cleansed the vision or restored hearing, teas for the common cold and teas to soothe ulcers; there was even – tucked away in a drawer apart from the other ministering potions, which were arrayed on a shelf like condiments – a tea which specifically addressed itself to the ovaries. All of them enjoyed religious patronage: on the white paper boxes, a Virgin gazed imploringly skywards and wrung her hands, suffering I suppose from one or more of the internal agonies treated by the teas.

To see Rosalina brewing them up was like straying into a sorceress's den. The boxes contained no mere nipped leaves; they were assortments of twigs and tendrils, roots and parched buds, twists of prickly wood like barbed wire, all the bristling casements of deciduous nature. On the stove, the ingredients had to stew for half an hour before they evacuated their secrets into the water. She then strained out the shrubbery and drank the brown liquid from a soup bowl; she always felt better for it, discreetly hiccuped as it percolated through her, and returned from her witchy cavern in the hills to the twentieth century and its kitchen appliances.

She took me once or twice on time-trips, excursions back to a past which lay just a few miles outside the city, where cement and asphalt and tarmac were peeled away and *terra* resumed. We went one autumn to a pig-slaughtering at Mafra, in the mountains between Lisbon and the ocean, hitching a ride in a battered taxi whose driver slept in its back seat in the city all the week, and allowed himself to go home on Sunday. The town cowers medievally beneath the intimidation of the church: a gaunt, granitic monastery on a cliff of steps in the main square, which like a baleful ancient inquisitor forced the houses to their knees.

In the hills behind, her relatives had their scrimpy farms. The valleys feuded, and the fields were seamed with invisible lines of fire. As the quarrels continued, factions came to personify the patches of land or stands of eucalypts (known as *clipsh*) they fought over. One venal sister-in-law, to whom Rosalina wouldn't speak, was always referred to as 'her from the Serra da Luz'; she was also dubbed the *cabra*, which made me think of her as an ill-tempered nanny goat, greedily grazing the disputed slopes. Currently the argument concerned care of the octogenarian mother – who was handed round between the farms, with interludes in a Lisbon shanty and detours to our house whenever it was thought she needed a confessor – and, more important, disposal of her pension. Also on the agenda was the matter of eventual rights to the few squares of earth she owned, and her embroidered bedspread. The clan convened over a butchered hog to haggle. By this time, I knew about such blood-smeared communal rituals: my colleagues at All Souls, I gathered, climbed onto the college roof once a century and trailed a dead duck round the ramparts, chanting a song about mallards.

I had met the sacrificial pig on a previous visit. In a yard of bullocks awaiting their division into beefs and rabbits with rheumy eyes and sick, scrofulous ears, it was the prize exhibit. It luxuriated in its stall, rolling in swill like a bubble bath. For months it had devoted itself to eating, and expected some putrid tribute every time the stall door opened. It wrinkled its snout at us in contempt when it saw we had only come to admire it. Already it was so resplendently heavy that it could not support that heaving pink body on its thin ankles and pointy trotters. It therefore gave up all thought of standing, and reposed in fragrant muck with the air of an epicure on a divan.

Adelina, the farmer's wife, made me promise to come back for its slaughter. 'It's a beautiful thing to see,' she said, and when she noticed my scepticism she added, 'for someone who likes to see that sort of thing.' I thought I'd ask for a preview. She described the scene, an annual rite. The men foregathered, and a deputation of a dozen or more paid the pig a visit. They poured a hearty swig of home-distilled brandy down its gullet – not to give it courage, but to perfume its meat. It burped in satisfaction. Then, when they set about nudging, teasing, tugging and hauling it from its couch of swinish content, it had a sudden realisation of what its pampered omnivore's life had all been for. It understood mortality that instant. Eviction from its excremental bed meant death. It writhed, kicked up spatterings of mud, rolled its eyes, squealed. Crossing the yard to the block on its back, it had no time to learn acquiescence, or console itself by rapidly inventing religion. At least, nowadays, it did not have to experience its end: they zapped it with electrodes before they hosed it down to lay bare the rosy flesh under crusted dirt; only then did their knives go to work on it.

I was happy to trade the actual sight for her description. We arranged to arrive the next day, for the feast. Planks and trestles made tables in the yard; there were boxes and barrels to sit on. The relatives carved up the old woman's acres and her monthly pension in a corner, with less surgical efficiency than they had shown in their dealings with the pig.

The matriarch herself, dressed in the black she had worn since her husband died sixty years ago, a handkerchief knotted on her head, perambulated with the aid of her stick. When she bumped into benches or great-grand-children, she wailed *Ai Jesus*, or rather – since that looks like a curse, not an appeal for intercession – *Ai Zhesoosh*. *Zhesoosh* is a better name for the figure she imagined than Jesus, the meek, mild, gentle invention of we Protestants. *Zhesoosh* sounded militant, like the *Bózhe* of the Russians, with his brazen Arab-sounding initial syllable and the furious whoosh, as of a chariot cleaving through the air, with which his other syllable was forced forth. He, it transpired, was the harsh but just cause of her tribulations: he had clouded her sight to punish her for some half-remembered sin. Her name was Aurora; she lived, however, in a permanent dusk and, knocking into me and poking me experimentally with her stick, asked the barn-door 'Is that a person?' She seemed not to mind that the barn-door didn't answer. She had grown used to obtuseness, to groping through a world of obstacles placed in her way by a whimsical deity. Next time I passed, she patted my bottom appraisingly, felt her way round my waist until she located a hand, then gave it a whiskery kiss, just in case it belonged to a relative or a potential benefactor.

Slices from the pig's ribs smouldered on the brazier. One of the women was feeding a minced reduction of him into an intestine, a if he had been revived to consume himself with no need of a mouth: the result would be sausages. The rest of the body lay about inside the house. The kitchen was an operating theatre. The sink bubbled with blood, due to congeal into black puddings; there were overflow pails and jugs. Unclassified cuts of pork covered the counters and a table.

Since I had missed the execution, it was re-staged for me. Assuming my protests were mere politeness, the farmer's wife cleared a section of the counter, dabbled and fumbled through the piles of meat to search out the constituents of the pig's head, then reassembled it for me: the halved nose, like an amputated trunk; the guzzling mouth; the flaps of ear. There were other ambiguous gobbets of gore which didn't quite fit the puzzle. But after a while she managed to piece together the face of the beast, as if re-suturing Frankenstein's monster. And having done so, and let me gulp at the effigy of drained wax, she then grabbed his features in handfuls and dispersed them again. The quaking buckets of blood, and the body successively slashed into fragments, reconstructed, then once more sundered: was this butchery or a Mass?

The question reminded me that, to compound my estrangement, I was an infidel here. The rumour circulated, I knew, that I was a Protestant, or an atheist (which amounted to the same thing).

At least I was not mistaken for a Mormon, pairs of whom – adolescents called Elders, moulded from bland plastic in some factory in the desert and sent here to practise subversion – prowled the Lisbon suburb, disingenuously asking directions from the maids and then engaging them in doctrinal debate. To the maids, these sets of Mormon twins were not so much strays from out there as drop-ins from outer space. Only one in each pair ever spoke. Could the silent one be a dummy, in whom a speech-box had not been implanted yet? Their eyes never blinked, or registered uncertainty; they didn't sweat, despite their antique underwear. Had the relevant glands been removed back in Utah? Theirs was the calm of cold fanaticism. They frightened me as much as they did the maids, who after the first campaign were warned against them by their employers, and hurried indoors when they saw the white-shirted crusaders with the sealed pores approaching. Rosalina paid me the compliment of assuming I was not one of them.

But then what was I? She couldn't conceive. For me, everything was relative, partial, fractionally true; she, however, had never needed to imagine an alternative to her own life. Beliefs also were absolute. How could there be another system elsewhere?

One day she worked it out. There weren't any Protestant churches that she knew of in Lisbon: this must be the clue. So she asked me, 'To be a Protestant – it means believing in God but not going to church? Is that it, Senhor Peter?' To spare her more mental vexation, I agreed.

I learned to be wary of stubbing my toe on one of her superstitions. I had already done so once, when learning the language by mimicry. I enjoyed being a baby again, elated by all the new gurgly sounds it was possible to make, much less concerned by sense: I would find out what the words referred to eventually, when I had more practice in piecing the world together syllable by syllable; meanwhile it was a pleasure just to vocalise. And it was fun to do without rule-books, first acquiring words, rehearsing them silently, listening for a context in which they could be used, at last triumphantly deploying them.

Thus in all innocence I collected a phrase of hers. I first heard her use it once in a rage against the pot-bellied, nimble-fingered grocer who sold door to door from the back of his van. He had cheated her of some small change once, and would not make amends when she pointed it out on his next visit. They raged at each other with haughty indirectness. He was *o Senhor* to her, she was *a Senhora* to him. The gentleman is a bandit, she shrilled. The lady is a cow, he replied. (They did not do business any more after that.) As he drove off, she clenched her fist and shook it at his van.

Then out came the saying I coveted, delivered with a machine-gun's clatter on the opening consonant: *Raios os partam!* she said. Or actually *Rrrrrrraios,* because a rattle-snake couldn't have stretched it out with more insidious menace. It was a drum-roll of doom. I had never been able to wrap my tongue round this sound. It flapped in vain against the top of my mouth; when I wanted to roll an r, I found myself whistling instead. Here was my chance to practise.

I co-opted the phrase, and was soon applying it to any domestic inconvenience, to buses when they were late, or to the postman if he did not have a letter for me. The first few times, she winced. My pronunciation, I thought; but I was bound to get better. Still, the more often I discharged it with its florid rat-tat-tat, the more perturbed she was. The corner of her mouth retracted in a spasm of pain. Once I was sure I saw her cross herself.

It was time, I thought, to find out what the phrase meant. It turned out to be a Grade A curse, which I had been homicidally misusing and – even worse – devaluing in the process. The *raios* were lightning rays, of which (together with thunderclaps) Rosalina had a holy terror; the phrase was a call for lightning to strike an enemy and break him. To her, it was voodoo, saved up for an emergency. How could it summon the forked fire out of the sky to punish the grocer if I was wasting and weakening it? I felt genuinely guilty – not because I believed in the malediction but because I believed in the power of words, in their effectiveness as spells, their magic capacity (as in the case of 'Hoi!') to open doors and induct you into society. Fond as I was and am of the phrase, I have never uttered it since.

Every society has its deity, its source of value and of legal exaction. In England the sacred idea was society itself, envisaged as cricket: a team game, with its silly but solemn rules and its compulsory uniforms. A colleague at Christ Church once loudly accused me, when I turned up for dinner without a tie, of 'letting the side down'. The match, as he saw it, was between us in our business suits and our pupils in their torn jeans. Any slackening of the dress code, and chaos would punctually come again.

In America a different faith prevails. The team and the side, those holy English notions, mean nothing there. The local god, as you discover once you turn on the talk shows, is the self, sovereign, autonomous, and generally in therapy to restore its conviction of its own worth. In England, a class (or, drawlingly, clarse, with the vowel itself a badge of subscription) is a group you belong to, just like a college. In America, clǎss refers to the individual's aura, created by clothes or hair-style or the clǎssy nonchalance with which you defy time, prosecution, paparazzi or whatever.

But the god of Portuguese society, or at least of Rosalina's experience, was God himself. I began to perceive that he presided over all our doings. Her sayings were formulae intended to assure him that we were aware he was eyeing us down the chimney or through the keyhole, and could revoke our existences whenever he pleased.

The last thing she said before going to bed was: 'See you in the morning, if God wills.' The proviso always made me shudder: were we clambering into our blanketed coffins, and switching the light off definitively? If I helped with the washing-up or cleared the table or did some other supernumerary chore, there was another chiming formula to reward me: 'May God pay you with good health.' He (rather than a high-fibre diet and membership in a gym, as New York believed) was the source of well-being. The dead moved into his care, as if into a retirement home. When Jorge's father died, she referred to him from then on as 'Senhor Doutor who God has'. For a year after the event, any mishap – a pan of rice which burned, or a plate which escaped her hand and shattered on the floor – was interpreted as God's castigation for her bad temper with the dead man during his illness.

God needed to be bought off with donations: hence her sacrifice of that rope of hair. Favours were besought with the earnest promise of future repayments. Grace was like a bank loan. If a relative survived an operation or recovered from some agricultural disaster, Rosalina would go on a pilgrimage to the mountains to pay back the devotion she had promised. Aeons of *Avés*, mile-long spools of rosaries; sometimes, as well, a classified ad inserted in the local paper (which God omnisciently browsed in) recording thanks for the gift; in extreme cases, a journey on foot to the shrine at Fátima in the middle of the country, where the Virgin had made an appearance; in a real emergency, punitive circuits of the church at Fatima, struggling round the stony yard all day on bleeding or bandaged knees.

You were expected to sin, if only to keep the priest in business. The matriarch Aurora was regularly brought to the house to be confessed: in the suburb, the priest made house-calls, though the pharisaical rich had little use for him. She waited in the kitchen, invoking *Zhesoosh* every now and then. When Padre Francisco arrived – moist with godliness and black round the jowls, the antithesis of those blond, non-sweating Mormons – they retired to the pantry, kept as dark as a confessional to stop the potatoes sprouting. How could I resist eavesdropping behind the door?

Padre Francisco addressed her as his daughter (she could have been his grandmother), asked how long it was since he had last confessed her, and then set about helping her to find some sins she might own up to. It is not easy for a woman in her late eighties who is nearly blind. Most of the vices require vigour, will-power, or at least eyes to lust with. She was always embarrassed by having nothing truly vile to tell him. When all the graver options were discarded, Padre Francisco always supplied her with a compromise. 'Perhaps, my daughter,' he would insinuate, 'some little acts of impatience?' Low-grade grumbling she could in all conscience confess to. He prescribed a penance, and God was appeased for the time being.

It all seemed as barbarous to me as the pig-slaying, a conspiracy to keep the poor and ignorant in submission by inventing crimes they could be punished for. I had not reckoned, as usual, on the capacity of the victims to protect themselves. Padre Francisco had a bad reputation among the maids of the street, because he was in the habit of picking his nose while handing out communion wafers. If Rosalina saw him behind the rail on Sunday mornings, she rapidly dodged into another queue of communicants.

The same religion meddlingly moralised illness, and pretended that a physical accident was a spiritual test. When Jorge's mother suffered a stroke, a nun from a nearby convent began to visit. Her name, or rather the title, was Irmã Inocência – Sister Innocence. She held the confused old lady's hand, and mouthed consolations she could not understand. The Christmas before a second stroke killed her, Irmã Inocência sent her a card, with a message fulsomely hoping that she would find the courage to continue bearing her cross. I almost ripped the paper in rage when I saw it. As if sickness and death had a reason, or constituted a plot like that journey to the mound!

Now a few years later, I am less intolerant, because I recognise the same motive in myself. The myth, the fiction, the persuasive, shaping lie: has anyone ever lived without them? Religion devises a metaphysical order; art organises and refines the view from the window. Both tell stories, because a story is patterned and purposeful, which the world is not. In retrospect I rather admire the cheating art of ingenious Inocência, who turned an affliction into a challenge, disabled helplessness into valiant endurance. It was one more case of that self-interested map-making which dreams up the idea of a centre and locates it here, now, in me. My only current objection to religion is that it insists on pretending to be true.

The time had come to test my own estrangement. Last spring, a Virgin visited the suburb. For a week there were processions in her honour, transferring her image from one to another chapel in the district, with a final peregrination to the monastery of Jerónimos at the bottom of the hill. Every night Rosalina washed up in haste, collected her candle, and hurried off to join the crowd of followers. On the last night, I asked her if I could come along. She looked doubtful at first, but relented when it occurred to her that she might be ushering an errant, protesting soul back into the fold.

Below the tiered embassies with their alien flags and their embattled gates, in streets as narrow as culverts beside the monastery, the parade had lumbered out of the last chapel and was milling to organise itself in the tunnel between the houses. From around the corner we could hear the chanted *Avés* and smell the dripping wax. A whole society had scrambled into the alley, and tripped itself up or reeled in disoriented circles as it tried to establish order and precedence. Priests bumped into teenage soldiers, dogs barked, lost children squalled, candle flames treacherously tongued someone's hair or molten wax slopped onto someone else's hand. Instructions stammered from police radios in a coughing fit of static. It was an unmade world of colliding atoms, lurching bodies, undirected energy. Above its hugger-mugger, on her shoulder-high catafalque of flowers, bobbed its more or less unmoved mover: the meek, implacable, immaculate blue and white woman, stiffly at attention though in danger of toppling over as the crowd broke like waves around her bearers. If it had rained then, we would all have reverted to that undifferentiated time before the beginning – mud, muddle, anarchy and swirling uproar.

Somehow, in the street where there was no room to turn round, the molecules steadied themselves, formed partnerships, arrived through mishap and experiment at the idea of degree and hierarchy. It could all be attributed perhaps to the wooden woman, but it happened around her not because of her, and she only just escaped submergence in the rivulet of flesh or singeing by the hand-held flames. The world created itself in homage to her, assuming that she was the creator's vessel.

A chain of spiritual and social eminence rose from the chaotic ground like the fakir's self-erecting rope, then lowered itself again so the procession – with everyone now correctly placed in relation to the creator – could sway off down the street, in time to those rhythmic *Avés*. The Virgin bounced along on a portable garden of lilies, inside a cordon of fire. The boy soldiers were her pall-bearers; scouts carried sparking torches. In the crowd, women held up candles, wrapped in cornets of wrinkly aluminium foil from the kitchen drawer like ignited ice-creams, or plugged into the necks of plastic flasks which once held detergent. The ecclesiastical ranks traipsed behind their totem: a bishop nodding under his silky baldachin, its poles supported by swarthy novices; priests absently signing the empty air with their index fingers; a fat, jowly nun holding up in front of her chest not an icon or even a prayer book but a transistor radio, broadcasting the event. The outer edges of the procession were flanked by the temporal powers: police astride their motorcycles blocked traffic so the raggle-taggle horde of wailing women, sleepy children and excited dogs could pass. A cripple rotated down the street in advance of the Virgin and the bishop to sell candles, veering unevenly from side to side with one leg shorter than the other.

Once there was a rabble of profane intruders, among them a giggling teenage girl in a leather jacket, who bopped along to the drone of the *Avés* and, having no candle, puffed out smoke from her cigarette. An old man next to me grabbed the cigarette, pulled it from her mouth and hurled it away. 'You see,' he said to me as she gyrated off through the ranks, 'God is good – otherwise he'd have struck her down.'

What I liked best about it was that the sacred image opened doors, exposed secrets. It possessed the creator's omniscience, the X-ray vision which the novelist aspires to. As it passed, the convention ordained that you should make your house ready for the spirit's visit, and place all your wordly goods on display in case the spirit called for a souvenir. It reminded me of the preparations for the Queen Mother's passage through my street in London. That too was an instance of an image's power, except that she vanished from one privacy into another, disappearing for a cup of tea with invited guests in the basement, whereas this travelling idol made everything public, and merged us all in the same boisterous throng. At last, thanks to her intercession, I saw into the houses which were always tightly shuttered against the sun.

All doors were propped open, all blinds and curtains pulled back, all light bulbs switched on (even the humblest apartments had chandeliers). The houses declared themselves transparent, like a spirit radiantly shedding its cement and furniture of bone and flesh. Everything precious in them which was usually locked up had been arranged on laden dining-tables and cluttered window-ledges or draped from balconies: candlesticks of silver or serpentine brass, ancient plates with cracks in the glaze, blood- or earth-red oriental rugs, lace-trimmed bridal sheets slept in once only. From one window, a pink snow of petals drifted onto the candles and the seething torches.

Everyone interpreted the occasion or envisaged the spirit as they chose. For an elderly woman, sobbing on her knees in the gutter, relatives sustaining her elbows as she worked her way through the beads, it was a summons to penitence. But when the chants and the flickering lights passed some shanties on a vacant lot near the monastery, the blacks streamed out in their turbans and aprons to smile, wave or – like the naked dirty children – jump up and down. To the woman in the gutter, the march was tragic: we follow the image because the deity has quit us, leaving only this replica behind. To the black families from the ramshackle huts, it meant carnival. And to me?

On the way down the hill, the maid from next door, Lurdes, had told me about this Virgin. Lurdes was an ill-favoured woman who had never married, lame, wall-eyed, not especially clean, patronised by Rosalina for her simplicity; she had no good physical features, and no bad moral qualities either. She also knew a fair amount about the world, at least as mapped by Christianity, having been on pilgrimages to Rome and the holy land. 'You know,' Lurdes said as we followed the trail of smoke, 'this Our Lady has been everywhere. She even went to Russia once,' and though she didn't finish the sentence for fear of offending me I could tell that she approved of a mission to reclaim the unbelievers there.

The insipid pastel-coloured figurine was as ubiquitous and immaterial as air, or as the human craving to imagine explanations. People abjectly credited her with power, and fell to their knees as she passed; but the only power she possessed was that which they had invested in her. She had been elected to deity, carved into symbolic status, just like the great-grandmother with the hat at the bottom of my street. Before we recreate the shapeless world we find ourselves in, we must create the idea of a creator. That was what we paraded through the streets.

As the mob droned and shuffled towards the monastery and the image inside its shield of flame dwindled into the distance, I remembered something Baudelaire noted about his rambles through Paris with its heterodox altars and its curiosity shops of toys which are divinities in some other country – 'I never walk past a wooden fetish, a gilded Buddha, a Mexican idol without saying to myself: maybe it is the true God.' He was right, and in all cases. A somnolent Buddha, an African stick man, this soppy lactic Virgin and the Greek athlete in the Oxford quad, even the basilisk with the beacon who rears from the New York harbour: they are all true gods, as long as anyone believes in them. Though shouldn't they be the ones to believe in the human mind, which has invented them in its own image? And there is a second proviso. Despite Baudelaire, the issue is not truth, but the necessity of fiction.

It was all too much for me – the flames, the fumes, the stench of wax and the snowfall of petals, the hypnotic moan of the *Avés*, the crone in the gutter and the jigging children from the slum. I was unaccountably moved; I began to cry.

My definition of ritual is an occasion which chokes my throat, interrupts my breathing, makes my eyes stream. I was used to having it happen in opera houses, and (for the most part) only there. Now it had overtaken me in the crushed, chaotic street. It was caused by the sudden, painless extermination of the individual life. We spend so much time defending our singularity, defining ourselves by placing ourselves outside things, apart from others – or at least I had always done so. But the instinct can be overruled, and in its place comes this feeling of merger: a sensation just like drowning, which I knew about because I had been rescued from it in the thermal pool in Death Valley. What I recall from that experience was the bliss of surrender; no struggle at all, until I was hauled out by the scruff of my neck and left beached and gasping on the ground as if newly born. Music induced the same prostration and the same absolute vulnerability. Wagner could be relied on to do the trick, when Parsifal and Gurnemanz march to the Grail temple through a threnody of bells, or during Elsa's long, tentative, interrupted advance to the minster in *Lohengrin*. The orchestra carried with it a conviction of attunement, membership in a community of emotion as buoyant as that hot spring water in the California desert. This pious, lumbering mob was just as oceanic. I may not have believed what they did, but I believed in their belief.

Rosalina was quietly gratified the next day, and kept me under observation for signs of change. She suspected, I was sure, that she had engineered a conversion. In a way, she had.

Later that year, in another world, I went to another religious procession – diabolical this time, with a throng of fiends, freaks, monsters, mutants, bogeys and disgraced angels: the Hallowe'en parade in Greenwich Village.

The true gods here were an occult lot. Priapus in a greasy raincoat, flashing a floppy trio of plastic privates; a consortium of Hair Stylists from Hell, electrically frizzing one another's fright wigs; Hitler with a moustache of mascara, a brown military jacket and arm upraised in a salute, who changed from a ranting dictator to a ballerina at the waist, for instead of the bottom half of the uniform he wore a pink tutu, and skidded through the streets on roller skates – a centaur coupling power and grace, mania and frivolity, authoritarianism and art. For the last few hours of October, to the sound of steel or brass bands and with ranks of tossing, twirling male majorettes, the Village became pandemonium, a congress of ribald devils.

The same festival in Oxford had a different, dourer meaning for me. Hallowe'en was the Eve of All Hallows, preparation for the day devoted to All Saints which follows; after that came the feast for all souls of the faithful departed, when the college founded to pray for them makes its elections. Every year as the nights turned clammier and the pavements slicker, with the lamps quavering through drifts of fog from the water-meadows, I remembered the anniversary with a shiver. The faithful departed rose from their graves on a carving above the front gate of the college; the gerontocracy inside might have been assembled from their teeming number.

Election didn't make you immortal, but nominated you for membership of the dead. An elderly historian stumbled in circles round the quadrangle during my first year at All Souls, and had to be dissuaded from straying out into the street. I came upon him once on the frosty grass, his eyes and nose watering, his mind babbling. All I could do was blow his nose for him, and coax him indoors. A few months later he sagged forward in his chair at a college dinner. The waiters closed ranks and, while everyone else at the table contrived not to notice, lifted up the chair, tipped it backwards and carried him out sprawled on it, as if in ironic triumph shoulder-high. I gathered that it was not done to express sorrow, or sympathy, or anything at all. To be distressed by death was as vulgar as to enjoy the food you were currently eating. Either way, you admitted you were alive, and offended against the rigor mortis of good manners. A collective grief was eventually signalled by the college flag, flapping at half-mast above the gate with the carved ghosts.

In the Celtic calendar, the year ended on October 31st. I always thought of it as the date when, for a while, my own childhood ended: from now on, it seemed, I would have to act prematurely elderly, and remember to wear a tie.

Sanctifying Hallowe'en and making it soulful, Christianity routed its witches, warlocks and irreverent imps. Greenwich Village preserves the pagan rite. Hallowe'en here is childhood's perpetuation and its revenge. At dusk, infancy turns malicious. Tiny ghouls convene among the monkey-bars and sand-pits opposite my apartment and spread out to extort sweets from harassed doormen and dog-walkers. Adolescents lurk in doorways with cartons of eggs under their sweatshirts. One year it was fashionable to inject the eggs with chemical hair-remover. If you were lucky, you merely got shampooed with congealing yolk; if not, when you wiped away the slime you found your head looked like a frayed carpet. The shops sell wounds, sores, deformities, wolfman teeth, capsules of vampire blood, liquid latex which can be sculpted into scars or warts or wrinkles, white make-up which glows in the dark, green scaly insect faces or porcine snouts. Play, for one night only, taunts and torments the reality which the rest of the time overrules it.

The Village reinvents itself for the occasion, and takes on the likeness of a bad dream. Down Hudson Street at the White Horse Tavern, all the white horses in the windows turn spectral suddenly, even though during the year they look chubby and cheery, like carousel animals out to pasture. Death rides a pale horse after all, so the steeds join his cavalcade, carrying grubby pumpkins on their backs. The antique shop a block away has changed to a haunted house. Cobwebs of stretched, strandy cotton wool entangle over some baronial chairs and a musty screen, or thicken round a suitcase from which two amputated wooden hands poke out, as if clawing at their suffocating tombstone. A mourning veil of thin wool shrouds the room, with black plastic spiders roosting in corners. At the pharmacy, the same webs finger the Epilady depilation kits, the packs of Seductive Musk Body Talk Cologne, and the aromatic boxes for trapping roaches. The chocolate shop sells edible heads, white, milky brown or dark, and a motorised witch with a crone's shrivelled face stirs up a cauldron of cocoa butter. The candle shop beside it exhibits a black patchouli stump next to a Dracula candelabra: six birthday-cake candles studded along the outstretched arms of a spook wearing an RIP shroud; except for his black and white sobriety, he resembles Liberace arisen from his piano seat, balancing his battery of candles on that billowing, engulfing, nocturnal cape.

Everywhere the skeletons are partying. A man without meat, all scoured bleached bone, lounges on the window ledge of a restaurant beside the eaters of bleeding burgers and chilli con carne, grinning as they cannibalise him. Other bags of bones try on new clothes. In one window, inflatable ghouls – white, with clear plastic rib cages containing air not organs – drape themselves in feather boas, sequinned flapper dresses or cloche hats. On Broadway, a corpse with a face mask crusted in carnage models its burial suit in an open coffin, one hand thrust over the edge clutching a pile of phoney garnets and junk metal brooches, avaricious even in death. In the leather supplier on Christopher Street, among rats concussed by traps and a belfry of gibbering bats, the skeletons are learning the unholy joys of sado-masochism. Swords pierce their cavernous heads, and an armoury of chains and handcuffs are looped through their empty pelvises. One of them – a Hell's Angel perhaps, when there was beef and sinew on him – still wears a skull ring around his polished knuckle. Hallowe'en lends itself to this kind of sexual theatre, where eroticism mimes extinction rather than outwitting it.

Round the corner, in another window, Freddy Krueger runs amok. Freddy, the killer from the horror film *Nightmare on Elm Street*, is the hero of this holiday. Here, in an obscenely fussy tableau, he is on the rampage in a suburban bedroom, slashing his way through a bloody wreckage of ripped pyjamas, wounded teddy bears and crushed, befouled packets of pizza chips. Pus drips from his fangs and hangs like stalactites from the open sores on his face. His raised hand ends in claws, with a scimitar attached to each finger; every blade is extruded further by glistening spidery threads of gore.

Freddy is one of the monsters bred when American reason nods off: the ruthless, hilarious opposite of everything the society holds dear, cutting a swathe through those quiet elm-lined streets and their chintzy dormitories, scattering scraps of brutalised fast food in his wake. All the novelty stores sell his slicing, bladed glove, and with a tube of liquid latex you can make a copy of his scorched, melted face for yourself. He has epigones everywhere, and when one of them turns up in the Hallowe'en parade, leering from under a felt hat and fencing with those lethal fingers, he always gets a round of affectionate applause. These are the machine-made incubi of the national mind, and this is the season when they take to the streets.

If Paul Bunyan was the first American folk-hero – the leveller of trees, the slayer of nature, whose axe hews civilisation from the rough ragged thickets of matter – then Freddy and the maniac in the skull-like hockey mask from *Friday the 13th* and the motorised killer in *The Texas Chain-Saw Massacre* are his latter-day descendants, chopping down and cleaving through the fabric he built up. No sooner has America constructed itself than it feels obliged to dismantle the structure in an angry frenzy of reinvention. The idealists need the anarchists and the assassins; there must be a constant turnover in Americas.

In the Lisbon streets, the bobbing, toppling graven image inside its herbaceous border and its cordon of fire managed to symbolise society's cohesion, its belief in itself. Freddy's murderous career celebrates freedom from all that. The man of violence, with no pieties to restrain him, pursues his own liberated happiness, and leaves cosy Elm Street in ruins. At Hallowe'en, in the Village where the city keeps its marginalia, America flirts deliciously with its own destruction. England too has its hours of licensed terrorism, which follow a few days later: Guy Fawkes' Night, when effigies are hurled onto pyres of burning rubber and London shudders to the sound of joky pyrotechnic explosions while the sky flashes crimson. I always imagine, lurking indoors or peering up at the bursts of flame from my yard, that the whole top-heavy officious edifice has been blown apart, and relish the seditious, improbable thrill of the idea.

In the tableau on Bleecker Street, Freddy acknowledges the date by wearing pumpkin-coloured boots (though they're soiled with the vital juices of his victims). All cults convene on this last, haunted evening: the hobgoblins and uprisen cadavers of the Celts, Christianity with its troops of drearily worthy saints, and the native American veneration of the pumpkin. Still, although it is autumnal, the pumpkin hardly matches the ghoulishness of the occasion. It is plump, globular, with a sweet pulp under its rind; to qualify as a Hallowe'en emblem it is hollowed out, with alligator teeth carved across it in an evil smirk. The ruddy face of Falstaff, gutted, becomes the grinning skull of Yorick. The shop-window dummies on Christopher Street sport pumpkin-coloured T-shirts under their leather jackets for a week. Even the Empire State Building valiantly tries, despite its lack of bulk, to be mistaken for a pumpkin: its shaft glows orange, and the spire is red, like the fruit's inflamed stalk.

Among all the icons and allusions and simulacrae, it comes as a shock to see the real thing, incongruously lolling among the gilded frames in a Christopher Street gallery – a pumpkin like a guillotined head reposing on a litter of withered sheaves, attended by ears of corn with grains the colour of decaying teeth. The mouth cut into it decadently smiled as the flesh ripened and rotted. I passed it every day for a week, watching the smile become fixed, anguished, while the orange skin turned blacker, or whitened into furry mould. At last its death became too life-like, and it was spirited away. Next time I passed, the decomposing head had been replaced by a fresher one, which could suffer through the cycle all over again.

On the day itself, the undead are too impatient to wait for dark. At the Asian grocer's on Eighth Avenue, I found myself piecing together my lunch next to the Wicked Witch of the West, hook nose, conical hat and all. Her diet alone was out of character: not filleted babies garnished with newts' eyes and frogs' toes but bean curd, lettuce and scruffy alfalfa. Along Fourteenth Street, the Phantom of the Opera strutted through the vendors at their oily food stalls. A mask protected his seared face (though enough of his nose remained for him to implant a stud in it); the icy wind from the river ruffled his home-made nylon cape; he stalked along, despite the demystifying sun, with the stiff gait of one whose legs had been too long cramped in his coffin. The men selling hot dogs at the corners didn't turn their heads. Nor would they have done so, probably, for a certified zombie.

Despite the plastic tarantulas in webs of cotton wool and the putrefying pumpkins, the parade when it jived into formation down the West Side Highway was short of spooks, ghouls and things that go bump in the night. People impersonated dreams, not nightmares. These were not the uprisen dead, but the unleashing of alternative, imagined selves: Chaplin trotting along with the jerky, jittery gait of bodies in a silent film, led by a non-existent dog; Carmen Miranda, hairy-chested, with a pyramid of paw-paws, coroneted pineapples and bloated berries on her head; Colonel Sanders in his ante-bellum white suit, dragging a rubber unplucked Kentucky chicken whose neck he had just wrung; arms extended to embrace the crowd, a Diana Ross whose sequinned sheath slid down her chest to reveal a pair of goose-pimply male nipples; Ronald Reagan inside a mask of furrowed latex with a look of good-humoured bewilderment incised on it, cupping his ear at the crowd's roar and the band's clatter to signal that he couldn't hear a reporter's questions because the helicopter on the lawn was rotating its blades.

Down the river, the Statue of Liberty with an aching arm and a frozen countenance managed to keep her beacon aloft. But here was her alter ego, who had slipped out of the metal carapace for an evening to tell the truth about the harbour she illuminated: a lank-haired, heavy-set girl in a filmy purple prom frock, holding a placard on which she identified herself as Miss Jersey Shore. Instead of the Statue's spiky helmet she had a syringe stuck through her head, and carried instead of an optimistic torch a bag of the medical waste – fouled bandages, phials of deceased blood, used hypodermics – which had washed onto local beaches throughout the summer. Miss Liberty glowered down the bay, loftily conscious of her allegorical mission. Miss Jersey Shore, however, smiled at the dirty, indifferent world in commiseration, and at the same time waved her free hand happy-go-luckily. Liberty – having stepped down from her pedestal, come to terms with her shame, tucked up her skirts and taken to the streets – now meant freedom, which was the ideology of the evening: the freedom to take nothing seriously, not even the sacredness of America.

Behind her trailed a pair for whom the city was still a paradise, so long as they could redefine its rules to suit themselves – Adam in a body stocking with a battery-operated banana at his crotch (a bulb winked on its tip every few seconds, like the neural trigger of desire), Eve dividing her attentions between his banana and the juicy, unforbidden Big Apple she carried (of course she had a moustache).

Others had re-created the creation in their own way, reconstructing their bodies in contradiction of biology. One man had engineered himself into contortions like a double-jointed cubist circus act, and hopped along both upside-down and back-to-front. Behind him was his back-to-front self, who had put both his clothes and his face on the wrong way round; looking forward, gripping the second self which began over his shoulders, was his upside-down identity, with boots where his brain should have been and a second smiling head grazing the ground. The two halves of him, their pairs of arms and legs interlinked, seemed about to turn cartwheels in the street. The creature told an unsettling truth: how can we ever know what happens behind us, or what rear-view variants we might be presenting to the world?

Further on, someone else had beheaded himself for the occasion. A giant in a soiled toga strode past with his head clasped under his arm. The shoulders and the clean-cut neck had been built up on a platform a foot or two above his head, which in the crook of that bulging arm still scowled at the cameras and greeted friends despite its plastery pallor and the line of blood, viscous as raspberry jam, where it once had joined the neck. 'I'm called Caligula,' I heard the head tell a reporter from the television news, squirming in the lock of that unflexing elbow as its upper tier swayed uncertainly; I assume he was hoping to relate himself to Dracula by rhyme.

Then there were those who had opted out of human being altogether, and costumed themselves as objects. A pair of puns on legs, for instance: a Sony Walkman as a walking man, his feet peeping discreetly from the slim black electronic box which encased him, his arms as headphones with padded hands to fit over his user's ears; a blind man as a Venetian blind, with a white tapping stick and the blackened lenses of some ancient spectacles poking through his slats. The body as apparatus, the technological extension of itself, and the body as furniture, its useless eyes usefully blinking over the view from some travelling window.

Or the mirror man, whose body had disappeared behind a kaleidoscope of reflecting facets and refracted angles. Stitched to a grey suit, he wore a patchwork of jangling, glinting glass squares, which as he walked bounced back the street lamps, the flash bulbs, and snatches of our own faces. He threw in the occasional pirouette, and in wheeling round he vanished into a column of sparks and spangles; he grabbed the world in handfuls – the ranks of dancers around him, the mob straining at the barriers on the sidewalk, the horns, the sirens, the screams of delight, the blasts from the next band still two blocks further north on the Highway – and flung it at us again in a shrapnel of light. He no longer existed: he was only what he saw, or what we thought we saw in and on him for a few seconds as he jangled past. Instead of the clump of carved, painted wood trundled through the Lisbon streets, this harlequin of borrowed brilliance fractured and jumbled what he took from us, then returned it brighter than before, as if hurling luminous coins through the air. The other image mutely accepted donations – prayers, petals, smoky candles. This one, more generously, bombarded us with sparks and sequins. The world as it rippled across his mosaic coat changed to a ballet of jesting, restless atoms. How could he bear to go home, close his door, remove the second skin of mirrors, and lapse back into solid, drab humanity?

Though the traffic droned past on the West Side Highway, the city might have been in suspension. Its daily regime laid aside, its rules waived, it had surrendered to a phantasmagoria. Dreams over-ran its streets, and the cars retreated timidly before them. For two hours the revellers swaggered, shimmied, sashayed past, as inexhaustible as thudding waves on a beach. Around the corner where Houston Street began, I had no way of knowing how much more was waiting to unravel down the Highway and turn towards us. Surely by now the first ranks could have reached Union Square, doubled back to the river and down the Highway to begin the route all over again, like soldiers in an understaffed stage army? But the ranting, roller-skating Hitler in the frilly dress, the girl with the used syringe through her head and the man stitched together from glass shards didn't reappear. Fantasy scorned to repeat itself. There was no limit to extravagant imagination, no letting-up in its campaign to confound what society decreed to be real.

Behind the barrier, I was squashed against an old lady who chuckled and clapped each new contingent. She guffawed with delight when a hatchet-faced latex George Bush, accompanied by a blowsy Barbara, strode over to shake her hand and present her with a souvenir abortion kit – a wire coathanger with a label attached asserting 'This is George Bush's Reproductive Rights Program for Women'. She was a noble, wintry New York specimen: bright-eyed, quietly feisty (she prodded a cop who blocked our view in the small of his back, and he moved on with a smouldering glance at us); she had the garrulity of those who spend most of their time alone, and are relieved for once not to be talking to themselves. In London her equivalent would have been sad, faded, sequestered in some dank distressed Victorian mansion block; here she was unapologetic, eternally hopeful, drowning solitude in the tugging, tidal street, ordering the cops around with an American confidence in her rights and an elderly conviction of her dignity.

She must have sensed that I didn't quite belong. At my age, she would have been on the other side of the barricade. As it was, I couldn't enjoy the scene for fear that I would forget the details of it before I got home to scribble them down. It all thronged past too quickly, before words had a chance to detain it. As I struggled to index all these flying figures somewhere in my head, like a worker on the production-line who finds himself unable to keep up with the conveyor-belt, I remembered Henry James's injunction to a would-be artist: Be one of those on whom nothing is lost. It was sad advice, suggesting mnemonic desperation. He had not said, Lose yourself. The imperative was, Lose nothing; make sure life doesn't rob you. I felt as nervy and insecure as the man in a foreign place who is forever patting the wallet in his pocket, checking the lump made somewhere else by his room key, making sure he still has the passport which will guarantee his exit, mentally rehearsing the sums in his last transaction to convince himself he was not cheated.

'Are you from the city?' she asked, as she felt me fidgeting, anxious to lay hands on the river of impressions gushing past.

I should establish my credentials, I thought. 'Sure I am,' I said, 'I live on Bank Street.' I probably even diphthongised 'I am' to 'I yam' in my desire to appear authentic.

'Why, you're a neighbour then. I'm on Christopher. So you know already about the party later.' I did not, but pretended to. The revellers made the rounds of the bars, competing for prizes, then celebrated for the remaining hours of the night on the street outside her apartment. 'I don't even *try* to go to sleep on Hallowe'en. You should come on down and join us. 165 Christopher. I'll bring a chair out of my house for you.' Touching, her assumption that I would need a chair: the watcher was accorded invalid status.

I'd be there, I told her. This indeed (as a walking subway carriage clattered past, crowded with strap-hanging internees bound for Far Rockaway Horror and Dead Stuyvesant, with another Freddy lugging a butchered torso, and an unseasonal articulated Chinese dragon advancing in a hail of crackers and sagely nodding its fiery head) was the great republic, the all-inclusive society. Anyone could be a member. Just pull up a chair.

I remembered it later, as I lay in bed a few blocks north and listened to the distant hoots, shrieks, screeches, the crazy jubilation of a city only a little more frenzied than usual. It is there waiting for me, I thought, on the gadabout pavement; it has my name on it. An empty chair.

6

The Strangeness of Strangers

A T NIGHT, MY NEIGHBOUR WOULD TURN ON EVERY LIGHT,
pull up the blinds, take off his clothes, and begin performing.
Between us was the narrow crevice of the New York street, filled
at the bottom with cries of 'Motherfucker!' or the wailing of dogs
tied up outside the supermarket or the cannonade of passing
suitcase-sized radios or the cadenza of an unheeded car alarm or the
perfume of charring hamburger puffed from the kitchen vent of the
restaurant on the corner. Up here, five stacked layers of lives above
all that, there was only the silent confrontation of windows. The
blotched pink brick and blistering sills of the building opposite
contained my picture gallery. The plaster had freckled or peeled,
like thinning elderly skin; by day the soiled glass stayed opaque. But
darkness switched on a two-storey wall of portraits.

Each rectangle boxed a life. In one, a girl who came home from
her work to resume her vocation toiled over a typewriter beside a
green lamp, maybe chronicling what she saw in the windows of my
building; next to her, an old woman, whose daytime occupation was
watching the street, perhaps in the hope that some long-lost child or
long-dead spouse would round the corner and walk forward into
focus, rested her tired arm with its lapsing flesh on the ledge. At
nights in the summer she moved her bed to a divan beneath the
window. I could see her there in her twisted sheets, trying to suck
oxygen from the motionless, syrupy air like a fish thrashing itself
to exhaustion on land.

Above them, a white crate which had been vacant for months
was finally occupied by a youth with an oiled quiff of hair like a

cock's comb, who made himself at home by spraying the wall with paint to represent hurled, congealing spaghetti, or possibly brains which a bullet had pulped; pizza cartons piled up on his kitchen sink. Beside him, on his own bright, solitary stage, the neighbour whose window directly faced mine – mostly naked, but sometimes dressed as a cowboy or a surfer or policeman – play-acted his fantasies.

With their lights on and their blinds up, I could do more than see into the rooms of these people: what they placed on view was the inside of their heads. Arriving home late, I would sometimes glance out. There they all were under the trembling spangly treads of the World Trade Center and the blinking planes like fireflies, mutely monologising inside their frames. The girl would be remonstrating with a worried parent or an intrusive lover on the telephone. The old woman mopped her brow and neck with a napkin, sticky despite the pale, frigid glow from her television set. The boy with the bristling crest stared at his wall, searching for pattern and meaning in the furry squiggles and smears of red and black paint. And in the next window, the cowboy shooting straight from the hip or the gliding surfer or the authoritarian black-leather cop – whichever persona happened to be on duty that evening – rehearsed his draw without a gun or cleaved imaginary water or swaggered and swung a length of invisible chain.

Voyeurism or projection, I sometimes wondered? If the windows had been empty or the blinds had been lowered, could I have dreamed up people to fit in those niches? Was the man opposite me only strutting and posturing because he knew someone was watching?

On my own wall, between the two windows which stared at the building across the street, I hung a poster of the film which taught me most about the public privacy of the Village, and about my own itchy watchfulness: *Rear Window*. It dated from a re-release in the early 1960s. At the top, Hitchcock himself inquisitively pulled up a blind and pouted over it with the smug propriety of a butler advertising a peep-show. 'See it!' he commanded, 'If your nerves can stand it after *Psycho*!' What we would see was touted below: 'the most unusual and INTIMATE journey into human emotions ever filmed!'

The journey, depicted on the rest of the poster, seemed to be travelling into the scabrous façade of the building which faced me. James Stewart sat in his wheel-chair, back to me, binoculars raised to point out of his window. He saw what I saw: the same beige, fading brick and powdery plaster; the same rusted zig-zag imprinted on it by the fire escape; the same lighted rooms, chambers of guiltless confession. Only his characters were different from mine. The poster labelled them: The Strangers, lowering their dog from the balcony in its basket; The Honeymooners, emerging briefly for a breather in their night-clothes; Miss Lonelyhearts, grappling with her gigolo; in the space where my cowboy/surfer/cop stripped off, Miss Torso wiggling in her underwear. One window remained dark, with only a white cross slashed across its black pane. It was this at which James Stewart's binoculars took aim. 'YOU' – said the poster – 'won't be able to tear your eyes away from this window!' Its capital letters pointed a finger as accusing as the binocular lens. Had we, by watching so greedily and by hoping for a crime, willed it to happen? Was that particular oblong the screen onto which the viewer projected his own bad dream, like my other neighbour spraying the wall with scrambled, murky graffiti?

Beside the poster I stuck two postcards, scavenged somewhere else, for the same film. In one of these it was called *Fenêtre sur Cour* or, in another translation on the bottom line, *De Man aan het Venster*. The man at the window: even more pertinent. Here the subject, and perhaps the culprit, was not the window but the man stationed in it. This time we look not over James Stewart's shoulders but into his face. He has lowered the binoculars, but images linger in them: in one lens the curving, gyrating rear of Miss Torso; in the other, that obligingly obscure bedroom where anything can be imagined. Above the binoculars, his eyes are wide with alarm, his brow anxiously crinkled. Is this the look of a disinterested witness or a professional spy? Does the observer relegate himself to the sidelines, impotently outside life like Stewart confined to his chair with a broken leg, or does he manipulate what he sees by remote control?

In both poster and postcard, the binoculars have swollen, elongating in James Stewart's hands. In the poster, they extend in front of him like an insect's protruding, globular eyes on stalks; in the postcard, the lenses are the size of satellite dishes, larger than his head. They work like magnifying glasses, to expand a doubt into a suspicion, espionage into incrimination. *Rear Window* is a fable about the observer's power. James Stewart plays the unmoved mover, the invisible *auteur* behind the camera who directs events in front of it.

The second postcard slyly demonstrated his power. The other images were vertical; this one stretched out horizontally, as if seeing things through an anamorphic lens. The windows across the courtyard had also expanded sideways. With their three panes of glass, they had the shape of Cinemascopic screens, playpens for dreams. James Stewart, binoculars raised, occupied the lower left-hand corner, gazing towards me. The brick wall of the apartment he scrutinises lay behind him. This was the point: a graphic sleight-of-hand made it clear that he didn't need to see the windows across the way, because he had filled and furnished them from his own imagination. Between his head and the two lighted rooms where his characters cavorted, the building's fire-escape clambered down the wall, just like the fire-escape I could see from my window. But instead of red metal against clay-coloured brick, the fire-escape in the postcard had been blurrily air-brushed to a shade of chilly, phosphorescent blue.

This was not the visionary African sky of the Lisbon slum, but the tone of the so-called blue hour, when the sun has sucked colour and vitality from things; the sickly blue of anaemia or frost-bite; the dangerous blue of gun-smoke. The rails of the fire-escape were heatlessly ignited by it, like neon tubes. It zig-zagged down the wall with the searing speed of a lightning-bolt, and discharged itself into James Stewart's head. Or was that where it began? For, connecting him with the windows he couldn't actually see, it represented the ladder of surmise and invention he had rigged up in order to invade those rooms. Instead of letting the occupants escape, it helped the deductive burglar in; instead of saving them from real flames, its cold blaze marked the advance of a fire which was deadlier for being quite without warmth. The blue spread like a contagion around Stewart's head: it dyed the dress of Grace Kelly, standing behind him with the knowing smirk of an accomplice; it made the lowest landing and the dark window opening on it glow radio-actively; it lingered in the two dilated glass eyes of the binoculars.

Apart from the fire-escape's use as a fuse, there was other evidence of the observer's guilt. James Stewart has apparently relocated the tenants across the courtyard to suit his convenience and to concentrate his obsession. Two windows are in view, each of them with a new occupant. In the film, Miss Lonelyhearts lives at ground-level; she has been moved upstairs to the room where Raymond Burr commits the murder, and here she cuddles her latest young man. Below, her apartment has been taken over by Miss Torso, who in the film lives upstairs in a separate house next door. She is, of course, bumping and grinding in her underwear. Is she the jazzy id of the previous tenant? Or has James Stewart, more a peeping Tom than a detective, transferred her there so he can keep simultaneous watch on his two favourite subjects – the starved spinster and her pick-ups, the party girl and her packs of drooling admirers – without having to switch back and forth between buildings?

Miss Lonelyhearts seems to have outgrown her inhibitions by changing apartments: downstairs she fought off attackers; upstairs, she nestles willingly in the young man's arms. But her fears apparently remain like an odour or a stain in the room below. Miss Torso, who in her previous lodging gladly entertained her gentlemen callers, is now a victim. While she dances with her back turned to James Stewart, who as if establishing an alibi has his back turned to her, a man can be seen in hiding behind the curtain in her room. His face is concealed by the fabric, but a hand pokes out into view and reaches, grabbing, towards her body. Is it one more extension, like the eyes elongated by binoculars, of the watcher across the way? The observer decides in advance what he'll see, and tampers with the innocent facts to make sure they gratify him.

At my window, I could manage no such feats of telepathic compulsion (and had no Grace Kelly to nip across the street to snoop on my behalf). Though I began to think that surveillance gave me rights over these people, they guarded their mystery even if they had no clothes on. I knew what my exhibitionistic neighbour's fantasies were; I did not know the drabber things which might have made him real – what he worked at, what his name was, what those books were (two of them hardbacks!) on a shaky shelf in the corner. To understand the girl, I would have had to read what she was writing. Yet why did I presume that she must be recording her experience, and perhaps authenticating me by mentioning the peeping Tom across the street? She could just as well have been typing someone else's manuscript, or a business letter. Prowling in their cubicles, they could tell me as little about their lives as zoo animals whose habitat is a cage. They were denied relationship, which means that you discover yourself by encountering the similarity or the incongruity of another person – except, I suppose, that the exhibitionist had a relationship with his audience in my building, and with the personal he impersonated when he undressed.

Apartment lives are short stories, tales of routine and repetition. The old woman sits on the divan sleeping fitfully. The boy contemplates the mess on the wall as if it were raked, smoothed, systematic pebbles in a Zen garden. I thought of inventing associations between them. The girl, Midwestern and ingenuous, hopelessly fancies the stranger on the stairs who changes once the door is closed into cowboy, surfer, cop. (She couldn't have known about his antics, unless she saw them reflected in the windows of my building.) The zonked boy robs the old woman to buy more cans of spray paint. Or the exhibitionist suborns him for a duet? A sweet romance between the boy and the girl, who soothes his upright hair, weans him from pizza, and repaints his incoherent wall?

None of it worked. The characters would not comply. When I saw them on the street or coinciding at the door of their building, they registered no interest in each other. And the old woman removed herself from the cast by dying during one of my absences from New York. Her successor in the room fitted wooden shutters, and kept them permanently closed.

The apartment's creed is apartness. The blinds may be up, your private life exposed to the street, but the door is double-locked and probably bolted too: no-one can get in.

Each building pays half-hearted dues to the idea of community. In mine, a Christmas tree and a menorah are set up in the lobby at the end of the year. Plastic pliantly stands in for both the pine needles and the five-pronged candlestick. Under the tree there is a pile of gift-wrapped beribboned boxes (the same every year), addressed to no one and presumably empty. The display hardly constitutes a hearth; people hurry past it to collect their mail, catch the elevator or hail a cab, and feel relieved when its winking lights are unplugged and returned to storage in the basement at the beginning of January. The compression of lives creates indifference not intimacy: we survive by not seeing, hearing, feeling.

On my floor, a couple who didn't appreciate the rules treated the corridor as the main street of a small town, a forum where their lives could be shared with others. When their child was born, they taped a placard to the door of their apartment announcing 'It's a girl!'

The corridor did not rejoice. Reactions I overheard while waiting for the elevator:

'Who gives a shit?'

'Yeah, and I bet she's called Kimberley.'

'Are they just in from Jersey, or what?'

'Bo-ring straights.'

'NOCD.' (Translated, this means 'Not our class, dear'.)

Upstairs, there was a death. A grumpy man in his fifties, with a purple complexion and boozy breath, had gone out one morning in January to buy the paper and returned to slump dead on the floor of his apartment. Three weeks later, the carpet around his door was pulled away so the corridor could be redecorated; the smell which leaked out told all. They were able to date his death by consulting the unread newspaper. The police took out the body at four in the morning, when they thought no one would be about.

I heard the story in the elevator, and cadged more details from our doomy Transylvanian doorman. 'Was already,' he said with a delicious shiver, 'quite discomposed.' But even before they broke the locks and bagged the remains for removal, the person who once lived in the putrid body and the infested apartment had been forgotten. Some decompositions are crueller and quicker than that of flesh.

Once over the tale of the discomposed grouch on the seventh floor, the doorman brought me up to date with his own troubles.

Dark, sly, gleefully morbid, he occupied his post in the lobby like a gentle Cerberus. He watched with a wise, regretful smile as we crossed over into the underworld of the streets; he always seemed faintly surprised when we made it back safely. Packing up to travel home to his own apartment uptown after midnight, he said good-night with ominous finality, as if drawing a line – and a blackly inky one – under the remark. There was no assurance, after all, that he would return in the afternoon. He regarded his own life pro-visionally: it could be rescinded at any moment on the subway ride home. In any case, he thought of himself as suffering through an epilogue to that life. He had left Eastern Europe twenty years before. He lost language, identity, social status in becoming a refugee; deracination in America was a post-mortem existence. He watched, in between announcing our visitors, for symptoms of the second death which would repatriate him, and took a dour pleasure in citing the calculation of Nostradamus, according to whom the world could not expect to outlive him for long.

Suspecting from my bag that I was on the way to the airport, he regularly seized the occasion to dramatise the idea of departure – his, not mine. If I said that I looked forward to seeing him again in a few weeks, he would solemnly contradict me: 'Oh no, I am dying.' That statement defied me to fret about missing my flight, and virtually ordered me to put down my bag.

'This time,' he needed to specify, 'I die for certain. I bought my grave already, on Staten Island. A nice grave, only it is for three. I ask the priest to find two orphan children to be buried with me. I am poisoned in my blood. Someone has poisoned me. They discover it in my hair. I am without one million cells of red blood: one million they have taken from me. The doctor says irrecuperable. He charged me six hundred thirty-seven dollars; cash. I do not know who gave me the poison. It is Satanic forces maybe, Communists. I write against them, maybe they poison me for silence.'

He kept a store of self-published pamphlets in his locker at the rear of the lobby; they explained the role of the anti-Christ in the Yalta peace conference, which sold his slice of Europe to Magog in the person of Stalin. Now the devil who swallowed half a continent was gobbling up his corpuscles. 'I have Satanic forces inside me, in the blood. But there is also angels, who want me with them.' He gestured upstairs, as if the angels travelled in our halting elevators. 'Satanic forces and the angels, both are pulling at me. I am torn apart here.'

I pictured his dismemberment, on the lobby floor which the super's wife scrubbed and shined every morning. He was thrilled by the imminent showdown, and his black eyes glowed like embers. I could also imagine the super's wife with her bucket, berating him under her breath in Spanish for choosing to stage a cosmic combat on her premises. Having rehearsed his end, he let me go. 'I am on Staten Island when you come back.'

When I came back, he was inside the front door as usual. I

expressed amazement and – I hoped – pleasure. 'Oh,' he explained, 'I am very much drunk. Every night, with brandy. And the red cells grow again. But I have now paralysis in the leg. I feel nothing here.' He pulled up a grey cuff to reveal a patch of unsunned, insentient, papery skin. 'It creeps from the foot. Now in the knee, nothing. I wait for it to move further. All numb. It is the end. I invest in the grave already.' And he grinned.

The apartment – being a mental state, a conviction of self-sufficiency – is a portable notion. Since its space is coextensive with your head, it can be transistorised and carried round with you.

My friend Arthur goes walking in Central Park playing tapes on his stereo headphones. I tagged along once, but I felt shut out as a romantic symphony dinned between his ears, with the occasional metallic overspill jarring me. It wasn't possible to talk, and the music (so far as I could second-guess it from the tinny climaxes) seemed unsynchronised with the swooping roller-skaters, breathless joggers and pert, begging squirrels. When he changed the tape, I asked him why he insulated himself this way. 'Because then I can come out here and feel just like I'm back in my apartment,' he said. The stereo was a mobile room which could hold one person only: provided he didn't leave home without it, it was as if he hadn't left home at all. Down the brawling streets he walked, inside a cocoon of sound as impermeable as a deodorant.

With his tapes, he orchestrated the city, and predetermined what he saw when he went out. There were seasonal variations in the choice. In the autumn, Strauss's *Four Last Songs*. The voice spiralled in slow motion through the air like a falling leaf; it described a European garden's wistful death, though in this American park the trees flamed in protest against extinction. Winter demanded something rigid, glacier-like, as hardened in postures or endurance as the frozen earth beneath the snow or those spars of granite by the lake – Sibelius usually, or Shostakovitch. For the gushing, torrential spring, it had to be (at least once a year) Stravinsky's *Rite*, whose rhythms hammered at the ice and made the joggers, sacrificing their own bodies to the idea of renewal and eternal youth, look more than usually frantic. During the summer he stayed away from romantic calories and made do with chamber music – cool, clear, precise, to counteract the city's torpor and its miasmal heat.

The soundtrack also depended on the route he took. If he walked across the field among the baseball players, it had to be loping, athletic, long-lined, American, which generally meant a Copland ballet score; further north, the shaded paths, warty mounds and glowering thickets between the lake and the Metropolitan Museum demanded tubas, trombones, chromatic menace and the growling of dragons (if not muggers) in the undergrowth – *Siegfried*'s threatening wood, with the forest murmurs timed for the lawn beside the museum and the combat with Fafner on the way back west through the shrubbery; on the pebbly track round the reservoir, with the city's ranks of mansions revolving behind the wire fence, it needed to be bleak, brutal, suddenly disenchanted as the wind raked the water and the dwarfed towers swivelled on the other side of the imprisoning wire: passages in Mahler suited.

He was always devising new itineraries, with new musical accompaniments. There was no use in my arguing that it was all artificial. That's how they designed the park, as he pointed out: its vistas were artful, organised like interior decor when the ragged farms were overlaid with a scenery of tousled knolls, faintly terrifying ravines and lily ponds irrigated by hidden water-pipes, with a dairy as impractical as Marie Antoinette's. The park was not countryside; it was a pastoral symphony. He half suspected that the twittering of the birds (which he could not hear through his head-phones) came from loud-speakers, and the begging squirrels had all been to charm school for a seminar on cuteness.

Of course, he had to do a good deal of impromptu editing as he went along. Not of sounds, which were preordained and mem-orised, but of discordant, obnoxious sights. A marauding squad of ghetto kids did not belong; nor did the howling police cars; the blown papers and crushed cans were not permissible either. Still, by overlooking all these he could conduct the view, as if it were a home movie flickering on the wall of his apartment.

His co-ordinated forays offended against my own hope for a walk in the city. I wanted it to yield advent, adventure, the unexpected: in New York the stroller could be an intrepid explorer, veering from splendour to squalor, traversing Italy, China and Puerto Rico within a few blocks, tracing the unkinked trail of a single street from one end of the island to the other and tallying every possible human experience on the way. I liked Central Park because, not knowing how its anthology of little landscapes slotted together – where exactly rustic dishevelment gave way to a stately mall, where the slate-grey escarpment of boulders relaxed into a meadow – I was always liable to get lost in it. If I went astray, there were minutes of sweet uncertainty as I pondered where I might come out: among the polar bears which splashed or snored a few yards from Fifth Avenue, beside Lewis Carroll's Alice and her tea-party of bronze gnomes, or at the fountain, paved, arcaded and staircased like a Victorian ballroom? His soundtracks abolished all such uncertainty.

Yet we were both, I suppose, defining and delimiting the world and the city in our own ways. For him it had to be held together as a score, braced and barred like staves on a page. For me it unfurled into stories. The avenues had careers, travelling through destitution, brash affluence and retired gentility like upwardly mobile citizens; Fifth Avenue began at a triumphal arch but ended, overtaken by a different fate at 96th Street, among strafed tenements, toppled hydrants, and the smell of frying. The apartment building opposite me was a digest of abbreviated lives, which you could read only if people stayed near their windows. Even getting lost in the park merely meant the postponement of an end or an outcome, like a story with three or more alternative conclusions. Would the ending be at the ice-cap, in stunted wonderland, or on the patterned floor of that roofless Victorian mansion? They were all foreknown; only the choice between them was playfully left to chance.

The city, like the world, is a voluminous chapter of accidents. This car may run you over, that person may gun you down. Hence the need to imagine you control things by ordering and organising them. Inside his apartment, the boy across the street concentrates on unscrambling the calligraphic mess spewed over the wall; out walking, some of us set untuned reality to music, while others cannot see a thing without automatically wondering how to describe – and thus revise or replace – it.

Does anyone take to the streets without some mode of self-defence, a medium through which to view the world? Shades will do. It startled me at first, this New York habit of wearing dark glasses on the dullest days of winter, in blizzards, sometimes even at night. Admittedly the light can be blinding, but the mannerism has nothing to do with the glare. It is the buckling on of armour: a visual shield. People in my building reach for their shades as the elevator arrives at the ground floor; once they step into the lobby they are on set, and they confront the street from behind the impregnable safeguard of a mask. The glasses like a two-way mirror allow you to look without being looked at in return. In addition they imply that your identity is worth the trouble of concealing. The blackened lenses confer an aura of stardom, which means an untouchable detachment.

The principle is perfected by those sinister hearse-like limousines with tinted windows which cruise the kerbs or park for hours beside the slick, sullied Hudson and defy you to guess who is inside them and – more important – what they're doing in there. I have often peered at the funereal glass, tantalised by the thought of a rock star shooting up, a cardinal canoodling with a hooker, or possibly Jackie Onassis biting into a double cheeseburger, her chin shiny with grease, a milk-shake gripped in her other hand. Here is the apartment on wheels: a strong-box of solitude, impenetrable because opaque, retentively private in these ogling public streets.

No doubt the back seats are mostly empty, like the Christmas presents in our lobby.

New Yorkers are incorrigible performers, straining to attain a personal mystique. The city resembles a thronged rehearsal room; it resounds to the tap of competitive feet, the flash of upstaging attitude. In the copy shop on Bleecker Street, everyone is xeroxing résumés. At the post office on Hudson, everyone is mailing manuscripts. Life, liberty and the pursuit of happiness entail a rage for self-betterment and for self-expression. Elsewhere people have jobs; here the menial, unmentionable job – waiting on tables or doing housework or typing the résumés of others or photocopying them – subsidises the career. Reality pays for the dream. One of the employees at the video store on Greenwich Avenue wears a tag on his lapel identifying himself as ERIK ACTOR. Actor, I realised eventually, wasn't his surname: the name tags of his fellow-workers said merely BRANDY or DOLORA or J.J. Actor was the self's parenthetical aspiration, and its capitalised advertisement. You never knew: a casting director might spot you as the right type while you took the money for a tape; your future might at any moment walk in through the door.

'What do you do?' I asked a psyched-up girl I met at a party. The dream burned in her eyes; she even chewed gum ambitiously, determined to suck the stuff into submission.

'I take class,' she said.

'Acting? Singing? Dancing?'

The blazing pupils widened at my dimness. 'Sure,' she said, 'all of those.'

Talent in the parable was a gift, as capriciously and unequally bestowed as the grace craved by Rosalina and her relatives. America cannot permit this inequality: talent belongs to us all, and to each of us in all its potential manifestations; we only need to keep attending class. Miss America one year – a violin-playing starlet, proud of her own emergence from over-weight teenage – arrived in New York after her coronation in Atlantic City to propound her gospel: 'Feel good about yourself, no matter what other people think of you.' And never lose faith in your own manifest destiny, in the contest you will one day win, the stage you will one day occupy alone, inside the nimbus of a follow-spot. It is the local religion. Original sin and all imperfection have been done away with: these are merely the penalties of not feeling good about yourself. Sanctity, likewise, has been redefined as stardom. We are all jogging or dancing or singing or weight-lifting our way towards heaven. No one will be screened out because they are spiritually ugly.

Behind me on the bus once, travelling up Eighth Avenue, I heard a girl console a young man who clearly was not making it as a model. 'My agent would send you out for industrial,' she told him. 'You've got a great face for industrial.'

It was all I could do to stop my neck from swivelling automatically backwards on its axis like a bird's, to catch a glimpse of that industrial face. But I could not invent an excuse for doing so, and had to imagine it instead. What could have been so industrial? A broken nose perhaps? The pock-marked lunar remnants of acne? I suspected that industrial was a euphemism for unaesthetic. Did he look like an industrial accident?

Then he spoke. The mild, resigned voice did not belong to the stevedore or hard-hat or trucker the agent would have sent him to audition for. 'Maybe,' he said. 'Nowadays all they want are prep

boys. You have to wear those eye-glasses with tortoise-shell frames
– it just doesn't suit me.'

'Perhaps your pictures are wrong. You should have new pictures
taken. Have you tried outdoors?'

'My agent says that's not the problem. What he wants is to drop
the last four letters of my name: he says it would de-ethnicise me.
We're talking about that.'

I set myself to puzzle out what the four offending letters of the
poor man's name must be – witz, vich, berg? The alternative
suffixes buzzed in my ears: aski, akis, alis, aert, ioli, tryj, czko, zagi,
zano. Or could he after all be a Wasp who needed to lose an
invidious mill or myle or wall or ford or knap or land or pont or
pton?

It was winter, it was snowing, I was late, but since my only way
of decently seeing who owned the industrial face and the ethnic
name was to get up, move down the aisle to the back door and leave
the bus, I did just that. The season cheated me: the out-of-fashion
face was muffled by a scarf, woolly ear-muffs and the kind of plaid
cap hunters wear. But I could see what his companion meant. His
features were chunky, Slavic. A thick, pugnacious nose, eyes sunk
in caves of bone; there might have been more brow, perhaps, under
the flaps of plaid. The name surely ended in owski, though I realised
that was one letter too many. Perhaps he was called Tadeusz
Rakowski, and the agent had it in mind to streamline him as Tad
Rako. Even so, from my glimpse as I got off the bus, I did not
foresee much of a career for him.

He was not right for Calvin Klein jeans, he could never be one of
those sleek bespectacled brokers in commercials for investment
banks; at best a petrol-pumper out of focus behind a smart car, or a
steel-worker advertising the virtues of cling-film bags for lunch-
time sandwiches. And if no one wanted to borrow his face to sell
things, he would have to return to the second-best business of
merely living in it. Meanwhile, what sacrifices the image required!
You changed your name for it, denied your origins, and all in the
hope that you might symbolise a dandruff shampoo, a cereal or a
fast-food franchise, until you reached thirty-five and became good
for nothing except a sufferer from haemorrhoids or a denture-
wearer or a heart-attack victim reprieved by daily aspirins.

Better to use the anonymous, featureless face as a cover from behind which, like James Stewart at his window in the shadowy back room, you could spy on existence across the court or the street, or eavesdrop on the unseen people behind you on the bus. The mistake was to hope that your perishable self might be the image, the idol. Images demanded a substance other than flesh: the grey-green metal skin of Mercury in the Oxford pond or the matronly colossus in the New York harbour, the carious, worm-riddled wood of the saints in the Lisbon alcove.

I stepped down into the slush and waited for another bus; he travelled on up the slippery, wallowing avenue towards his dream, or towards the exit from it.

Sex here, for a few years in the late 1970s, became a performing art. By this I mean that it took place in public, under the scrutiny of a critical audience. The performers, of course, had to be strangers. If they had loved or even known each other, the transaction would have been compromised by emotion, tamed by endearments; instead it was a display of technical grace and stamina. With someone you knew, the encounter would be an episode, one incident in a continuous story, tenderly habitual. Unexpected and unrepeatable, it had a different urgency, and a quality of blatant self-revelation. It also acknowledged the opportunism of the New York streets: intersecting eyes, the friction of passers-by, the chance to assign identities to strangers who will never disillusion you by answering back or crossing your path a second time.

The decrepit piers along the river at the bottom of my street had a second life as orgy rooms. Where freighters once unloaded and liners docked, in long concrete halls with metal stairs to the upper offices, among clods of plaster, felled timbers, puddles fed by the leaky roof, and the blown litter of the West Side Highway, the dancers stalked, manoeuvred, gelled and dispersed all day and most of the night. You stepped off land – wriggling under a corroded door of corrugated iron or edging along a slithery rim of wet, crumbling wood above the water – and out of reality. In the dim, labyrinthine ruin, people enacted their dreams.

I remember one scene, like a frame retained and singled out from a long, whirring, flickering film of approaches, connections, dis-connections. A muggy afternoon, langour not lust in the air. Men saunter through the passages of heaped-up rubble where the roof has fallen in, kicking pebbles and eyeing the flayed walls with the lazy absent-mindedness of walkers in the country. 'Nothing doing today,' someone says. But in one of the office cubicles, ankle-deep in pulverised plaster and soggy paper as if in grass, a copulation is in progress. A boy grips the window ledge and looks out through the smashed glass in the vague direction of the all-licensing libertarian lady with the torch; behind him, a man with his pants down but his shades still in place slaps and slams into him; a dozen or more watchers rub their groins or listlessly masticate gum. Tour boats pass on the river, with snatches of amplified commentary about the Village as an artists' colony straying through the air towards us. On the stilted remnant of the highway outside, joggers chug along, too intent on their quests for personal best to glance this way.

It had all been going on for a long time. Some of the watchers ambled off, others arrived and jostled for position. The incongruities of the scene became painful. I began to understand why sex and the theatre both require the ritual extinguishing of lights. The man who had been panting and grunting through clenched teeth let loose a sigh, retracted, buttoned up his jeans, gave a valedictory whack to the boy's flank, and said to his public: 'I mean, sure I'm an exhibitionist – but this is ridiculous.' Non-consummation by reason of stagefright? No one could ask for their money back; still, he looked apologetic rather than annoyed, and it was the onlookers he addressed, not his partner.

Next time I returned to New York, the coffee cup still wept blood across the river and the beacon still glowed like a green match down in the bay, but the piers were gone. The sheds with their concave roofs and drooping gantries and avalanches of crumbled brick had been puffed away like spider-webs; only the floors remained, without their superstructure of fantasy, now debarred behind a fence. Occasionally, looking at these concrete runways to nowhere, I wonder whether any of it really happened.

Everywhere in New York you are liable to meet monsters: by that I merely mean self-created characters, bodied forth from their own unaided imagination and imposed on the rest of us by sheer bravado. Such a marvel was Mrs Bernstein, who sold me some blinds in her alcove at the top of an encyclopaedic department store. At every landing on the escalator's way up, girls with cosmetic sunsets on their cheeks, and boys whose tortoiseshell-rimmed spectacles (the broker look) were fitted with clear glass offered spritzes of the latest fragrance. The rolling stairs ascended through a series of tiered, congested worlds: a country store furnished with quilts, comforters and piously stitched samplers; a mocked-up junk from Hong Kong harbour, ridden by dummies lounging on bamboo chairs in sweaters emblazoned with Chinese dragons; an electronic command-centre, all percussive boxes, shiny silver discs and screens on which a hundred bland, beautiful, styrofoam people emoted with the volume turned down.

Above this cosmos of commodities, Mrs Bernstein presided in a salon made of multi-coloured slats and fluffy ruches. Ransacking a bin for new blinds (from behind which to conduct surveillance of my neighbours) I heard her before I saw her. She was concluding a sale with some satisfied clients. 'What I need, girls, is a cuppa coffee. No, what I need is a good-looking man. I'd even settle for an average-looking man. OK, all right already, I'd take Paul Newman.' Her vowels had the authentic Brooklyn gravel in them: the girls were goils, the coffee was cawfee, and Newman got turned into Nooman.

I peered through a window-frame of half-cocked Venetians and there she was, seeing off the two ageing girls and settling down to muse about Paul Newman. Her face was tired, without the strength to support its pursy skin; the rest of her was as indeterminate as a sack of potatoes. But she clearly had a resplendent idea of herself. It was written across her mouth in a crimson smudge of lipstick, and on her fingernails in the same colour; it glowed from the dye she had used on her hair, as brightly dark as a raven's wing. Red and black, she smouldered like a neon sign among the screens of white, beige and alabaster blinds. Now she was giving advice to another customer. 'Mrs Bernstein's my name, honey. If I get famous, I don't intend to change it. You can call me 9 to 5. Sure, I do stand-up comedy. With my arches, siddown comedy I would prefer.' And she slumped into a chair behind her desk, momentarily defeated by fatigue. But the trouper in her rallied when I approached and mispronounced her name.

'I'm Steen, dear, not Styne. Not like the conductor. He's a different branch. People are always mixing us up. But he can jump higher than I can. You know wad I mean?' I did: as she led me away to find the blinds she thought I should have, I began to understand the verb to shlepp, and to pity her poor arches. Mrs Bernstein onomatopoeically shlepped or slopped across the floor, her body rocking sideways as those feet, flat as the vowel in Nooman, hit the ground; she winced at every step. 'I always say,' she said, 'that they'll take me out of this store feet first. Sooner that than I should have to walk.' Then began the return hike to her desk, as painful as if barefoot on scorching sand. Lowered into her seat, the body descending with the awkward delicacy of a weight dangling from a crane, she recomposed herself. A hand raked through the wiry nest of hair; she checked the aggrandised mouth in a tiny mirror. 'Excuse me, dear, while I do some repairs here.' Then she had gathered the energy for the next scene.

With the matronly girls, she had been giggly and adolescent, mooning about a dishy movie star. With me, she perceived that she needed to be maternal. Having found my blinds, I also bought a gadget with seven rotating fingers to clean them. A great invention, I commented. 'Believe me, dear,' said Mrs Bernstein with the hint of a wink, 'an even greater invention is someone to use it for you.' Did she do marriage-brokering as well as comedy? Would she send me to Mrs Mahoney on the seventh floor – to whom I'd heard her refer – to buy a bride? In the event, she pulled the credit card form from the machine with a croupier's flourish of the wrist which set her charm bracelet jangling, pushed the voucher across the desk towards me, handed me a pen which professed to ♡ N Y, and said, 'Just sign here like a good boy. Bet you ain't had anyone say that to you in a long time.' A lawng toime. No, I hadn't. The years stretched backwards like the lawng and the toime. I wanted to give Mrs Bernstein a kiss, but was wary of the incarnadine mouth. Nor was I sure that she'd appreciate it.

She bagged my blinds and tied up the parcel. 'All you need now,' she called out as I left her little fief, 'is a pair of ambitious elbows.' Did the chuckle in her tone mean encouragement or scepticism? I could imagine her wrist dismissively flapping and her lucky charms dancing as she estimated my chances of getting the blinds hung. 'Klutz, honey, is not the word.' Would she say that to her next customer? Or would she go into my marital prospects? 'Honey, I ask you: a grown man buying his own blinds, *and* cleaning them too – is that right?' Allowing the escalator to waft me back to ground, I still felt myself to be in her power. Her dyed hair, her painted mouth and the spiel which issued from it were her protest against anonymity and effacement. She had invented herself – the wise-cracking star of the blind department, for whom retail was another of the performing arts. Why shouldn't she invent me as well?

A recommendation to those unable to bring off such self-engendering stunts: get yourself a dog. On the streets of New York, dogs are psychological accessories. Trotting along at your side, intent on its own trails of private detection among the fossilis-ing pizza crusts and black-bagged cornucopias of litter, the dog is your secret and unashamed idea of yourself.

The sybil who tells fortunes on Bleecker Street has a bull-dog in her consulting-room. Rheumy-eyed, jowly, his tongue drooping from his black gums like a rolled-out red carpet, he glares at the sidewalk or snorts and twitches in a deep, dreamy sleep. I can see the point of her professional choice: inside his creased skin, gathered into folds like Mrs Bernstein's ruches, he resembles the Buddha, somnolently wise, regarding the street with sorrowful red eyes; I'd sooner trust his divinations than hers, since I once saw her reading on the sly one of those supermarket magazines which feature nonogenarians in Arizona giving birth to triplets with wooden legs, aliens with pea-green heads visiting Reagan in the Oval Office, and exclusive interviews from beyond the grave with the double who died for Elvis.

On Hudson Street, in the window of an antique shop, a crimped and pomaded white poodle stretches out on a re-upholstered chaise longue, and snaps at anyone who contemplates buying it. The owner of the poodle fusses and preens in the background, not having the courage to sprawl on the chaise longue himself; he shares the dog's vocal pitch, and its air of withering disdain.

The fledgling lawyers and brokers walk designer dogs around the block – Jack Russells, or Sharpeis whose puckered skin has to be dusted as if they were Staffordshire ornaments.

The young undaunted would-be actors, who still look collegiate and wear their shirt-tails outside their pants, favour mongrels, bargain-basement rejects crossing a chihuahua and a Yorkshire terrier or a Labrador and a German shepherd. Such dogs, mere generic specimens without a brand-name, are companionable because they're grateful to be loved, and their very shagginess and innocence recalls a life elsewhere: the suburbs, the mid-West, paper rounds, basketball hoops on the garage door, mounds of raked, rotting autumn leaves; the distant world which will reclaim you when hope or money runs out.

These people lead their spirit-animals through the city. Every dog is the incarnation of an idea: your infant self, as yet unwarped by reality; the image you would like to see in the mirror.

Through the air-vents in my kitchen and bathroom, I can hear the lonely familiars, locked in apartments below and above while their owners spend the day coping with odious actuality. The chutes carry their mingled growling, howling, yapping – overlaid with the chirp of caged birds or the screech of tropical parrots – and their joyous hysterics when the doors open in the afternoon and their human other halves return. Outside the building is the untuned orchestra of the street, all clashes of metal, keening klaxons and engines with heartburn; inside, travelling down those internal wind tunnels, the wordless voices of solitude and then of yelping happiness. Even if I do not look out the window, the apartment is an acoustic shell, rumbling with surface storms and sending up whispered messages from underwater.

One of the animal surrogates is a spaniel called Oliver, owned by a woman on an upper floor called Mary. I encounter them sometimes in the elevator. If she's alone, she is ungainly, flinching, awkward. Her walk is stiff; having pressed the button for her floor, she backs into a corner and stares intently ahead. Instead of shades, she wears a second skin of pink make-up, beneath which she is fading. What is her story? – I have often speculated. What disappointments does she acquiescently carry round with her?

One day, after I had lived in the building for seven years, she spoke to me as we waited in the lobby for the elevator. She did not look at me, so I wondered at first whom she could have been addressing; but there was no one else. She was frowning. 'You know,' she said, 'I think they're getting better about predicting the weather. It was supposed to rain today. And it did.' The tone was earnest, as if these were the opening remarks in a debate. Her eyes, concentrating on a neutral zone of wallpaper, registered the effort it took. A trivial remark, if uttered aloud, became portentous to her. I was quick to agree about the weather-men. Still, next time we coincided in the lobby, she was jerky, startled, almost blushing with shame. Had I propositioned her? Had she propositioned me? I was a stranger with whom she had, for a moment, been guiltily intimate.

Yet when the dog accompanies her, she is transformed – as ebullient, bouncy and keen to please as he is. In the elevator, on the way to or from his laxative tours, he strains on his leash in his eagerness to grovel at your feet. He is all licking tongue, muzzling nose, caressing paws and fawning eyes. If allowed, he will roll over flat on his back and wait to have his belly tickled. Like Mark Antony's sycophants, he spaniels you at heels. His owner's instinct is to rein him in, to cramp his abject affection in her corner of the elevator. So much emotional energy, unleashed in this tight metal box, could be dangerous. Besides which, his paws are often muddy. But if you tolerate the dog, she lets the cord slip gradually through her clenched hand until he pounces, grips a leg and performs frottage. The furtive discomfort on her face gives way to a smile as he goes to work. Ollie, her ulterior, has taken over.

'All he wants,' she said to me half in apology the first time I reeled backwards from so much wet, frantic spanielling, 'is you should love him a little.' I consented, aware of what lurked behind her pronouns, and touched too by her little feat of fiction-making. Mrs Bernstein had prepared a character with which to outface the world – a comic mask, with the corners of the bright mouth turned clowningly down when her feet hurt her. Mary, characterless, cringes in the corner of the elevator, but allows the spaniel as he tugs at his restraints to stand in for her. He even speaks on her behalf, like a loose-lipped dummy on the terse ventriloquist's knee. 'Yes,' she will say if someone takes the trouble to kneel down and rub his chassis, 'that's what he likes best of all. Ooh, *isn't* that nice?' And she shivers with second-hand pleasure. He is her alibi, her alias; like every art-work, he unbinds a fantasy and fulfils a wish.

He has now scampered off in pursuit of his own career, romping through white looped mazes of toilet-paper or appreciatively gobbling dog food (probably with his ears pinned back). 'He's gonna be a model tomorrow,' Mary told me last time I admired him. 'He's getting fifty dollars for a morning's work!' I had the feeling that she would deposit the fee in a separate account, and would not regard it as her money.

All over the city, machines are reporting on the secret lives of their owners. Dial a wrong number, or even the right one, and you're liable to find yourself eavesdropping on a solo of self-definition.

A man's voice – thickened, almost choked by his excitement at hearing himself solicit strangers – says, 'You know I'm on for anything, so let me hear your pleasure. Tell me what's on your mind after the tone.' The electronic squeak is your summons to collaboration. (This one was a wrong number.)

Or you might catch, to your puzzlement, one side of a conversation between two dirt-dishing girls, reviewing events of the previous night: a voice, tantalising you with the pauses between its little cries, reacts in monosyllabic shock or glee or wonder to the scandalous reports you have been left to imagine – 'What? . . . No! . . . Who? . . . Him! . . . Her??! . . . Where? . . . Wow! . . . Yuk!! . . . Gross! . . . Barf! . . . And? . . . Oooh! . . . When?' There is a punctuation of sound effects: a spasm of discreet retching after one of the tangiest unheard revelations; an incredulous whistle; a weary sigh; a fit of giggles, the music of conspiracy; whooping laughter at a joke you can't share. And then at the crescendo of these exclamations, the voice steps aside from its cooing, oohing, aahing dialogue and says in a different register (lower, flatter, bored by your importunity, no longer with that breathy high-pitched eagerness), 'I'm talking to someone else right now. Leave a message and I'll get back to you after I hear the rest of this story.' It is an essay on the nature of telephonic contact – always one-sided, a substitute for dialogue, with imagination having to make up for an absence – and on the crossed lines, snarled connections and chance encounters of urban relationship.

The message which the medium passes on to you is something overheard, like confessions muttered through the grille into the ear of an unseen priest inside his dark box. The telephone line seems to plug into a mind whose never-ending conversation is with itself.

'Why don't you call me?' said Joseph, a chubby actor whose physique (he thought) misrepresented him. Despite his well-fed jollity, he was always trying to starve himself into tragic heroism. 'I've got a new message,' he added. 'It's very *me*.' But when I telephoned, he answered in person. This wasn't the point at all; we had nothing much to say to each other. 'Wait a minute,' he said, cheery as usual. 'I'll turn the machine on, then you can call back.'

I dialled again, and the telephone answered itself, as he sat in his apartment and watched the tape turn on. It was not his effusive I which spoke but his invisible, internal, anorexic me. 'O that this too too solid flesh would melt,' the voice began, as tremulous as a violin string. 'O God, O God' was not morose though: it had the genuine rage of the city in it, and shouted a reproach at the sky for having assigned his soul to the wrong body. I held my breath as the recitation continued. Would he do the bit about incestuous sheets? What if his mother, left behind in Milwaukee, should ever call him? But he spared her Hamlet's accusations, and signed off after the verdict that the world was an unweeded garden, province of rankness and grosserie merely. 'That it should come to this,' he moaned, and tutted in self-mocking disapproval.

Then, unlike Hamlet, he got down to business, gave his real, irrelevant name, and promised to return your call promptly: after all, it might be his agent on the line. Prodded by the beep, I could not think quickly enough to leave a message, so after a few awkward seconds hung up.

He called me back later to remonstrate. 'And why don't you get a machine?' he asked. It was as if I had failed to honour a contract. Others let me listen to them thinking or dreaming out loud; why didn't I do the same?

'Oh, I don't know,' I said. 'No one calls me anyway.'

'If you had a message, then they would. They'd want to hear your message. Why not get a machine and see if I'm not right?'

I thought about it. Suddenly, remembering another of Hamlet's problems (apart from the over-weight which Joseph sympathised with), I understood my reluctance. I didn't have a machine because I wouldn't know who to *be* on it.

Meanwhile my neighbour across the street was still indefatigably dancing. He had no problem knowing who to be. Once when he was doing his act, a psychologist I knew came to call on me. Glancing at the spotlit stage a few yards off, his eyes widened. 'Will you look over there?' he said (which I was already doing); 'that's what I call conceptualisation of the self!'

In fact, a repertory company of selves hung round the corner in my neighbour's closet. Accessories told you who the naked body belonged to tonight: chaps (leather pants cut out round the privates) for the cowboy, a helmet and a truncheon for the cop, a head-band for the surfer (who might, on reflection, have been a tennis ace, wanting to keep the sweat out of his eyes).

He would emerge from the walk-in closet already kitted out, chemically primed, pumping away. The cowboy swaggered in time to some silent rhythm through the cramped room, reached the window, then suddenly wheeled full circle to gun down an opponent behind him, the bullets fired by pelvic spasms. The phantom enemy presumably popped up into life again, like a cut-out target on a rifle range, because the duel would need to be fought a dozen times in the course of the evening. The surfer's routine – if that's whom the head-band belonged to – was more free-form. He swerved, slithered, went with the flow, shook the spray from himself; there was some frugging and twisting which seemed appropriate for a Californian beach party. But I'm not certain: it was a difficult charade to guess. The cop, who must have specialised in traffic offences because you could almost see the bike he bestrode, was easier to decipher. He had an impressive record of arrests, to judge by the pantomiming of domination and the flaunting of that night-stick. I gather that, along with the helmet, he wore boots, which got an oral polishing from all those humbled culprits.

Mostly, throughout these marathons, he jerked off – always inconclusively (I suppose the drugs guaranteed that); it was just a matter of keeping his courage up. More often than that, he also talked on the telephone, though doing so interfered with the cowboy's draw. Perhaps this was his job? Phone sex had become an industry: the mouthpiece was safer and more sterile than any prophylactic. Could he be talking clients through to climax as Randy the raunchy cowpoke, Skip the beach-bum, or Butch the cycle-cop? The phone company's motto in its folksy advertisements was 'Reach out and touch someone', which was precisely what you couldn't do over the telephone. The medium deflects its erotic messages; it assumes that sex takes place in the privacy of the head and is the conjuring of an ideal, non-existent other. If this was so, I admired his exhausting dedication to his art. Truman Capote once remarked that the good thing about masturbation was that you didn't have to look your best. My neighbour – preening in costume, punctiliously blow-dried – refuted that. After all, he could have served his customers while slumped in an arm-chair, wearing slippers and watching television with the volume (as well as the blinds) lowered.

Once at least, the encounter concluded in person. I could tell that he was talking to someone in my building. He usually behaved – and this was the performer's grandest illusion – as if his potential audience outside the window was not there; he did not even recognise us by granting a curtain-call. But this night, the caller was nearby, in view. His contortions suggested to me that it was someone on the floor above mine, but further along. My window faced his frontally; to see the person he was talking to, he had to lean backwards, crouch down, even press his face against the glass, with an eagerness unbecoming the aloof characters he played.

And then, abruptly, he slammed the phone down. What had disturbed the dream, I wondered? A real policeman keeping watch from the street below? The sudden arrival home of his imagined partner's actual partner? He disappeared into the closet round the corner, shed his skimpy uniform, and returned in jeans and a flannel shirt, struggling hastily into a wind-cheater. Despite our tropical apartments with their chugging, tingling heaters, it was winter in the street, with an icy gale buffeting the lamp-posts. He left the room without turning off the lights. Was he leaving town in terror? Had he just remembered a dinner engagement?

Neither, as it happened. He almost vaulted down the four flights of stairs, because a minute later he was outside. I expected a dash to the corner for a taxi; instead he crossed the street, and disappeared again under the awning at the entrance to my building.

I remembered Raymond Burr in *Rear Window*, aware that he was under observation, exploding from his frame across the courtyard and stalking round the block to invade James Stewart's apartment. Stewart, the paralysed voyeur in the wheel-chair, had only a camera and some blinding flash-bulbs with which to defend himself against the vengeful assault of reality. It was dangerous when your subjects realised they were being watched. I half-expected an angry knock on my door. Would the amateur cop have a search warrant? But the elevator, I was sure, went straight to the floor above.

Upstairs, the conversationalists met each other at last. The rest can't be reported on; it has to be imagined. Since it took place inside my building, I couldn't see it.

Across the street was a neighbour I could see but whose earnest, unstinting talk on the telephone I couldn't hear. Next door to me in my own building was someone else I could hear but whom I never saw.

The voice was my only evidence about her, and she used it – so far as I could tell – only to vocalise, not to talk. She seemed to have no telephone, no television, no radio, no record-player. The life on the other side of the wall was nunnishly muffled. But her room must have contained a piano, because every morning she tapped out scales on it, warmed up a voice which sounded froggily middle-aged, and set herself to labour through an aria.

It was always the same piece, from Puccini's *Manon Lescaut*: the heroine's account of the gilded opulence in which she lives as a *poule de luxe*; her piercing appeal for sexual release. My neighbour warbled or wailed through the opening bars. Then, just as the music began to lift and swell, buoyed up by Manon's desire, she promptly cracked. At once she went back to the beginning, and took another run towards the hurdle of that first high note. Another strangled squawk announced that she hadn't cleared it. Occasionally she would allow herself to go on, but the misery of her defeat reduced the voice to a whimper just when Manon should have been urgent and impassioned; mostly, however, she crept back to the start, took a deeper breath, and ventured again up the treacherous incline of tones. Sometimes she made twenty or thirty tries at a climax she couldn't manage. It was an unremitting penance she subjected herself to: she was Sisyphus the soprano.

Eavesdropping through the layer of board between us, I became first intrigued, then obsessed by her. I could overhear her most intimate dream – of being a singer, and perhaps also (since she never sang anything but this one aria) of being the bejewelled wanton Manon in a rococo bedroom, not a solitary failure in a bare apartment. But still I could not see her.

When she went out, she scurried down the corridor like a fugitive and used the fire-stairs rather than waiting for the elevator. For exercise, or to avoid observation? She came up to the fifth floor by the concrete stairs as well: her door closed behind her once or twice as I stepped out of the elevator. She was right to avoid it. The elevator was an arena for the giving of attitude. People used it to languidly model new outfits, to leaf through shiny Caribbean travel brochures, to complain of jet-lag or ho-hum about the trials of a freelance life. Her chosen theatre was inside her room, and she came alive (briefly, before the shaming crack) only there. The one territory in which she could not prevent herself from being glimpsed was the building's lobby, and the few feet of corridor between the stairs and her door. I began to listen for her exits, so we might casually coincide in the hall. I would hear her leave, but by the time I had unlocked myself top and bottom from inside she was out of sight, with the door to the fire-stairs swinging vacantly to tease me. When there were strangers in our corridor, I pretended to fumble with my keys in the hope of discovering if this was her. The snazzy corporate type with the briefcase? No, surely not. The distracted lady with the greying pony-tail and the determined, sniffy terrier? Maybe; but not. Anyway, the dog was too self-possessed.

I gained one item of info from her mail-box in the lobby. She was called Miss Brown. Or at least she was Brown; I supplied the Miss myself. The name didn't quite seem trustworthy, though. In England it would have been drably ordinary, as subfusc as the colour itself. But in New York, in this building, where the tenants were Silver, Stein, Silberstein, Schexnayder, Gonzalez, Rivera, Fujikawa and Smuga – among others – its ordinariness was the most exotic thing about it. It must be an alias. But why hadn't she chosen Ms M. Lescaut?

Meanwhile, through the coy wall, the rehearsal continued. Always the tentative pitch-setting cue from the piano. On your mark, get set, go. The quaking ascent; the trembling hesitation; the squawk as the note turned sour, or the squeak as it omitted to come out at all. Once she got triumphantly beyond it. I applauded, even stamped my feet. Then she went astray a few bars later.

By this time, having heard that interrupted melody for an hour or more every morning for weeks, I was trying extreme tactics to bully her out of hiding. Some days I loudly, tunelessly sang along with her. I even bought a recording of the aria, and taunted her with some velvety competition. The singer's voice on the record winged along indomitably, while Miss Brown went back to begin the faltering uphill struggle again, undaunted. Soon the needle wore down the track, and the challenge lost its force. She had lived with failure for so long that she refused to be hurt. The curse through the wall, which I longed for in reciprocation, never came. Did I dare to climb out onto the landing of the fire-escape we shared and peer in? If I had known the eurhythmic cowboy's number, I would have called to ask what he could see inside her window. Steady on, I finally had to tell myself.

She simply vanished. I wondered how they got the piano out of there without my hearing it trundle across the floor. The rest of the furniture concerned me less. It didn't sound as if she had a great deal. All she needed, like the dancer's tormenting barre, was the piano. Or could it have been a tape? The scales she shrilled through were always the same; perhaps, when she came to grief during 'In quelle trine morbide', she just pressed a button to rewind. She took dictation from the machine, and it could make no adjustments when she slumped out of tune. No, there never was a piano. We had both imagined it.

Once I realised the apartment was empty – as I passed, a realtor opened the door on an oblong scoured by the winter sun – I began to hunt for remnants or relics of Miss Brown. Down the corridor was a tiled cubby-hole with a door like that of every other apartment, except that it had no number on it and lacked the usual battery of locks and the squinting pupil of the peep-hole. You left your rubbish there. Edible scraps were launched down a chute, and plummeted straight to the furnace; solid objects were stacked in a corner. I made a habit of checking the room daily; sometimes more than once, on my way back from the elevator. Among the jumble of dry-cleaners' wire hangers and empty bottles, there were occasional treasures. My first television set originated there, and my desk-lamp too. It was my source for day-old tabloids, in which I could read about the murders *The New York Times* thought unfit for print.

The room was, in its way, the most sociable place in the building. Neighbours who otherwise ignored each other's existence donated their cast-offs – electric typewriters when they were overtaken by word processors, records when perishable vinyl was superseded by those shiny flying saucers which only a laser could play, unfashionable coats or obsolete video machines – to the common good. Hardware was quickly recycled. Every item dumped there was a bequest, and we all pieced our lives together by recomposing what others had left us. Those without such depositories inside their houses placed their donations on the sidewalk. Once, further down the street, I saw an armchair appealing for adoption, with a sign pinned to it saying 'Please give me a home'. The words had turned bleary, tearful in a flurry of snow. I couldn't be of help to it; it was too heavy for me to tackle alone.

When people move, they shed skins: what had Miss Brown left behind? I began digging through the legacies of the day. The high-gloss magazines surely were not hers, and neither was the pair of hiking-boots. Likewise the Vuitton bag. If only I could find the score of her aria, with some self-critical marginalia! Maybe she had quit the city, resigning from that dream and symbolically discarding the evidence. Already worried that someone would arrive to send their egg-shells and chicken-bones down the chute and find me scavenging here like a tramp, I suddenly felt sad and shameful. My grubby hunt seemed to sum it up: one stranger pursuing an elusive other, confronted by a door left swinging as the prey has rushed through it; deduction conducted among the debris.

Then, crushed under cartons of bottles, an ironing-board with a burnt pad, bundles of newspapers which blackened my guilty hands and a roll of mats for the building's dogs to pee on, I found my souvenir of Miss Brown: a metal music-stand, as rickety as a broken-legged flamingo, at which she had given her make-believe concerts. It could no longer stand upright, so it had no use. But I took it all the same.

The Eighth Avenue bus seemed an unlikely place, at the time, for a love-feast. But inside it, for half an hour, the city's enmities and estrangements were suspended. Passengers climbed on to find themselves taking part in a communion.

The bus starts its career opposite my building. This time, it pulled up at the spot where I was standing, rather than making me sprint half a block or splash through puddles to reach it. When I dropped in my token, the driver said 'Good evening'. I looked behind me: there was no one else getting on. I looked down the bus: there was no one else aboard. It was me he meant. Startled, I looked at him. Craggy, with one of those American faces carved in planes like the presidents on Mount Rushmore or Dick Tracy in the cartoons; straw-coloured hair and sky-coloured eyes. He was grinning. I at once ran through his possible ulterior motives, and by the time I had canvassed them all, the bus had pulled away and it was too late to reply.

He eased it into the avenue, idled to a red light, and began to sing – not bored humming or crude caterwauling but real singing, with all the tenorial tricks: vowels teased out like chewing-gum, throbby rhythmic undertows, swellings and diminishings of volume. 'Shine on,' he sang, 'shine on harvest moon, up in the sky . . . I ain't had no lovin' since January, February, June or July . . .' I was alone in the bus. Could this be addressed to me? As it happened it was harvest-time, somewhere behind the Erie Lackawanna sign across the river. I tried to look pleased; he went on warbling.

The next stop – past the two-way mirror of the private eye, the park with the bums sleeping or classifying their troves of tin cans, the donut shack at the corner where the street people loiter in the hope of sneaking a squirt of ketchup – was on 14th Street. Now, I thought, the serenade would have to end. Once all those people boarded, I could safely merge with a crowd again. There were chuckling black women, Spanish-speakers with cartons of hi-fi equipment from the bazaars along the street, and a group of deaf and dumb people, chattering silently with their fingers. And every one of them, as they paid their fare, got a greeting, always slightly different, customised so as not to seem uniform or machine-made. 'Good evening to you. And how are you tonight? Good evening, ma'm. Good evening, my friend. Howdy. Hi there. Welcome aboard. A *very* good evening to you.' The black ladies simpered, the deaf people signalled amazement to each other.

The driver smiled, but gravely, knowingly, compassionately, aware that politeness was more shocking than abuse, and as we bumped out into the corrugated avenue he began to sing again. Still the harvest moon, still the lack of loving since ice-bound January. I looked out of the window, as the silent street bounced past: tenement-dwellers on their stoops, swigging from paper-bags; the Vietnamese grocers pulping oranges or clinically shaving the stalks of flowers; an upstairs room – a studio for aerobics, as it called itself – with a squad of women jumping to unheard music; a Western bar, Rawhide, which served Chelsea's ranch hands. It all seemed, for once, benign and relaxed. The sidewalk like a pageant exemplified America at play. And there was even a harvest moon, glowing alight in a grey September dusk to the east as the sun burned through the gases and fumes of New Jersey. The driver sang to the season, the city, the world, not to me.

By 23rd Street, the greetings had mellowed out. 'Mm, looking good. Hello my lovely; yeah. Come on in, honey.' The yeah was almost a yawn, a delicious exhalation of breath, a soothing crooner's caress. The new passengers were mostly oldies from the gloomy gabled towers of London Terrace down towards the river. They basked in the compliments, as if snuggling up to an electric fire. One of them worried about the LIMITED sign on the front of the bus. Did he only make limited stops? No, the sign should read LOCAL. He punched some numbers on a computer board, angled a microphone towards him, and sighed into it: 'Well now, for you ladies and gentlemen who might think I'm limited – I'm not limited at all, I'm local. I'm real local. Yeah. I'm so local I'm completely *un*limited.'

Along 23rd Street, above the Y where I'd had my surreptitious showers two decades before, beyond the corner where I'd run for my life down those black corridors and smelly stairs, a gold pyramid floated upwards, hovered in the crevices of consecutive streets, and was snatched away as the bus started up again. It belonged to an insurance company on Madison Avenue, but had taken off from the building. It seemed to spin towards the brightening moon; then it was gone.

While the driver was explaining his unlimitedness, someone he knew got on. He received his greeting, and shuffled to the back of the bus. Now he was hailed out of hiding. 'Hey Frank, come on down and visit a while. Sorry, but when I see all those pretty ladies board the bus' (he meant the beldames of London Terrace, with their sparse hair as blue as the moon) 'I just can't think straight . . .' The pretty ladies tittered. Frank sidled up the aisle to visit, with the microphone turned tactfully off.

We chugged towards 34th Street. The pompous façade of the Post Office, with its vaunting promise on the pediment to deliver your mail despite rain, sleet, the wind-chill factor, the sabre-sharp gales of the New York winter and the sodden heat of its summers. A block-long slope of empty steps with two guard-rails marking out a single narrow lane up them: only one of the revolving doors functioned. I remembered my daily visits to General Delivery in

1969, and my diminishing hopes. Next, the Art Deco wings and flutings of the New Yorker Hotel, now propped up by scaffolding. A neon sign above the avenue, never switched on any more, spelled out NEW YORKER vertically, but without the first E and with the final R dangling shakily askew. Inside, in rooms lit by bleary unshaded bulbs from the ceiling, Moonie cultists have their cells. Once in a while they tumble mysteriously down an elevator shaft. Opposite, three avenues away, the silver needle of the Empire State still took aim at an empty heaven.

'Coming up to Madison Square Garden,' said the driver. 'We've got a Grateful Dead concert here tonight, for those who like *that* kind of music.' The pavement was awash with Deadheads, demon versions – in their tie-dyed T-shirts and moth-eaten jeans – of the blissed-out Moonies in the hotel across the way. They had been camping there for days, selling south-of-the-border hempen bracelets and serving falafel to passers-by. 'Jerry Garcia's on the bill, I see,' said our host. 'Hey, Jerry's been around for a hundred years. Jerry's a survivor. He's been around as long as Sinatra.' Which was of course the cue for a song. 'I did it myyyy way,' he wailed, vibrating the 'y' like piano wire; and then 'New York, New York, Nooo Yaawk. Mind yourself getting off. Take care now. Have a good one.'

Over 34th Street, he coasted up a section of the avenue clogged by day with trundled racks of furs and puffed-up, apparently inflatable down jackets. He had eased into his act. 'Are you all settled back and relaxed? Would you like another song?' Collectively, we were too timid to request one. But he helped us with a corroborative 'Yeah!' and jollied us along. 'If you care for refreshments, just step down to the rear of the bus and fix yourselves whatever you'd care for. It's the happy hour. Yay. Did the piano-player come to work tonight? He isn't here? We'll just have to sing without the piano tonight. And what would you like to hear? What the world needs now . . . Yeah, love is what we need. And a smile. Keep up those smiles as you exit the bus: we need 'em out there.' The crowd was warming, overcoming its shame at such unsophisticated delight. His farewell greetings became more extravagant at every stop. 'Easy does it. Come ride with us again soon. Keep smiling. A pleasure to have you aboard. Peace. Shine on, shine on.'

At 42nd Street, among the stalls of skateboards, gold chains, fingerless gloves and triple-X videos, the shoe-shiners lazed off-duty in vinyl armchairs with their squares of carpet furnishing the pavement. There was a turn-over of passengers as people spilled out at the bus terminal. He was neighbourly, in a city which usually execrates cars with number-plates from the next-door state. 'Good night to all our friends from the great state of New Jersey. Have a safe trip home. You folks still have Brendan Byrne as Governor over there in the Garden State?' He preserved a hint of New York chauvinism by getting this wrong. 'What, you folks let him go?' We were soothed across 42nd Street, with its bomb-blasts of neon and its midnight suns. The teletype above Broadway blinked out share prices. The Chrysler Building prickled a sky which was dark now with its circumflexes of light.

Above 42nd Street, the avenue abandoned itself for a while to sleaze. Drugged seedy somnambulists; a cinema called The Adonis whose feature attraction was a non-Greek god alleged to be *Hung like a Horse*. Two of the old ladies from 23rd Street were worried about getting to the theatre on time, and about quitting this communal cocoon for the accidental insanity of the street. 'We've got some fire-engine activity up ahead,' the driver warned them; 'hold on while I segue into the kerb.' And then, 'Goodbye my darlings, parting is *such* sweet sorrow. Enjoy the show.' The greetings continued as people got on. More flustered, refugees from these crowded blocks, they looked affronted by his welcome. Where was the catch? The soothed, beaming faces of the rest of us seemed to be relishing a snide private joke. 'Thank you for flying the bus tonight,' he said, 'and please observe the "No dancing in the aisles" sign.'

Someone getting off wished that God would bless him. 'What a friend we have in Jesus,' he agreed. 'Oh yeah!' Before 57th Street he had convened a gospel meeting. Everyone sang along: 'What the world needs now is love, sweet love.' I found, to my surprise, that I knew the words of the whole song. 'What we *don't* need,' the driver editorialised, 'is nukular missiles. We got enough of those already.' On the sidewalk, people waiting for the traffic lights gaped at the cheery, chanting bus as it shunted past – a ship of fools on tempest-tossed, careening Eighth Avenue?

Between verses, strangers began to talk to each other, as they'd otherwise only do in a crisis.

'What a nice man! He should be working with people, not his hands.'

'Everyone says New Yorkers are so mean and rude. We know different.'

'He should be on television.'

Overhearing this, 'I am,' he said. 'You can see me next week on *Good Day New York*, channel 5, 7 to 9 in the morning, I'm not sure which day, but tune me in. And I'm going to be on an NBC day-time drama one afternoon. See, they even wrote about me in the paper.' He passed back a sheet of tabloid newsprint, sealed in a plastic folder. There was such a scramble for it that I had to read it over someone else's shoulder. I picked up some of the details: Irish and Scandinavian ancestry, mixed up in the melting pot – hence the joviality combined with the hair of flax; wife and two lovely children in Queens; ambitions to perform, and the chance of a bit part in an NBC soap.

Behind me, there were disbelievers.

'What's he *on*?'

'He's a lobotomy job.'

On 57th Street, some cowed Midwesterners boarded, and apologetically – having had previous rebuffs – asked directions. 'You folks from out-of-town? Hey, never mind, we're all out-of-towners, one way or another. We're all just passing through here on God's earth. We get on the bus, ride up the avenue aways, get off when our stop comes. That's why we've got to help each other out. Let's see those smiles back there! Life's a positive, that's what I say. A positive high. Yeah' – this eternal affirmation, breathed out with a faint, delicious sigh like the purring of a stroked cat. And when he released the sigh, he shuddered as if the word left him tingling, like the cat arching its back in sensual delight. We were on 59th Street, with the silhouette of the Hotel Pierre at its end, a skeletal sorcerer under a peaked hat casting spells on Central Park.

At once, the avenue changed its name and nature. Having been sordid for most of its length, it became sleek, grand, patrolled by top-hatted flunkies blowing whistles for taxis. Henceforth it was to be known as Central Park West, and so long as the assumption held good – until 96th Street, when it abruptly lost its assets, its respectability, and its obsequious doormen – I enjoyed my glimpses through the windows of privilege. It was early enough for lights to be on, too early for curtains to be drawn. Usually I longed for the bus to dawdle or stall, so I could add to my collection of purloined interiors: rooms seen, never to be visited. In one there would be a wall of spotlit Impressionist picnics – maybe paintings of an arboreal Central Park with young girls in flower, so unlike the actual wood of error and danger with its jutting spars of granite below the window. In another one, there was a four-poster bed, draped in red velvet. Some millionaire slept there in a gaudy, curtained catafalque. Inside the bus, I was wary about catching the eye of other passengers: they might stare back, angry and accusing, treating observation as an invasion. Those windows were my consolation, places you could safely look at because no one returned the look.

This time it was different. No need to gaze at an unattainable life outside, upstairs; the riders on the bus had become a congregation and a choir. Their guards lowered, as if enticed to creep out from behind their shades, people were almost fearfully grateful. The driver kept up the team spirit by swooning into another song, luring us all to follow. The deaf and dumb people lip-read the tune, and sang along with their loquacious fingers. It was, while it lasted, beatific.

For me it lasted only as far as 72nd Street, where I had to get off. I even smiled as I tripped over a suitcase in the aisle. Then the door folded shut behind me, sealing in the music.

Two weeks later I had the same driver, going downtown on Broadway this time. He took over from someone else above Times Square with its yellow novas and fizzing meteors. I expected an anthology of show-tunes and theatrical gossip as we cruised down the gorge walled with hallucinogenic light. But he looked tired, sullen. It was late at night, and the city had withstood his daylong efforts to outsing it. He hummed through his teeth, and rationed the greetings.

Outside my apartment, I was his last passenger, as I had been the first two weeks before. 'Thank you,' I said as I got off; he grunted. I was almost relieved. Had I imagined the journey a fortnight ago? Or were things happening backwards, as the physicists say time does? This might be the first trip, disgruntled and joyless; then, two weeks further on, he would recover, steer the bus round the corner, and head uptown again serenading the moon. The best option, I thought, would be to write it all off as a daydream. Then reality – the bag people brawling in the park over internecine thefts of beer cans, the clangour of a fire-engine, the car-load of louts yelling at the street – would be easier to return to.

7
A House of Fiction

M Y FIRST FOUR WINDOWS FRAMED A WORLD I HAD NOT
chosen. From the front of the house I could see a ragged,
pitted hill, and the steaming chimneys of the zinc works; to one
side, the window showed the gruff profile of the mountain rearing
over Hobart; at the back, beyond the race-course with its twiddly
Victorian grandstand, another picket of hills and burned, twitching
trees; to the other side, from my bedroom, a neighbouring kitchen,
its domestic rows and drinking-bouts lit by a bleary neon strip on
the ceiling. The sun appeared from behind the zinc works (and
rubbed out the plumes of snowy smoke which flared from the
factory sheds all night). It toiled across the sky as if doing a job, and
set in the back yard: it had other worlds to awaken somewhere else.
In the morning it returned to its track above the mountain, and like
a compass pinched at a niggardly narrow angle it triangulated my
sliver of world.

My parents moved when I was two or three years old to this new
house in a new suburb: weatherboard shell, lid of crinkly iron,
internal divisions of ply-wood; the smallest of the available models,
since they had only one child and would not be having any more.
The house was what the English call a bungalow. One floor only,
no attic or cellar, no up and down: the kind of dwelling which, in
England, is reserved for the retired, too infirm on their pins to cope
with stairs. Inside, the arrangement of space was open-plan with a
democratic vengeance. My parents never shut their bedroom door;
it took pitched battles and a war of nervous attrition during early
adolescence to secure myself the right to close mine and keep the

light on after they had turned theirs off. They suspected something shifty and criminal in this desire for privacy, I suppose. In fact all I wanted to do was read. It was a house which legislated against the inner life, and was inconsistent with mystery.

Even when I won on the issue of the door, the view from that bedroom window remained a problem. Neon glared through my blinds late at night, voices roared or cursed or merely droned in boozy loquacity, and finally bottles were piled up, clanking and rattling, on the back porch. During the day, the sun as it trudged on its rounds anatomised the yard of these roistering neighbours: unplanted rubble, still scratched by the teeth-marks of the bulldozer which first felled the trees; limp, punctured rubber tyres; the stacked crates of brown empties. What if this were to be my only world?

One day, experimentally, I shut out the view. I had a store of foreign magazines a friend of my father's had passed on to us – *National Geographic* with its gaudy russet deserts and happy savages, *Saturday Evening Post* with its snug New England autumns, *Life* with its earnest statesmen, *Look* with its film stars whose legs were insured for dizzy sums. I spent an afternoon cutting them up, arranged a collage of scenes and celebrities on my bed, then taped them to the window-pane. The scabby yard and the squabbling kitchen disappeared behind my own design for a world: golden maple trees shading Zulu dancers, a red Pennsylvania barn in the Himalayas, a bullish Churchill and a pouting Marilyn Monroe, candy-coloured cars with fins and a liner's prow knifing through foam. This map of multiple, overlapping Utopias stayed in place until evening. Then my mother noticed it, and I had to peel it off. There were some beery cheers from the next-door kitchen as I dismantled the screen of images, screwed them up one by one and threw them away.

My earliest memory is of something our house did not contain: a staircase.

I can see it clearly, though without a penumbra. Interrogate it as I might, it won't open further out, or vouchsafe other details. I am looking at the staircase from below. It arrives at a landing, and veers away somewhere else. I can't follow it.

The little scene, excerpted from a story lost to me, looks yellow. I find a yellow staircase hard to accredit. The colour must be sun, filling the narrow hall at the foot of the stairs like a bright, seething swarm. This is where it all begins. The treads with their thinning carpet – I have added those – climb into possibility. After the landing is the future. It's a variant of the view from the chapel in Lisbon, with worlds potentiating beyond the point where sky and sea vanish into each other.

The staircase belongs, I guess, in the house where my parents rented some rooms before moving to their own half-acre in the northern suburbs. It was on the edge of the city, running steeply up a hill; the houses were Edwardian, tall and fussily ornamental, with glazed tulips in the front door – perhaps the source of that tinted light which warms my memory and keeps it alive. I have never been back to check: only the indistinct mental snapshot remains. I'm told you are given back these earliest years – which seem to pre-date the retentive worry of remembering – when you're old and the mind goes wandering. It might be something to look forward to.

Meanwhile, the move north to the new suburb had taken my staircase from me. Our life out there was flatly horizontal. Stairs were the preserve of those my parents deferentially referred to as 'the higher-ups'. We had no rituals, and therefore no need for different levels.

Even so, after a few years I chanced upon a likeness of my staircase, in the house of an army mate of my father's. Thought he was well off, and had both a migrant bride from England and a yacht moored at his own jetty, war had equated him and my father; the friendship didn't last far into the peace-time prosperity of the 1950s. But it survived long enough for me to visit the house, which unravelled in terraces down a slope into the harbour. At the end of the garden was the jetty with the tethered yacht.

That impressed me less than the heady abysses inside the house. You entered it across a concrete bridge jutting out from the street. Beneath was a shaft which dropped two storeys into a paved yard. I never crossed that bridge without clinging to the hand-rail in self-engendered alarm. When the front door opened, you were on the top floor of the house; you descended into its poked-out layers on a series of staircases, the last of which conducted you out to the garden, along a pontoon of planks, then down a rope-ladder into the water. To stand inside the front door was to feel those successive floors raised on stilts from the rock tremble beneath your feet, or bounce like diving-boards angled above the depths. Vertigo overtook me before I stepped off the doormat. The house declined like a continental shelf. My first staircase I had seen from below, and it spiralled resiliently upwards; this one plunged, digging through the subsoil in a shaky pyramid of Zs, skidding irresistibly over the wet boards into the harbour which the gulls bombarded.

Of course its terrors were imaginary, but that is one reason we grow an imagination: to frighten ourselves with knowledge of the unknown. Long after I had passed the crawling stage, I always insisted on bumping down the stairs in that house on my bottom.

At home, grounded, there were no such giddy dangers. A removable trap in the corridor between the two bedrooms opened into the cramped loft beneath the undulating iron roof; but the ceilings were squares of plaster-board, and you could put your foot through them if you went up there. I never thought it worth the risk – had I slipped off the timber beams – of knocking a hole in our perishable box-top.

Denied an attic, I contented myself with inventing a cellar. The land under the house sloped unevenly. One side of the building rested flat on the ground; the other was propped three or four feet above it. That left an angular cave under the floorboards, reached by a bolted door in the foundation. I colonised it at once. It was my bolt-hole, with a hessian bag daintily spread on the dry clods of earth and knobs of gravel. Into one of the piles which held up the house I drove a nail, and hung there a bashed-in tin cup which had once contained a bicycle lamp. I never put anything in it.

There was little I could do in this dark corner, so low I had to crouch. But it was a place from which surveillance could be maintained. I could see the sunny, unsuspecting outside world through slits between the concrete blocks of the foundation; I could hear my parents making the boards creak inches above my head. I had my symbolic sanctum, my fictitious facsimile of a house, and after thirty years there are still chalk marks on one of the unshaven cross-beams where I once staked my domain: OFFICE– KEEP OUT. The embargo was hardly necessary. I wasn't pestered by importunate drop-ins down in my kennel with its carpet of sack. The snarling sign is still there, because no one since has ever bothered to unbolt the door and crawl in.

When I left home in search of my imagined worlds, I dragged along a suitcase overloaded with ambitions. They underwent amendments through the years, but the first and most urgent of them never changed: when I finally grew up, I reminded myself every so often, I would live in a house with a staircase, and a cellar too. And the views from its windows would be placed there by me.

After a decade, my tally included an attic in Oxford and a slice of fire-escape in New York; still no staircase to commute between strata on, and no below-ground bunker to retreat to.

The Oxford attic was actually the interruption of a staircase. When the new layer of rooms for students was tucked in under the roof, the stairs which twisted up to my front door had nowhere else to go. They buried their head, therefore, in a no-man's-land of rafters between my ceiling and the next floor. I had the bonus of an attic without even being at the top of the building. Behind a battered makeshift door of pine, the stairs continued for a while, reverting from stone to wood. Then, around the last turn, they gave up. A water-tank was stowed here, swathed in a blanket, and a battery of flicking tongues and implacable dials telling tales on the electricity users in the quadrangle. Once a term, two men from the Steward's office arrived with a torch, a prison warder's bundle of keys and a much-thumbed notebook, to read the meters.

I ventured up with them once or twice, and they introduced me to the staircase's modest mascot: a dead bat, which years before they had pinioned with its wings spread between two cables on the wall. They checked on its decomposition on their visits every quarter, and thus counted down the time to their own retirement. It was the size of a cameo brooch, and had died with its pin-prick black eyes open. A colleague of Bob, I wondered, escaped from the Reverend Dodgson's tricksy belfry? No, it was organic matter: when I touched it experimentally, its nether regions collapsed and drifted to the ground in a thin dry rain of sediment and leathery speckles. 'Mind out there, sir,' said the man with the torch; 'he's an old member of the college, and we wouldn't want to lose him.' I understood the reproof.

After that, I checked on the mortifying bat from time to time, but didn't touch. Sealed in this tomb at the top of the stairs, with no ants or flies or earthworms to feed on him, he slowly resolved himself into air. His brown fuzz went first, floating away as spores of dust. The squashed, harmlessly malicious face hung there for a year or two more, until it had hollowed into a mask, a membrane. It maintained a twisted grin a while longer, then gave up the effort and relaxed into nothingness. At this point, I found that the little bat's elemental undoing wasn't funny any more; I didn't go back up there again. The men with the torch and the clanking keys on a hoop and the dog-eared book of account meanwhile retired. Once the memories which held the bat together dispersed, it had no choice but to follow.

My attic at least contained a corpse (and now, a ghostly transparency of atoms). For a time I thought it might also yield a cache of secrets. My six rooms, secularised for me, had always belonged to the college's chaplain. (A chaplain needed this many, someone explained, in case there was an influx of undergraduates in spiritual distress: they could be simultaneously but separately accommodated and attended to, without having to queue up in embarrassment on the stairs.) Upstairs I searched for the remnants of all those temporary clerics, who held the job for a few years before being redeployed. I longed to turn up something incriminating, and even crawled across the rafters groping – for what? All I found – stuffed behind the water-heater as wadding, then dragged back down the flight of wooden steps and banged on the floor to dislodge their crust of clotted grime – was a bundle of ancient issues of *The Church Times*. Evidence perhaps of bad faith, I thought: a true believer would have taken them with him to the next parish. But on balance, the attic was unmysterious. It was dark without being obscure, dirty without soiling anyone in particular. Once the bat disintegrated, the ticking, punctilious meters had it to themselves. If I wanted psychological plunder I would have to look elsewhere; or invade my own filing cabinet.

The New York fire-escape couldn't console me either. It was not a staircase but the parody of one, let down by a hook from the sky, as the New York buildings, suspended above the streets, seemed to be. You connected it to the earth yourself, and then only in an emergency, letting down the last hitched-up length of rungs when you reached the bottom landing. (The windows above would be belching smoke and spitting flame.) I disliked the fire-escape on principle: the building wore its disbelief in itself brazenly on the outside. Like an organ-donor card, it prepared for a disaster which was all too possible. That ladder defined the pile of bricks it was braced to as an inflammable carton, mere tinder.

Nor was I likely to annex the landing outside my window as a balcony. In the tenements, people used to haul mattresses out and spend the night on their fire-escapes during the steamier summers. I climbed onto it a few times, to wash the sooty windows or to pummel rugs, and always crawled back across the sill with the relief of a feeble swimmer regaining land. The metal slats swung like a cage above the rumbling street, and bounced as lorries bucked over the potholes. Up here the air thickened around you in a weft of smuts, spores and feathers from the lecherous pigeons which preened on the roof of the building opposite, in mimicry of the citizens on the sidewalk five storeys below; sometimes, when a gale scythed off the river, there were even squares of crumpled news-print, shredded by fingers of wind. Already, at this height, every-thing was flotsam, harried by those invisible capricious tides which coursed between the cliffs of stone and glass.

The fire-escape was a chute for plunging onto the street, where all the litter which the wind juggled would slump in the end. My staircase was to have the opposite function. I intended to ascend it. Not that I planned to arrive anywhere: it wasn't an express route to self-promotion. I wouldn't have minded climbing it in perpetuity like a treadmill, or like the exhausted insect figure in the Piranesi print I had in Oxford, grappling with a coil of steps which twists upwards forever, ending miles overhead and centuries away in a chasm. On the Tube in London, I didn't mind if the lifts weren't working (or sometimes didn't mind, since they mostly weren't), since there was then a reason for trudging up those clanking iron spirals towards the surface of the earth.

I knew all about the Gothic perils of the staircase, which conceals an incubus round the corner of every landing. Any Hitchcock character who ventures up encounters at each gradient the image of his or her gruesomest fears: the slavering watch-dog in *Strangers on a Train*, the cowled, faceless nun in *Vertigo*, the creaking icicle of light beneath the door in *Psycho* and the lunging knife. None of this warned me off. The unknown didn't frighten me; the known, however, did, and the staircase promised escape from that.

At last, down in the basement and along the tunnel in my house or cottage or garden shed in London, I found a staircase I could own. It was green not yellow – a thick coat of carpet had been tacked to it, so it slunk up the wall more like a mossy forest path than the pillar of sunlight which burned off the floor in that dim Tasmanian hall – but I didn't mind revising my dream. Childhood with its Midas touch can turn anything to gold, or at least to daffodil yellow; nowadays I was reconciled to seeing the world in darker colours. As it bent round the landing and trudged up the incline to the first floor, it represented the way ahead as overgrown, brambly, maybe infirm underfoot. There was no longer any question of soaring directly upwards, afloat on some aerodynamic scrap of rug, which the scene I remembered seemed to promise. Puffed out by the time it attained the first floor, where it opened into my bedroom, the staircase then gave up the effort. But since the head of my bed was fitted into a corner by the banister, I could lie there looking down at the landing and taking stock of its progress; I could even, if I left a light on downstairs, see my entire miniature domain reflected in the glass of the pictures on the wall beside the stairs.

Later I devised an extension for my unambitious, out-of-breath staircase. Above the landing was an inexplicable doorless cupboard, big enough to fit a bunk bed in: a sort of tree-house propped on top of my green, tangled, indoor hillock. For at least a year I avoided looking at it or thinking about it, and had to train my eyes to pass by on the other side when I crossed the room: it was putrid with damp, and the plaster-board on its walls first mottled, then started to curl and peel, disclosing colonies of mould. The analogy with a forest – seeping moisture, the ripe odour of earth – became uncomfortable. The room-sized, suspended cupboard was hacked to pieces and re-cemented. Then I had to decide what to do with it, or in it. Its ceiling somewhere concealed a trap-door, but I didn't fancy a view of the sniffling, rheumy London sky. Why not an empty tabernacle? I extended a lamp into it, and had it painted slick, liquid white. The skin of vinyl shone when the bulb was turned on: it was my glossy, clean, well-lighted place; my abstract, imageless chapel.

I only needed a step-ladder to reach it, but I found instead another staircase, the detachable kind they have in old libraries for retrieving books from the higher shelves. It was taller than me, and almost broke my back as I staggered home from the junk shop underneath it. Still, its disproportion pleased me. It was an overstatement:

ascent rendered triumphal. But it did no harm, because apart from that immaculate, uninhabited oblong it had nowhere at all to go.

My staircase, I thought, needed some protective presences, to unseat the terrors which Hitchcock installed on each step – the snarling dog, the avenging matron with the cleaver. Since it resembled a trail through clammy woods, I began to search for animals whose habitat it might be. If I could find one for every tread, I would make it safe (though I might always double the cordon of guards by starting another file of them down the opposite side of the stairs).

The genii I began with, which snapped and growled on the bottom stairs, were dragons. One was Chinese, bought in Hong Kong, carved from a grey-green boulder, its ravine of a mouth occupied by a rattling pebble so it wouldn't bite my ankles as I passed. Chinese dragons are benign creatures, mainly concerned to keep warm their hoards of loot. Positioned at your door, they guarantee a blessing. A monster in papier-mâché, discovered in Barcelona and set just above the Chinese beast, acted as the blood-thirstier rear-guard. Chinese dragons like to splash in water, prefer-ably paddy fields, and therefore don't need wings; the Barcelona specimen had a pair of them, green as algae, their struts spiky, spread for take off. Its scaly neck, thin as a lizard's, suffered a genetic accident halfway along, and suddenly forked into three heads. Each of them had singeing coals for eyes, a grate of teeth, and a tongue which furled like a licking flame.

A pottery Portuguese devil kept watch on the third step. Actu-ally, since to name the devil directly was to summon him up, he should be referred to as 'the dirty pig'. It took centuries of super-stition to compile him, with his pile-up of disfigurements: eyes crossed, horns twisted, one tusk protruding through his upper lip to pierce his snout. He was painted fire-engine red, the colour of inflammatory fear, though the chunky pitchfork he gripped in his hands was silver, cold as impaling steel; he raised his pronged tail as contemptuously as a bull about to unload his bowels. Above him, another Portuguese animal, which he might have stripped to the bone. This was the iron skeleton of a goat, the scratched and rusted bone of its elongated back intended as a boot-scraper; a scapegoat, rescued from its encrustations of mud and put out to pasture in its own green field.

Next, the last of the Portuguese totems: a cockerel with heraldic comb, flapping wings and a rudder of resplendent tail feathers. Its eyes protrude like fried eggs, its beak is open to make an announcement. Instead of feathers, a stipple of dots has been painted onto the clay, adding up into a set of red and yellow hearts. There's one on its breast-bone, where its real chicken-hearted organ should be, two more on its agitated wings, another pair on the sides of its arrogant tail. Paint has made a flaunting peacock of it. Or is there a meaning to its surplus decor? All those exterior hearts symbolise resurrection, and commemorate a miracle in the town of Barcelos. A pilgrim, passing through on his way to Santiago, was accused of theft, and sentenced to hang. Hauled off to execution, he made a last appeal to the judge, who was about to sit down to his dinner of roasted cockerel. The judge was in a hurry to eat; the pilgrim vowed that heaven would send a sign on his behalf, and promised that the bird would rise up from the judge's plate in protest. The cockerel promptly untrussed itself, reassumed its feathers, collected its severed head and feet, scrambled upright and crowed. The judge reprieved the pilgrim, and I suppose had the cockerel killed all over again so he could dine. Anyway it now carols silently on a perch of carpet.

After the diabolical pig, the skeletal goat and born-again rooster come two cranky, smirking English grotesques. First is an elderly metal gnome, who would lurk in the grass if the carpet pile were thick enough to conceal him. He might have been a faun once, in some kinder climate. Now his whiskers are wintry, he's arthritic with rust, his conical hat is an invalid's bed-cap, and he dislikes life in the damp garden. A slit between his shoulder-blades suggests that he used to be a money-box; he has the tight-lipped look of a teller behind a grille. I shook him experimentally when I bought him, and his innards rattled. But he had lost his key to foil future owners, so I can't prise him open. He protects the secret he has swallowed, and his appointed stair.

On the step above him, like a gargoyle growing out of the floor not a wall, rears a crookback cast-iron Mr Punch, in retirement from a career as a door-stop. He must have resented that stolid, stationary occupation: his mouth is malevolent, his mountainous nose belongs to a defamatory Victorian Shylock, and he raises a knobby finger to beckon under-age Judys into the bushes. Under his ribs, in the cavity hollowed out by the hump on his back, cowers his dog, a mongrel as abused and vindictive as the one which hounded Bill Sikes. If the gnome is an elderly English faun, Mr Punch is the national version of a satyr, still ripe – despite his deformity – for lust and skulduggery. He and the dog (rabid, I dare say) man my landing. Punch will trip up intruders, the dog will maul them when they're down.

With all these fanged familiars on duty, the staircase as it turns the corner can afford to lower its guard. A pair of American totems take over: a rubber Mickey Mouse, seamed and cracked with age, and a Superman made of felt whose volatile cape needs vacuum-cleaning every so often. The mouse's balloon-shaped face is fixed in a rictus of permanent good humour; the man of steel has a face as square and chiselled as the petrified presidents on Mount Rushmore, betrayed slightly by the black kiss-curl pasted on his forehead. With his locked jaw, his clenched fist, his taut thighs under their blue and red tights, Superman is immobilised inside his armour of muscle. Only his cape moves. Mickey Mouse's limbs, by contrast, are articulated and rotate inside their sockets. His arms and legs twist with double-jointed fluency, and wherever you press him – his clown's nose, his dish-like ears, his knees or elbows – he squeaks and emits a puff of air through one of his crevices. Superman stays as taciturn as a punch-bag.

Two aspects of America: its nostalgia for an infantile past against its relentless manufacture of the future. The squeaky, pusillanimous mouse in everyone; the man-machine who swoops down, jet-propelled, to whisk us out of danger. The mythologies ranked on the lower steps mould figures which represent ancient fears: the dragon, the pig, the randy English satyr. Superman is in the business of reassurance, and propounds freedom from fear. Cartoon characters are fired from cannons or chewed by lawn-mowers or hair-raisingly electrocuted, then bounce back into shape with the rubbery elasticity of Mickey Mouse; the man from Krypton polices any offence against truth, justice and the American way.

The next step is the last to have been occupied. Its tenant is a Japanese Buddha, paunchy and contentedly asleep. I know that Buddhas aren't supposed to be idols; they have no magic powers, and should be used as meditative aids. Still I include this one on Baudelaire's principle that you can never be sure. Half a dozen vacant steps remain. I hope there are enough gods left to inhabit them.

It was the Portuguese who coined the word for my step-ladder of fetishes, straggling skywards on the green carpet. Fetish is *feitiço*: a made thing. The Portuguese explorers, adding new worlds to the world in the fifteenth century, wondered at the charms and amulets worn by the natives of West Africa. The chips of bone and carved wood they strung round their necks, bestowed by magicians, supposedly fended off evil. A spirit was thought to reside in those trinkets. The very word which the explorers made up hints at their doubts about this process of making. If the symbols were so patently invented, manufactured like toys, how could they be believed in? And the very immanence of the indwelling spirit underlined the fictitiousness of it all. The true god of the invading Christians was invisible, unknowable. Symbols deputised for him, but didn't pretend to contain him. The fetish was, by definition, an idol unworthy of worship.

Freud understood our need for these tokens, whether the force they condensed inside was a god or a charge of erotic energy. Items of wispy lingerie, skewering high-heeled shoes, leather gloves, any souvenir of an absent, coveted body – the trophies of fetishism are descended from the talisman the savage deems divine. So are all the objects we live with, since we bestow a character on them, fill them with ourselves, like the clothes we wear or the house we construct around us. Our world consists of dumb, solid objects into which we wish an intangible, probably non-existent soul. Hence the fetishist's closet of garments made sacred by association; hence my menagerie of stone, metal, clay, wood, rubber, felt, of every substance except flesh. The symbol is always a substitute for something else, something mislaid elsewhere, desired but unattainable. And who makes the made thing? A wizard, whom the Portuguese call *feiticeiro*. My staircase – when I look back down askance at it from my bed, feeling its spells solidify below in the darkness – is both circus and altar, put together by a combination of ageing playfulness and pensive sorcery.

Concerned to find sentinels for my steps, I almost forgot the extra requirement of a cellar. It seemed illogical: if the staircase meant escape, why did I have this contradictory hankering after a dungeon? Perhaps because they were complementary angles, the bird's eye view and the worm's. The world didn't need to be a platform; you could live dizzily above it, or burrow into safety underneath.

The Tube trains rattled beneath my floor, in gritty shafts which had a hot, subterranean weather of their own. But I had no trapdoor leading down. Then, after a few months, I began to speculate about a padlocked gate in the basement where I unlocked the first of my three front doors. The gate was made of wooden slats. Since one had come unstuck, I fiddled with it and squinted inside: nothing to see. Yet if it led nowhere, why padlock it? My curiosity itched until, deciding not to worry about who owned the gate and what lay behind it, I sawed off the lock and tugged the slats open. There was no entry to the underworld, only a tiled recess the size of a shower stall. It must have been the coal-hole once, though the chute down which deliveries tumbled had been closed off and cemented into the pavement above. My only option was to fit a new lock and leave the cubicle to its own sooty devices. Even so, I have my cellar, and – in another city – the use of an attic until I reach the age of sixty-five.

My painter was telling me about his previous employer. I knew the woman in question by sight. Her name was Enid, and she kept a knick-knack shop in a nearby street; surrounded by the leavings of a disgraced, too recent past – mugs from minor royal weddings, strings of lack-lustre beads, lamps from the 1950s trying to re-semble helical DNA – she simpered under a succession of fluffy angora bonnets, and turned misty-eyed with vagueness if anyone tried to haggle. Apparently all her soft, puckered flesh hardened when she got home. She was a gorgon to decorate for, he assured me.

'What she *doesn't* want done in that place!' It was a frowning, frowsty villa in Kilburn, desperate to win back a long-lost gentility. 'First there were the mirror-frames in the dining room. She told me she wanted them *after* I'd put up the wall-paper. I said to her straight off, "If you wanted mirrors, why didn't you say so before I papered?

Now I'll have to spend tomorrow stripping." But no, she didn't want the *mirrors*. Glass didn't come into it. It was only the frames. Six of them, without the mirror bits. I suppose at her age . . . She had them copied from some French castle she said she saw in a magazine; some tart's place, I shouldn't wonder. So up went the frames, *over* the striped paper. And then they delivered the chandelier. She got it cheap in an auction, she was so carried away she didn't bother about whether it would fit or not. When we got that up, it drooped so low over the table that if she ever ate there – she never does – she'd have had the bits of glass stirring her tomato soup. Well, almost.

'And then there was the loo. To start with she wanted it red, all lipsticky. I tricked her on that, I said my supplier no longer made that colour paint. So she toned it down to midnight blue. Then when I'd finished it – and I can tell you I was *never* so glad to get shot of anything; with the door closed it was a midnight blue nightmare in there – home she came one day from the shop and gave me a packet. "I want those on the ceiling," she said. I opened the packet and I fell about. It was stars. She wanted these gold stars on the loo ceiling. She'd worked out exactly where each one was to go. I know, but what could I *do*? Up the ladder I went, with the stars in my pocket and her propped in the loo door supervising. God knows if it was her birth-chart she wanted sticking up there. Or she probably liked to think she was space-travelling when she sat down for a tinkle. I almost told her, "You'd be better off putting some thunderclouds up there if Granny's going to use it." But by then she had *that* look about her, and you always know when that happens she's slipped the jack-boots on.

'The worst was the bedroom though. The higher you got in the house, the more over the top she went. She'd dug up this lamp somewhere that she was determined to have over her bed. Four shades, in different colours of glass, frilly like petticoats: I ask you. But that's not all. Holding the lamps were four – cupids! I am *not* making it up. And the expression on their faces! You wouldn't believe how bored they look, it's all they can do to keep from nodding off. Not a lot worth staying up for has happened in that room inside living memory. Even before poor old Athol croaked, she used to send him to sleep on the divan in the spare room; said he snored. I wonder she didn't cut his nose off for him.'

I sympathised with his tribulations, but while he was talking I pictured the astral loo and the heaven of blasé putti gripping lamp brackets, and I thought, Why not? Why shouldn't a house imagine itself to be a little universe? Though Enid's cupids might have been misplaced, altars are indispensable.

I remembered the upstairs oratory in Lisbon with its chipped bits of miracle-working bone, and felt the need of some fireside gods of my own. The staircase already had its troop of ogres; now I began the search for some out-of-work saints, and niches to lodge them in. They would insure me against malefactors, or perhaps just appease my sense of temporariness: if they lived on the premises, if they consecrated their corners, then I might – sooner or later – come to feel that I belonged as well, and stop believing that the place capsized or caught fire or simply blew away as soon as I locked the last of the doors, walked down the street and turned the corner by the church. More than once, flushed with shame at my own insecurity, I came back round the corner for another look, just to make sure. Occasionally, for no good reason, I would travel down from Oxford to check that the doors were locked, the power-points off, the roof intact; having done so, I'd go straight back, briefly happier.

A year later I had persuaded a trio of more or less sacred figurines to take up residence. The first was a Brazilian holy man, Saint Onofre, bought from the carver in the market at Ouro Preto. Saint Onofre was wild and unworldly. He had the mad eyes of Savonarola or Rasputin, but unlike them wore no monk's habit: his robe was his own lank, matted, ankle-length hair. The chisel had discovered him holed up inside the stump of a dark, sappy, aromatic tree, and it hadn't altogether disengaged him from his habitat. The harder it tried to gnaw him into a human form, the deeper he wriggled into the wood. The blade traced the grooves of his tangled locks from head to toe, but they were still grainy timber: hair which had hardened, along with his leathery skin, into spines, barbs, the mantle of austerity and apartness. Though Christianity may have thrust sainthood upon him, he remained impervious inside his thorn-bush of hair. He was a shaggy masculine dryad of the jungle, a personified bough. Better so – if he had been made of martyred, malnourished flesh, he would have stunk, delighting (as saints are supposed to do) in the privations and purgative obscenities of the body; instead he exhaled all the fumes of the rain forest, an incense of leaf-mould, juicy wood and fecund earth. Since the staircase was a green, overgrown path, I built a ledge for him on top of it, where he could look down as if from a tree-house.

He was joined after a few months by a more cultivated customer, who had long since cast off the rudeness and ripeness of nature: a baroque baby cherub from Oberammergau, all chubby knees and fledgling wings, whose pudgy fingers plucked a trainee harp. Then in France I found him a trumpet-playing angel to concertise with. They belonged, admittedly, to different races. The Bavarian cherub was six inches tall, and made of a wood which looked like sponge cake. The angel was fully grown, with a body of white biscuit pottery, put through the fire but left unglazed and so more fragile than skin. He tilted his head jubilantly backwards, and pointed his trumpet in its coat of gold-leaf at the sky. A gust of drapery, also gold, whirled round his middle.

The cherub could be picked up by the scruff of his neck like a kitten: there was a hook between his wings, so I attached him to the low-lying firmament above the staircase. The angel, however, posed a delicate problem of balance and decorum. While soaring through the air and brandishing his trumpet, he had somehow managed to cross his legs. His bottom jutted out with no visible means of support. Had he been resting on a cushion of cloud? And, if he expected to sit down, how was I going to hang him?

The answer lurked in a hole between his buttocks. He was not meant to be suspended; he expected impalement. A spike inserted here should poke into his hollow chest and hold him upright. The spike in turn would have to be driven into a shelf. Comfortable on his internal mast, he could then play silent trumpet voluntaries forever. Now all I had to do was to find a London carpenter willing to carve me a stake to sodomise an angel with. No one advertised this service in the Yellow Pages.

I decided, with my usual cowardice, to transfer the operation to Lisbon. The angel travelled inside a wad of old flannel pyjamas. I unwrapped him in a shop which dealt in religious bric-à-brac under the concrete span of the bridge over the Tejo. The elderly proprietor was called Senhor Beato: Mr Blessed. That augured well, I thought. He sold saints, and parapets to sit them on; he understood my needs at once, solemnly assumed that my motives were devout not sadistic, and asked me to bring the patient back for a fitting at the end of the week.

The stick he whittled was embedded in a semi-circular mantel, which I could then hang from the wall when I got the whole torturing apparatus back to London. He eased the stick between the angel's thighs with the soothing deftness of a proctologist. It must have come to rest inside the cavity of his head. Adjustments were necessary, and Senhor Beato carved two notches in the mantel so the angel's calves would fit securely. Then, worried about the junction of those biscuit buttocks and the gilded wooden platform, he took me round the corner to a shoe repairman he knew, who huddled behind a counter under shelves of snapped heels and worn-out soles, hammering away with hands and forearms blackened by boot polish. Senhor Beato explained what he had in mind: a square of hide, like those from which heels were made, cut into a circle with a hole at its centre. The pad was slipped over the stick, so the figure reposed on that rather than risking splinters in his rear. Senhor Beato shook my hand at the end of the transaction, and wished me good health. It was his tactful way of reminding the angel to intercede for me.

I bandaged the angel in pyjamas again, and carried him to London as tenderly as an egg. I even treated him to a taxi home from the airport, which I had never permitted myself. He now aims his trumpet at a joist I suspect of being damp. His infant colleague harps celestially under a patch of white enamelled sky. The wild man of the woods, his arms like creepers clutching through the thicket of his hair, exhorts whoever climbs the staircase. Surely I'm safe, I tell myself.

Of course I laughed, hypocritically, at Enid's flying circus of go-betweens. But as for her glassless mirrors – didn't she have the right, like me, to surround herself with images which altered the truth or else omitted it; to live in a house of fiction?

Fiction needs a house to inhabit. Fiction itself is a shelter, a domestic fortress built to defend the private life, like Wemmick's suburban villa in *Great Expectations* with its shallow moat, its painted battery of pop-guns, its 'queerest Gothic windows (by far the greater part of them sham), and a Gothic door, almost too small to get in at'. The cottage, stranded between ditches and vegetable patches, protecting its ordnance under an umbrella of tarpaulin, is the lair of individual autonomy. Wemmick fancies it besieged, and likes to think 'it would hold out the devil of a time', since he grows his own cucumbers. Once you wriggle in through that tiny trap-door – and have earned the right, as I eventually did, to close it behind you – you can look out of the windows. It doesn't matter if they're mostly sham, as blind as Enid's mirrors. What you can't see through them, you paint onto them.

'Let us go into the house,' proposes Sterne in *Tristram Shandy*. It is the invitation of all novels. They make up together, ranged side by side, an estate of solitary dwellings, semi-detached from reality. Sterne builds his own house according to a see-through psychological design. The window he looks through has been inset 'in the human breast'; he draws up a chair, he says, and observes the naked machinations of the soul within. The house is the box of 'uncrystallized flesh and blood' which protectively hides the mind.

For Jane Austen, the house measures the lonely, crowded space of society. Fanny Price feels both shrunken and clumsily outsize amid the grandeur of Mansfield Park. 'The rooms were too large for her to move in with ease; whatever she touched she expected to injure, and she crept about in constant terror of something or other; often retreating towards her own chamber to cry.' The public rooms are laid out as obstacle courses. The private ones may be used only for weeping.

At Wuthering Heights, the house, now haunted, harbours the guilty, fantastic contents of a brain. The dead Cathy scratches at the window from outside, begging for accommodation in Lockwood's mind.

Henry James's Poynton is the house as a citadel of civilisation, the mausoleum of its spoils. Perhaps only Oscar Wilde, who exerted himself to be worthy of his blue china, would qualify to live there.

Virginia Woolf sends the furniture whirling weightlessly into space: the philosophy of Mr Ramsay in *To the Lighthouse* is likened to a kitchen table come to rest in a pear tree, with the additional specification that this happens 'when you're not there'. The lighthouse beam rakes through a house which is empty of people and therefore full of thought.

This is the English lay-out: each fantasist has painted his own slice of terrace a different colour, and has his own back garden. But all these novels could just as well be packed into a single, multi-chambered, groaningly overloaded house, like the New York apartment building with its seven floors of solipsists.

The mad Mrs Rochester is locked in her attic. Clarissa's prison is her bedroom, though the bedrooms Fielding imagines – like those at the Upton inn in *Tom Jones* – are cheerfully open to all comers. Henry James, corpulently doubled up as he kneels on a doormat, peers through the keyhole. The interior he spies on is a peep-show of devious, deceptive intelligence. 'What is life, indeed,' asks Gertrude in *The Europeans*, 'without curtains?' Every carpet has an emblematic figure woven in it.

Downstairs Jane Austen waits in the living-room, relying on a loose floor-board to warn her of intrusive callers. Next door the characters of Peacock gourmandise on stuffed turkey, those of George Eliot debate reform and don't notice what they are eating, while Virginia Woolf's creations commune over a sacramental pot of boeuf en daube. The study, set apart, is the preserve of solitude (Mr Bennett in *Pride and Prejudice* bans his wife from his library) or of secrecy: the carpets and cushions of Carker's rooms in *Dombey and Son* betray him by being 'too soft and noiseless, so that those who move or repose among them seem to act by stealth'.

Below stairs, as Thackeray learns in *Vanity Fair* when researching the lower reaches of Becky Sharp's mansion, the servants bide their time and, at the first sign of marital discord or bankruptcy, don't answer the bells. Further down, in the cellars at Horace Walpole's Otranto, freaks and ogres like those locked in the attic run free and pursue their victims. Since *Ulysses*, other amenities have been built onto the house: the privy where Bloom relishes the sweet odour of his refuse and the bath where he studies his shrivelled penis.

The trouble is – as I often think, lying in bed as the rain splashes on the tiles outside and wondering if the roof will leak, or listening to the hammers from the demolition down the street, feeling a thud and waiting for a seam to open in my wall – that the house of fiction knows it is merely fictitious.

Imagination has cobbled and clamped it together, like the hut Robinson Crusoe improvises from whatever materials lie to hand. It may have a lock to keep out the killer rats, like the travelling box which the Brobdingnagians carpenter for Gulliver, and it may even be quilted 'on all sides, as well as the floor and the ceiling' to protect its tenant when it is loaded onto a coach; it can even have a sound-proofed lining of cork, like the cell Proust wrote in. None of these precautions can seal it, or make it safe from invasion or inundation. It bobs about unsteadily, like Gulliver's furnished hutch when the eagle drops it in the ocean, or one of Joseph Conrad's sea-going houses, held together by rivets, bombarded by typhoons.

On second thoughts, though fiction asks for a house, the best it can usually manage is a tent. Or perhaps a lifeboat.

Not all houses of fiction are protected by three doors and four locks, with blinds you can close and curtains you can draw. Some of them have gone out of doors, and wander through the streets. The shelter is invisible: you see only the person inside who has imagined it, who trundles or trudges along in a small, portable world like one of those fluffy cumulus thought-clouds which puff from the heads of characters in cartoons. It may be made of vapour, but whoever occupies it has to believe it is a bunker of impregnable concrete.

I had a friend in New York called Saul, who used to walk his dog in Riverside Park early each morning. He was a worried man, a professional worrier. Personal anxieties didn't bother him: it was the geopolitical ones which kept him awake at night. The dog, an impatient terrier, didn't share his temperament or his hours. It had no sympathy with his insomniac brooding; it demanded relief precisely at seven a.m. He tagged along behind it, still seeing fire in the sky, blizzards of black ash, the grey sluggish Hudson beneath the park boiling. When the terrier danced in a circle, staked out its ground and settled into a squat, he remembered to open a plastic bag for its droppings. Turd in hand, he followed the dog back towards Grant's Tomb.

That particular morning, it chose to honour a clump of bushes beneath a tree, padded with autumn leaves. First there was the investigative sniffing; the circular dance to define terrain; then the straightening of the spine at a sixty-degree angle, to expel the missile. Afterwards, the hectic scratching of the paws to cover up the mess before Saul could rescue it in his plastic bag. He bent down, the bag inside out on his hand like a glove, only to find that the bush was moving. It rolled over, shook itself, scattered its cladding of leaves. Then the bush stood up; it spoke; it said, 'Hey mister, get your fucking mutt outa my house.'

The bush had once been a woman. Blinking, Saul saw its gnarled face, its thorny hands, its brown foliage of muddied cloth. Its house was its unhoused body, wrapped in layers of insulation. His dog, he queasily noticed, had shat on the woman's skirts. Should he invite her home for a cup of coffee while he laundered the garments which she held together with a belt of rope? Would she allow him to wipe off the remnants with his plastic bag? That she permitted, though she spurned the offer of coffee and the washing machine. 'Forget it, mister,' she said, magnanimously releasing him from blame, though she gave the dog a kick when it returned to check on what species she was; 'I'm going back to bed.' And she disappeared into her clothes, spluttered and grunted as she re-embedded herself in the roots of the tree, and became a bush again.

Saul accepted her as a client, a claim on his worrying time. The next morning he carried some money to give her, but she had moved on. The weather was frosty; she had probably gone to hibernate in the warren of cinders underneath Grand Central Station. Down there, in the darkness of the tunnels, another fictional house barred its door for the duration.

The homeless are never without a home. Their appalling pathos, which makes me shiver with recognition as I pass them, lies in the way they fantasticate houses for themselves, conjuring them magically out of air or assembling them from cartons, wagon-trains of shopping trolleys, screens made from garment racks. Imagination raises walls around them, supports the beams, holds the roof in place. On the pavement or in windswept parks, they deploy all the arts whereby we live, and convince ourselves that we are at home in the world. They solemnly trust their flimsy barricades and tottering ramparts, yet at the same time – with an honesty the rest of us can't afford – they admit they are inhabiting an illusion.

A colony of these people camps underneath some concrete stairs outside the concert halls on the South Bank in London. The space is dry, but cramped: they can only sit, not stand up; some of them have to spend the time lying down, as if in their coffins. You can see them arranged in a sociable circle around a camp-fire (also imagined), gossiping, disputing, playing cards, passing a bottle. To keep the wind out, they have made a fence from panels of cardboard, one of which remembers whatever valuable item it once boxed: FRAGILE it says, illustrating the idea of vulnerability with the imprint of a wine-glass. On nights when I see that, I lock my own doors behind me with less confidence than usual.

Man unaccommodated would be a fearful sight. But we never give up our campaign to domesticate the universe. I find myself guiltily envying these people their faith in the street, and in the rivery, forgetful current of chances which gushes down it.

On one of my tracks through Greenwich Village, in the jumble of triangles across Seventh Avenue, an old woman occupies a door-way. She has been there for years, long and patiently enough to qualify as a monument, like Mercury tethered to his pedestal. She demarcates her terrain and declares her tenancy by sitting. I pass her every day, and have never seen her standing up. But though she doesn't move, she commutes in imagination before the rooms of a many-mansioned house. The narrow doorstep, only inches deep, is sometimes a salon. She organises the magazines which passers-by donate on a coffee-table only she can see, and entertains stooping callers. (They bring the coffee.) When she stretches herself across the step and wriggles into her coverlets, the door is a bunk bed. In summer, when the tarred streets bubble like lava and the city sweetly reeks as garbage swelters on the corners, she extends the doorway into a sun deck. She stretches out on a towel, commands a pedestrian to fill up her water bottle, and undresses to a greying satin slip. Sometimes the straps sag off her shoulders; she is as brown and wizened as a gipsy, and she roasts herself on the pavement as lusciously as if the street were her pool of chlorinated coolness. On humid evenings, you can see her seated at a toilet table she has blithely imagined, brushing her hair in a mirror which the truth won't ever splinter. Against her tanned skin, the hair is white like scoured bone. She spends hours weaving identities for herself with it: schoolmarmish plaits, knotted with remembrances; a lop-sided beehive; a crown of thorns. She ponders its ends and often sucks them, amazed at the way these white filaments unreel from inside her.

I have heard her talking – alone, or to her doubled-up guests – about the asininity of the Mayor, the barbarism of New Jersey, the virtue of neighbourliness. 'Stop by again soon,' she shouted after one departing visitor. '*Two* sugars in the coffee.' Once she was loudly deploring the degeneration of the block. A crack dealer, it seemed, had his eye on her doorway. 'I swear to God,' she raged, 'I'll relocate.' In the event, she outsat the crack dealer.

Last time I saw her, it was the onset of autumn. She had produced a bathrobe from somewhere: she must have had a crate of belongings in storage in one of those warehouses of cast-off lives over on the waterfront, since she changed clothes regularly, though she never left her post. Now she hunkered down in a clump of quilts, with a box of tissues at the ready in case of sniffles.

'And how are *you* today?' she shouted as I walked past on the opposite side of the street: it was a challenge as much as a greeting. She was wise to my habit of checking on her out of the corner of my eye. She herself, after all, qualified as a fulltime watcher. To her, my purloined glimpses broke the rules. I wanted to see without being seen, or without making a donation. She was determined to frighten me into visibility.

'Not too bad,' I whimpered across the traffic. 'How about you?'

'I'm *great*,' she shrieked, and fired off a sneeze. 'I'm rent-controlled!'

The wind scythed along the street from the river. I left her blowing her nose and waiting for the first storm of the season to lash her, or for a blizzard to clog the avenue and turn her block to a quagmire of slush. Then she would consent – reluctantly, ashamed of her feebleness – to move her house indoors for a month or so. Her return to the doorway would be a sign of spring, like a crocus cracking the frigid soil. On her step she symbolised recurrence, resilience, the doggedness of survival: the sitting tenant of her own body, and the microscopic square of world it occupied.

Her sedentariness is unusual, and is responsible for her air of luxurious repose as she lolls there and barks out orders for breakfast in bed or for a glass of water to be delivered poolside while she files her nails with an emery board. More often, those who live on the streets – once they have imagined their houses – go on to devise chores for themselves, or daily occupations. Their lives are a course of busy self-justification.

A woman in her forties, with morbid, thought-haunted eyes and a brow tied with twisted nylon scarves, has come to live in the park which I look down on from my apartment. Installed there, she paces for a living. All day she stalks back and forth like a harassed sentry along a line between the benches with their inlaid checker-boards. She is quiet, preoccupied with a private duty to maintain her world's particular perimeter, to tread it into the obstinate ground. She pauses to beg cigarettes in an undertone; once she has lit up, she goes back at once to her routine. Hers is not the gait of a caged animal, walking off frustration and rehearsing escape. Its deliberation suggests a mission, a military drill. She is charged with holding the line; she will guard it until she drops. She has known for a long time that no one will ever come to relieve her.

Days, nights, weeks of pacing have persuaded the dozing drunks and nosy dogs with whom she shares the park that the line is real. It divides the benches like a hedge, a fence of barbed wire, a battlement. No one crosses it any more. Even the dogs walk around it, tails retracted between thin legs, for fear that it might be electrified. She never looks up from the line while walking it. If she did, might it disappear? Or is she looking down into gulfs and roaring cataracts beneath the paved, downtrodden brick floor of the path, studying the deep as she balances on her tightrope across it?

Others have chosen to be caretakers to their chosen segment of street. The black woman outside Rockefeller Center, for instance, beneath the moon-shaped signboards which label an infinity of other Americas, who brandishes a lilac umbrella without a handle. Disabled umbrellas, blown inside out like crippled cranes, their stitching snapped so the fabric recoils along the spokes and mocks the idea of shelter, pile up in New York gutters after a downpour. Among the casualties there are even some perfectly hale specimens, dumped in corner bins among the bags of dog droppings: New Yorkers buy umbrellas whenever it rains, and when the sky clears discard them like outmoded identities, inconvenient memories. The black woman would have had dozens to choose from; lilac was no doubt what she had in mind, and she was prepared to wait. Usually it is the riggings which perish, battered by gales. Her little lilac roof was intact, but she had amputated the umbrella's lower half. With the handle unscrewed, she could use the teepee of lilac upside down. She advanced down the avenue holding it in front of her and using it as a duster, to brush the pavement before she walked on it.

This was her living-room, and she prided herself on keeping it clean. The metallic prongs scratched at stains which worried her, and whisked away scraps of paper. A song babbled from her lips as she worked. By contrast with the fretting sentinel in the park below, she was the very image of a happy 1950s housewife, humming as she made her home shine – except that her hair was a patch of thistles, for a house-coat she wore a shift of sacking, and the floor she swept or waxed in her house of fiction was the trampled turf of heedless Sixth Avenue.

My London neighbourhood has its own self-elected custodian, who goes about her duties inside the oblong box of streets fenced off by the Marylebone and Edgware Roads and Baker and Oxford Streets. I have come upon her at all four outer limits, looking across the causeways of traffic to the extra, unintelligible worlds beyond; she never crosses over, always shuffling back into her own domain, which is her disassembled, disparate house – this bench is her bedroom, the tap in that basement is her bath, the streets in between are all her corridors and horizontal staircases. She drives no train of shopping-carts, and hauls no bags. All she owns she wears. She is swaddled like an onion in a succession of adhesive skins, held together around the waist with the cord from a dressing-gown. You cannot see her face. It has disappeared inside a hood of bundled paper, knotted scarves and knitted hats which bulges above her shoulders: she is the shape, as she lumbers round a corner towards you, of a man-sized bulbous mushroom.

The last time I saw her she was pausing on one of the park benches which serves as a day bed, eating crisps and swigging from a carton of milk. She tipped the food and drink back into the hood, as if shovelling provisions into the mouth of a cave. I would see the face, I thought, as I passed. But when I got abreast of her there was only that black hole in the hood, gaping open in an unvoiced scream as the crisps and the milk crackled and glugged into it. The person had been obliterated, perhaps had fallen apart in the darkness which her vests and skirts and cardigans and coats wrapped up like a parcel and tied into coherence with the dressing-gown cord. The black hole defined life simply as need: a hungry desperation. Perhaps there was nothing behind it but a larger orifice, the echo chamber where humanity silently moans. To whom did the grubby hands which stuffed crisps and poured milk into the cave's mouth belong?

Soon the hands, directed by whatever obscure mind lives in the hollow of clothes, would be back at their business. She has a job, which is to tend a shrine outside a locked church behind one of the Oxford Street hotels. Above the railings is a war memorial, with a roll-call of names and a nailed, writhing Christ. She has set a jam-jar on it, and every day she tours the parallelogram of streets selecting flowers for it: geraniums or pansies from window-boxes or baskets dangling in basements; failing that, ivy dislodged from a wall, or the branch of a shrub which she breaks off by reaching into the garden sequestered in the square for key-holders. It may take an entire day to piece together a posy. By the time she reaches the shrine in the afternoon, the first blooms have already lost their petals. But the wilting sprigs and snapped tendrils only need to survive overnight; in the morning she discards them, rinses the jam-jar, and plods off in search of replacements.

I am not sentimental enough to suppose that it is all in tribute to one or another of the dead names on the list. This arbitrary task is the vindication she has settled on: her ruse for situating herself in the world, and for proving that she is necessary to it.

While she tends her unkempt altar and the umbrella-wielder on Sixth Avenue dusts the sidewalk, the men have more abstruse missions. There is one in London whose beat is South Kensington, sometimes Belgravia. He trundles a cart down the narrow streets in defiance of taxis, too well-behaved to use the footpath – and in any case, he regards his tumbril as a vehicle. It is a home on wheels, its attics and outhouses and extensions protected under a tarpaulin. If, like a magician, he whipped the shroud off, a miniature villa would surely be exposed. Roped to the side is a votive emblem, guarding the sanctuary like the plaster saints which the Portuguese prop in niches on their outside walls: a broom, with the broken green spout of a wine bottle stuck on its handle; in the mouth of glass, a candle which the rain has quenched. He is black. Outside everything else, he is adjacent to gender too. Though his face is stubbled, his voice is shrill; a chieftain's turban is wrapped round his head, but from under his grimy overcoat trail the hems of filmy layered skirts.

He walks along talking in numbers. Calculation is his hobby, his avocation, his esoteric science. 'Six plus one plus twenty-eight minus three hundred and seventy times fifteen,' you will hear him say. He sometimes writes this dance of digits on a square of cardboard, and attaches it to the side of the travelling house like a banner. The equations never have an equals sign, the promise of solution. The proof is still in the balance for him. All the numbers which have ever trooped through his brain are reeling in the direction of an ultimate sum; he pushes his cart towards it.

He has a colleague in Oxford, whom he has never met. This man has been stationed intermittently on the High Street for months now. The colleges debar him; he is mostly to be found on a seat outside a church. He is wiry, emaciated, with eyes which swivel in his head, rotating indifferently across the surface of whatever he sees before him and travelling on to scrutinise the contents of his skull. He arrives at his perch early, and spends the day there in the shivering winter sun with a trouser leg rolled up to the knee. He has a project: to pluck the hairs on his leg, tweaking them out one by one between two thumbnails, wrenching his body with each tug as if he were ripping leeches from his skin. Once a hair is extracted, he blows or brushes it away with a shudder, taking care that it doesn't attach itself to his clothes. He operates systematically from left to right and from top to bottom, like the eye working through words on the pages of a book; I have been watching him remorselessly progress towards the ankle. After that there is a second leg to pluck, two arms, a chest, assorted tufts in other hiding-places. Will the scalp be included?

It is a mystical preparation, like a monk's tonsure or a marine's crew cut, all the more efficient for its pain and for being self-administered. Mild as he is, absorbed in his campaign of depilation, he frightens me. He is picking apart the first house the body grows to hide in. Man unaccommodates himself.

They have resigned from ordinary life to concentrate on a vision. Patrolling a line drawn in the dust, mapping the universe by mental arithmetic, replenishing a roadside altar, they are fanatically true to their fixed idea. Their lives are exercises in computing how much we need, what we can do without.

Other people they can dispense with. The calculator in South Kensington talks only to himself, and if addressed he blankly asserts your non-existence: a person is too globular and amoeboid to be a number; a human being is a nought with clothes on. Still, the calculator has his draped cart with its soggy candle. Possessions are essential, except to the man who is plucking himself like a dead, scrawny chicken. Things are extensions of us, our means of commandeering extra space, our investment in immortality. The last item we surrender is illusion. Hence the house-proud woman who lives under the tree, or the one on her patch of West 10th Street. A house matters to them more than society, because it stakes out an imagined freedom, the inviolable space where they do their thinking. On the streets, they personify solitude. They are sole tenants of the desert islands they design.

Cities are built to deny the isolation and the fragility which these people almost blasphemously declare. But the armature of iron and steel never quite convinces us that we are safe or solid. Inside every bulwark there are other houses, as paper-thin and provisional as skin or as the screen of images I taped across my first window to alter the view.

In New York, twenty-four storeys above East 48th Street, a man sits in a tent. It is a designer tent, imported from Italy, modelled in shades of aqua and peach on those which Bedouins pitch in the Sahara. Its occasional occupant is the Libyan representative at the United Nations, prohibited by the State Department – because of his government's terrorism – from moving beyond Manhattan and the four other boroughs.

He can only glimpse America in the smoggy distance, beyond the river which he can't cross with its lachrymose coffee cup and the faded arches of the Erie Lackawanna. Tied to the city, he has recreated in mid-air his own landscape of unstable sands, where home means a fugitive, fictitious roof of canvas. In the tent on the top of Libya House, armed with his Bedouin axe and a cup of caradom-scented coffee, he muses on dust storms, aerial fire, and the toppling of worlds.

8

Planting a Tree

O UTSIDE THE WINDOWS, EVERYTHING MOVES: IN LONDON, the spearing and splashing of rain or the bluster of reflected clouds or the dive-bombing raids of sparrows on the look-out for crumbs; in Oxford, tour-guides administering their flocks with umbrellas and crowds filing in and out of the cathedral for the incessant, repetitious routine of prayer; in Lisbon, maids flailing rugs on the balconies, the knife-sharpener striking sparks from the grindstone attached to the back of his bike, the drivers employed by the Zaire embassy languidly polishing a patch of chrome; in New York the the world hurtles by with sirens keening, tyres screeching, and the blaring expletives of car horns.

Inside everything is still, except for a hand scribbling over a piece of paper. Silent too, except for music dispensed by appliances to contradict and muffle the outdoors. How is it possible to feel alone when there are so many voices written into grooves of plastic waiting to sing for you, and so much instant electronic transport on hand? And every book on the shelf is an optional life, another alternative to the view through the windows. My world, self-made and despotic, is in here; out there is the wilderness fought over by everyone else.

At least that is how I thought for a long while. I suppose the end of my little autarchy began when I let the tortoise into it.

I discovered the tortoise among a tribe of relatives, scattered like mottled pebbles through a landscape of wood shavings in a pet shop at the Oxford market. Buying it was one of my life's most gratuitous and inexplicable acts. I chose it more or less at random, persuading myself that this particular one – because it had been crawling over the back of a colleague, before it forgot why it was doing so and dropped off again into an abysmal, inert, centuries-long sleep – was livelier than the others. It cost roughly as much as a paperback book, and was the same size as one as well. On the way back to Christ Church, it dozed off in its cardboard box. Now, I thought, there would be something in my domain which was alive, which moved. Or which was supposed to move. When I put it down on the carpet, it remained comatose. I could hardly expect a cocker spaniel's bombardment of yelps and licks and grateful nuzzling, I told myself; and anyway, since this was my first experiment in adopting another creature, it was probably wise to begin modestly, on a lowly rung of the evolutionary scale.

After several hours, the tortoise did move. Its black eyes with their leaden lids blinked open: I can guarantee as much, because I was lying down on the carpet staring at its blunt reptilian head, willing it to betray some vital sign. The lids were hauled up, like dusty velvet curtains with sagging sash-weights, but the eyes looked through me, or took me for some twisted obstruction on the jungle floor which, in the remote future, it would have to negotiate a way around or over. The eyes registered only fatigue at the idea of such effort, and threatened to retire again behind their shutters of scale.

But since it was awake, it decided to circumvent me, and raised itself painfully on its clawed flippers. Its talons fumbled on the carpet; one or two legs managed to prop themselves up, while the others slid back to their swimming position; the shell which it was trying to lift pressed down the prying head and grappling legs like an oppression from above, the hump of deformity or hod of cumbrous, inherited bricks we all have to lug around. The long-ago up-hill labour of horizontal man attempting to be vertical was fought out all over again before me, and with no certainty about the outcome. Aeons of evolutionary strain were compressed into five minutes.

The assistance I offered was refused: when I grabbed the shell to steady it, all four pincer-toed legs retracted, its head was jerked into its entrails, and only a grey-green point of tail stuck out across enemy lines; when I let the shell go, it flopped to the floor like the stone it was pretending to be. Agonies later, the hydraulic process began again. Wobbling and lumbering, never able to keep all four legs erected at once so that it keeled and pitched like a raft on a stormy sea, it managed to cross a few feet of floor and then slumped back to sleep under a bookcase. It was still there the next morning, with the addition of a small white milky pool drying on the carpet under its tail. I cleaned up after it, feeling quite parental.

During the winter which it spent roaming torpidly through my rooms – snuggling while the centuries passed in a surf of paper in one corner or hesitating for all eternity on the edge of a step until I made up its mind for it, withdrew it from the brink and turned it back in the direction from which it had long-sufferingly, lethargically come – I fed it on leaves of lettuce which I slyly pocketed from my lunches in college. No one knew I was filching greens for a tortoise, but the underhand habit provoked no comment. One of the canons of Christ Church Cathedral, a generation or so back, was notorious for collecting toast and carrying it back to his lodgings. When he died they cleared out desk-drawers, wardrobes, commodes, bookshelves full of curling, carbonised bread. The college servants, watching me finesse a slice of cucumber or a crinkled leaf into a paper napkin, clearly thought that I was heading in the direction of the canon with the antiquarian interest in toast. Sooner they should think me unhinged – I calculated – then they should know I was harbouring a tortoise; I would rather be thought dotty than soppy.

Behind locked doors, I unpacked the salad scraps, lowered myself to the floor, and tried to buy a demonstration of affection with the bribe of cucumber or lettuce. Sometimes the ancient, cynical head, the size of the last joint on my little finger, would lunge like an adder about to bite, flash its scissory incisors, and leave a scalloped frill on the greenery. The morsel, translated through peristaltic ages down the length of the body under the shell, re-emerged a day later in the form of white spittle from the barnacled tail. More often the food would excite no reaction at all. The tortoise seemed to have outlived all appetites. While I tickled its insentient nose with lettuce, it looked steadfastly through me. I withered in that gaze; so did the limp, dejected lettuce.

I often thought, during these abject sessions on the ground, about the wonderful coda to *Tristes Tropiques* where Lévi-Strauss imagines that we might somehow gain access to the patterns and purposes of the savage, sophisticated tribal mind: his faith that this can happen is sustained less by his own anthropological skills than by 'the brief glance, heavy with patience, serenity and mutual forgiveness, that, through some involuntary understanding, one can sometimes exchange with a cat.' My tortoise and I never exchanged such a glance. Instead of patience and serenity, it had an infinite tolerance for tedium, so it could afford to wait for the moment when I became cramped or cold or remembered the absurdity of my position and hauled myself back onto my feet; I must presume that it never forgave me, though I regularly forgave it its trespasses, its messes, its stone-age stony-headedness. There was no chance of requital. I had chosen as a pet the animal most likely to confirm my sense of inadequacy.

During the spring, I sometimes smuggled it across the quad in a shopping bag, unlocked one of the innocuous doors beside the cathedral, and set it loose in a garden. I usually couldn't stay to watch over its rambles, and mostly returned to find it had strayed out of sight. All the anxieties of childhood returned in a panic as I ran up and down the cinder paths or groped through the flower-beds and even considered calling out for it or whistling: I was back in a world where things promised to be inalienable, and if you lost a possession – usually a marble which had skidded off course, or a tennis ball guzzled by a drain or held hostage in the backyard of hostile neighbours – then a part of you was amputated, your tenuous identity was disassembled and dispersed, blown away by the winds . . .

I always found the tortoise, which hadn't the ambition to travel far. It tended to skulk under a bush, pretending to be a clump of rock and no doubt relishing the distress which blinded me to its presence. I remembered thinking once, when I noticed where it was hiding and scooped it up with a spasm of happiness, that that is how life should be: all losses are restored, and sorrows end; the eternal return; the fragments of the golden bowl fly back into place and weld themselves together; you are allowed a second chance. I probably gave the unfeeling shell a hug.

Since immobility was the tortoise's mode, it took me a while to realise that it was dead. It had paused on a straw mat under my kitchen table. A lettuce leaf I had not been able to tempt it with turned brown and tortoise-shell-coloured beside it. Beginning to worry, I stretched myself out on the floor and stared into those open eyes. They returned no acknowledgement, but then they never did. I decided to wait another day. Perhaps it hibernated with its eyes open?

After another day I decided that the eyes had remained open to accuse me. I picked up the tortoise and shook it – gently at first, then furiously – like a stopped watch which with the help of some violence might start up again. It didn't tick.

Ashamed, and having anyway to teach, I hid it in a kitchen cupboard. During the day I brooded about the business of disposal. It couldn't be flushed away, like a goldfish or those unloved New York alligators. I didn't like to risk consigning it, even wrapped up, to my wastepaper basket. The tipsy scout who came in to empty it in the morning tended to spill its contents in doing so: I could just hear the clunk of the corpse on the floorboards. Perhaps I should leave it up in the attic with the pulverising bat? The more minutely I debated the formalities, the more like a shifty murderer I felt.

By the evening I had decided on a water burial. I would take it down through Christ Church meadow and ease it into the river. But it was spring, the rowing season, and I didn't want a crowd of hearty, laughing mourners. Luckily next morning it was raining, so there could not possibly be rowing practice on the river. Yet equally wouldn't it be thought odd if I set off in a downpour for a walk in the meadow, carrying a brown-paper bag which might have contained my lunch? Though I plodded down the sodden path unchallenged, the soaking bag felt as heavy as a suitcase; I felt sure I was walking lopsided, as if my old psychosomatic limp had come back to fetter me.

The river was gushing, a torrent of muddy tea. I took the beast out of its brown-paper coffin, gave it one last chance to revive and roll the sleety skies back, then leaned over the bank and dropped it onto the water. Onto not into: the current seized it and spun it away before it could sink; a few yards off, it spiralled under.

Squelching back to the college, aware that I was wet through, I began to feel sorry for myself. A good sign, I thought. I must be recovering.

When the short story of my tortoise ended, I realised that it reminded me of something. Des Esseintes had adopted one as well.

Des Esseintes was the solitary, dandified, decadent hero of Huysmans's *A Rebours*, the book which is blamed for Dorian Gray's moral decline. He turns his villa in the Paris suburbs into a palace of art. Like a more neurotic, precious and affluent version of Wemmick, he uses the house as his buffer against the vulgar reality outside. Proust insulated the ego by lining his chamber with cork; then, inside its muffling crypt, he could write the book about his journey in quest of lost time. Des Esseintes more ingeniously arranged to live inside a book, and therefore didn't need to write one: he bound the walls in Morocco leather. Trophies of connoisseurship recomposed the world inside his house.

Once Des Esseintes considers a venture out into noisy, unredeemed actuality. He plans a trip to London, which attracts him as a symbol of the modern world: sooty, stinking, industrious. He has himself driven to the Rue de Rivoli to buy a Baedeker. There he finds fog, slush, mud, smoke, and a swarm of plebeians. He is surrounded, he realises, by London already. He has had the experience in imagination. Why bother to drag his body and his luggage across the Channel? He returns home at once, feeling weary and sated as if he had come back from a voyage as arduous as those of Ulysses or Phileas Fogg.

Dorian Gray reads Huysmans's novel, though Wilde archly refuses to name it. To Dorian, it is the story of his own life: a parable about art's defiance of nature.

It was not quite my story. I would not have exchanged the sight of London for a vision of it; and my experience with the tortoise was different from that of Des Esseintes. He acquires the animal as a decorative feature. He wants it to set off an oriental rug, to mobilise – as it wanders about on its blundering primeval errands – the glints of bright thread in the weave. The scheme doesn't work. The dull brown shell tarnishes the lustre of the rug. Des Esseintes decides that the carpet is anyway too crudely bright and new; it needs subduing, and he redesigns the tortoise to achieve this effect.

He sends the creature off to a jeweller. It returns with its shell inlaid with gems, like a shield of jewels: turquoises, sapphires, rubies. He is delighted. But the burden of such luxury and the onus of such exorbitant symbolism are too much for the lowly crawler. It cannot live up to its glorious costume; it expires beneath it. Prodding it when it does not budge, Des Esseintes realises that it is dead. Still, why should he mind? It has compliantly become what it was always intended to be: a figure in his carpet. He declines, for the moment, to consider the possible moral, which is that art might be an agent of death, the revenge of one who has no talent for living.

The tortoise Des Esseintes introduced into his tomb of finery proved unworthy of him. With mine, the blame was differently distributed. I proved unworthy of it.

Or perhaps I was too intent on using it as a substitute for something else. I envied the creature its compact world, the tank-like armour into which it could withdraw head, legs and even its stub of tail. It didn't need to transform its body into a weapon, like the hedgehog with its quiver of poison pens. It could simply return into itself, and once all feelers were retracted it couldn't be hurt. But neither, as I discovered, could it be reached in there, by any amount of mute pleading. With an apathy I considered almost saintly – the perfection of passive resistance – it died to escape my emotional impositions.

The next attempt to animate the space inside my windows was the incident of the owl. Except that the idea of animating the owl wasn't mine. It was a practical joke, so ingenious that it turned out to be impracticable.

I had a barn owl in Oxford, which perched on a specimen branch in one of my bookcases. It was stuffed; I bought it as a joke about the fusty trade I plied in those rooms. Wasn't a stuffed owl a synonym for bad, pompous verse? Also perhaps for the taxidermic business of history, making corpses presentable? Other driftwood accumulated on the shelves and tables and window-seats, and began commingling in corners; the Zen stones and a cargo of pearly abalone shells stood guard round an old green brandy bottle in which a silver plastic rose was somehow growing. The walls grew new skins, and the Piranesi prints of mouldering Rome were placed by photographs of sleeky, shiny New York. After a while, I forgot about the owl, and remembered it only when I noticed puzzled students looking in its direction. It was an outgrown toy, a joke I no longer found funny.

Still, it refused to decay. Hooked to its perch, its glass eye focused in predatory fixity, its wings unfolded to swoop, it was death's exact simulation of life: like the aesthete's tortoise; like art itself.

Only the membrane of soot which had gathered on its feathers – a stuffed bird is not easy to keep clean – gave away the truth of its condition.

One of the students, who kept the owl under observation during tutorials, devised a scheme for returning it to life. He told me about it years later, after having escaped from my tutelage. He was an actor, with a sly gift for funny voices and experimental identities. Once or twice he exercised these voices on the telephone to excuse himself from a tutorial, claiming to be a worried room-mate or the grave, stern father of a friend with a sudden illness to report. I took the bait, and would not have minded the deception if he had spared my shame by not admitting the trick. When I saw him next after the second episode, I asked him how he was feeling. The friend's father had made the case – some gastric disaster – sound grim. I was glad he had got over it, I told him. A delicate calculation flickered in his eyes, a grin twisted on his lips as he tried to decide whether the pleasure of telling me what a fool I had been was worth the price of my outrage. He decided that it was. And besides, he could rub it in by presenting his triumph as an act of contrition: he was after all only making a remorseful effort to be honest, so what was I shouting about? The more I ranted, the more insidiously jubilant was his smile. I had a holy terror of him ever after. That puckish migration between identities broke all the rules of psychological decency and social peace. I now never answer the telephone without a twinge.

Because he knew the damage he had done, he operated after that on the assumption of my quivering alarm, waiting for the next magical, malicious voice to materialise from the air. It was in this spirit that he described his project for the owl.

'What put me off was the bribes. I'd have had to tip your scout to let me into your room, and I drew the line at that. No, not on principle; because of the cost. And there were all the other expenses: the second owl, the drugs . . . Oh, don't worry, I wasn't going to drug *you*. I had it all worked out. I'd get hold of a live owl, exactly the same as that stuffed one of yours. It wouldn't even need to be exactly the same. Yours has been there so long you don't notice it. Then I'd get into your room, take the stuffed one off the perch, put the live one up there in its place, and sedate it. This was the part I wasn't sure about it, but I bet I could have found someone in

Pharmacology to tell me how you knock an owl out. All the same, I had to be exactly sure how long it would take for the drug to wear off, so I could time my next tutorial for the moment when the owl came to. And you'd be sitting there droning on about Milton when suddenly you'd hear those wings beat and the owl would lift off for a lap of the room. You'd have freaked out! You know, I wouldn't have minded being sent down – just to see the look on your face when that old feather duster started to fly. Now you've *got* to admit it was a lovely idea. Just too much trouble to set it all up.'

He defied me not to admire the beauty of it. I made a tuneless effort to laugh, while shuddering at the thought of my totems, my familiars, my dead substitutes come whirringly, angrily to life. Would the Zen stones start pelting themselves through the windows? Would James Dean lollop out of the poster and dawdle off into the distance? Would Bob the Bat flutter down from Dodgson's alchemical hideout upstairs? Would I be shot down in the crossfire of uprisen things? When I went back to the room, my hand hesitated on the light switch inside the door. I needn't have worried. In the toyshop of the heart, not a thing moved.

There was an epilogue, years later in London. When I imported some greenery to my sunken yard – an emaciated tree in a tub, which performed miracles of self-overcoming to reach up to the sun; geraniums drooping from pots on the wall, and some ivy which I taught to writhe round a drainpipe – the local sparrows recognised my existence at last. First they perched on the roof and speculated about who might occupy the burrow below. Then the boldest was sent down on a reconnaissance mission. It descended in steps, using the thin tree as its ladder; it hopped about on the tiles, jerking its head back and forth like a tiny camera. Inside, behind the glass door, I was invisible, blotted out by reflections. It summoned four or five others, and they began assaying the dust for crumbs as if panning for gold, tossing rejected grains away with contempt. The squares of baked clay which I tried to remember to wash down were to them a field of nutritious grits, a meadow fertilised from the air. They pecked their way systematically across it, shrilling with pleasure at the discovery of another compact world to alight on. Eventually I had to turn a light on inside to resume my own life; the moment I did so I loomed into sight behind the reflecting wall, and they spun back to the roof in terror.

After that, I accepted them as an obligation. They announced themselves noisily every morning, and I left them daily harvests of breadcrumbs. Like children, they assumed it was my duty to supply their needs; after a week I was enslaved, distributing not only left-overs but also samples of food I hadn't eaten yet – they were partial to water biscuits, ground in my fist into powder, and to soft clods of fruit cake. I took their chirping and shrieking on the roof as an order, and would ransack the cupboard to see what I had for them. They allowed me to spy on them, so long as I remained behind the glass door with the light off: if I ventured out of this self-effacement, they scattered at once. Being scared of me was tiresome pedantry, I thought; it was like assuming that all policemen are thugs. Could they not make an exception in this one case? They didn't mind accepting my charity, but they would not be enticed into a relationship.

Perhaps they resented my envy of them, my creeping usurpation. Birds were professional observers, perched like these sparrows on television antennae or like my barn owl on a crook of wood, enjoying a supercilious bird's-eye view of the tethered, weighted terrain beneath; they touched base down there only to feed, but were not constrained by the dulling gravity of the ground. Shelley admired the skylark's ignorance of pain, and Keats hoped by listening to the nightingale to forget what it had never known: weariness, fever, fret, groans and death-agonies. Birds are blithely outside our world or above it. They must know the designs we have – when we try to buy their favours with bread – on their oversight or their indifference.

For whatever reason, things soured between me and the sparrows. The more servilely I catered to them, the more negligently they dealt with me. I began to leave wedges of bread or shards of crust rather than crumbs. This, however, merely freed them from having to eat under my unseen supervision. They swooped down like Jove gathering up Ganymede, gripped the quarry and made off with it to the roof where they could enjoy it in peace. After that, I frustrated them by reverting to crumbs. They in turn spotted the window ledges with their droppings, and idly sampled leaves from my starveling tree.

The breach came when I strewed the tub with phosphate to feed the tree. From above it must have looked like a banquet of day-old bread. The birds bombarded the yard while I was out, and when they found the phosphate indigestible took their revenge by spitting it, along with a layer of compost, out of the tub onto the tiles. I came back to find the yard manured, while the birds chortled from their look-out on the antenna.

Inside, temporarily defeated, I set about constructing my own tame aviary. I found corners on the stairs for a pair of more obedient birds: a shining polished parrot from Ecuador, its branch, its body, its nest and the eggs inside it all carved from the same chunk of tree; a gaudy, slangy Brazilian macaw, wearing its plumage as ostentatiously as a carnival costume, which lived on a crooked perch torn from a real tree, with a wire to suspend it from my ceiling – but as a precaution against its flying back into life its feet had been replaced by nails, drilled directly into the bough.

Under the banister I strung two more birds, whose wings of board creaked and flapped like some desperate flailing Icarus when you tweaked a thread beneath them. One was a seagull, the other a migrant Canada goose. Just above the goose, the gull rode on its back: I got the idea from watching television pictures of the space shuttle glide back to earth in the Californian desert. Unless I taunted them by twitching the thread, like some infantile tormenting god who has all of his creation on strings, they hovered there in a prison of breathless air, with only stray draughts from an open window to excite them.

Above the gull and goose, suspended from the same nail, I found room for an owl. This one didn't moult on its perch like the feathery yellowing ghoul in Oxford; together with the gull and goose it was flying, its claws extended in its grey undercarriage to snatch up some nocturnal morsel. I made this owl myself, or rather pieced it together from a kit of stiffened paper with some nail scissors and a tube of glue. Over several tense evenings of microsurgery, the flat painted cards were bent, interleaved and persuaded into the likeness of a body, with hooked beak, talons sharpened by my scissors, and phalanxes of feathers the colour of gun-metal.

Labouring away at it and cursing my clumsiness, I wondered why I should be treating a childish hobby with such grim adult seriousness. Once, when the scissors slipped and made a meal of a section of wing, I let out a cry of inordinate rage or grief. What game could this be, and why did it matter so much?

It was the game invented by the man in the cave at Lascaux, who painted on his wall an image of the galloping animal he had failed to kill or which perhaps he secretly, uselessly wanted to admire, detaining a bright shadow of the live, elusive reality. He discovered the occult fascination of the facsimile; his cave, a cage for images, was the first alternative world.

Meanwhile, in my ersatz zoo, the rabbits went on multiplying. Not by the usual methods. They didn't reproduce; they belonged to different families, races, species with no biological model in common; unable to be born, they had to be made. On shelves and tables, cowering in corners or scratching on vacant stair treads or even dangling from the wall, they motionlessly overran my house.

They joked about their own fabrication, in little fables concerning the difference between the birth of life and the creation of art. One of the rabbits, which I found in the back of a shop in Lisbon, inhabited the blue shell of an Easter egg. Rabbits, I know, don't hatch in eggs, but their proficiency at mating and the multiplication game has always involved them in the rites of spring; the goddess Eastre, who looked after matters of fertility before Christianity deposed her and counselled abstinence, chose the lustful hare as her favourite animal. Which might be why this rabbit has gone to live in a blue egg, whose shell he is careful not to crack: instead he opens two shutters in its thin, gritty case, and pokes out a head which has no body attached to it. His ovoid house rests on a green garden-bed, like the world-egg itself which is supposed to balance on the back of a tortoise.

Elsewhere two other rabbits conducted an experiment in cloning. Standing back to back, they were the twin halves of a metal candy mould, acquired at a garage sale somewhere in America. The indentations on the hollowed tin filled in the imprint of their absent bodies, pressing the flour into shape: streaks for the fur, eyes like buttons, alert upright ears, the marshmallowy pompom of the scut. As lookalikes, they might have been the start of an infinite series. In fact they were the two sides of a single body, which would be united when the mould was clamped together, locked, and put into the oven. Meanwhile they couldn't even admire themselves in the mirror like Narcissus, since the mould had made them face in opposite directions. If they were twins, they were the Siamese kind, shackled together by the mould's clips where their ears and tails converged. I didn't use them to generate a population of identical sibling biscuits. I found the idea of buttering their interiors and filling them with lumps of amorphous dough faintly repulsive. It was too much like making a person, as the raw material in that suit of armour was subjected to heat and hardened. I opened out the empty mould and pinned it to a wall. There it couldn't snap shut: nothing would be trapped into form inside it.

Along the shelves, other rabbits invented themselves by metamorphosis. Almost any object, it seemed, had a potential rabbit somewhere inside it, or on its surface. One had been rescued from deep in an elephant's tusk. It was Chinese, scraped from ivory, rearing with red ignited eyes. Another was painted onto a stone. For years the stone must have lain on a beach being lapped into smoothness, innocent of all resemblance to a rabbit; a few licks of a brush were enough to make a metaphor of it. One rounded snub end was a nose, the other a tail. Ears couldn't be accommodated on the even ridge, so they were painted in lying flat on the rabbit's back. The stone had a hump half way along, where the waves had worn it away: the rabbit therefore hunched its back, lowering its long ears and raising its spine in alarm. On the outside of the impregnable stone, a shrinking trembling fugitive creature lived. Underneath, in the matted fur where its testicles should have been, the brush had scribbled an illegible name – the painter's, not the rabbit's.

The animals had foregathered from all over the world. One of them came from the Philippines, and for a skin wore a layered paste of comic-book narratives in its native Tagalog. The little dramas, which Filipina housemaids read on their days off in every corner of Asia, unravelled in torn strips along and around its body. A bearded man emerged from a cabin under some palm trees on one of the rabbit's paws; a girl with a beehive hairdo wept a glycerine tear in close-up on its back. The characters exchanged abuse or affection in bubbles: OKEY LANG YON! said one of them, and another began a diatribe by declaring PERO HIRAP NA HIRAP NA HO AKO before the exposition was cut short by an overlapping stripe of scenes from somewhere else in the story. A single word, UAMALIS, floating inside a cloud to indicate that it was thought not speech, whispered in the cavity of the rabbit's ear.

KERBOOM, international onomatopoeia for an explosion, ricocheted through the air in separate red letters like quoits around the crook of the rabbit's hind legs, as if it had scampered onto a landmine.

I sometimes remind myself to have this rabbit professionally translated. Meanwhile, where the ripped edges of the cheap comic-book paper have come unstuck, it has begun to reveal an underbelly of English. The tatty coloured scenes were pasted to a cladding of pulped official documents. 'Dollars' and 'benefits' and 'investigation' and 'depreciation' peep through crevices between the frames where the men blow each other up and the girl with the pink face and the blue hair sheds her tear. This was no rabbit: it was a palimpsest of uproarious images and chattering words. It couldn't move, but the syllables frisked on its pelt like fleas.

About an Italian souvenir there could be no doubt. This was a rabbit, not a skittish papery alphabet: a little votive bronze modelled on an Etruscan animal, as pagan as Eastre's salacious hare. Caught in the act of elasticising its body to leap, it had been screwed to its pedestal just in time. Its ears poked up as aggressively as spring buds, and it even managed a pronged wagging tail. Its hindquarters reared, as sprinters do when bent forward on their mark. It was launching itself into a landscape whose overflowing energies it embodied; it scorned the idea of burrowing, of dressing up in smocks and jackets with brass buttons like Beatrix Potter's bunnies, or of drinking camomile tea.

Near it, however, were two English rabbits which advertised the domestic virtues. Elderly and genteel, they sat side by side in arm-chairs. The female, tucking her ears under a night-cap, nursed a lapful of knitting; her husband, with spectacles on his twitching nose, dozed over a book. They rested their hind legs on footstools: their hopping days were over. Demoralised, housebound, they had given up being animals, and were now the tamed copies of their human captors, or creators.

One last rabbit leaned against a line of books, a temptation and a reproof. Its body was chocolate; it might have been pressed inside the candy mould pinned to the wall. It wore a skin of silver paper, which dressed it in the style of an Edwardian schoolboy. Its ears stood to attention above a squashed, fearful face. I was given it one Easter, and should have eaten it at once. In fact I had begun to unpeel the paper, finding a join at the rear where the scut stuck impertinently through its tunic. Then I thought better of it. Compunction or cowardice intervened: was it this easy to unwrap a person? Was identity just a sliver of coloured foil costuming a blob of food? I told myself I would eat it later, and for the time being added it to my collection.

Since then I have occasionally considered it, when suffering from midnight starvation with nothing else in the house to gnaw on. But eating an image always seemed somehow more gruesome than eating something which was once alive. By now, in any case, it is inedible: last time I peeped through the tear in the trousers, the chocolate was turning chalky, whitish and dry. Decay has saved it. Shelved, it preserved childhood and its appetites – unsurfeited and unspoiled – inside that mummy-cloth of silver.

The proliferation of the rabbits is a mystery to me. Why have I allowed it? My only clue is that the single nursery rhyme I remember from my own childhood concerns a rabbit. I had a blanket known as a bunny rug, and the rhyme explained its origins. I can hear my mother humming it to pacify me:

> Bye baby Bunting
> Daddy's gone a-hunting
> To fetch a little rabbit skin
> To wrap his baby Bunting in.

I'm still not sure that I understand it. The first rabbits introduced into Australia had increased with a will and were eating the continent bare; a disease was invented to destroy them, and this was the proud heyday of myxomatosis. But if the rabbit was a hated pest, why swaddle the child in its ripped-off mantle? Was there a transference of guilt here, or just an enlargement of sympathy? If I became the rabbit when snuggled into its rug, did that mean I was the next victim; or could this have been my earliest and most painful lesson in fellow-feeling?

For whatever reason, the rhyme unfailingly sent me to sleep. Even at this distance, there is a primal comfort in it. It could be describing a family in a cave: the mother inside at the fire with the infant, the father stalking the dark outdoors; the mother explaining the father's absence, the father violently plundering food and shelter from nature; the mother singing, the father killing. Everyone's childhood is the early history of the world all over again. The rabbit seemed both to vouch for the security of home and to admit its snatch-and-grab precariousness.

Later, at school, I had to learn a mawkish poem about a rabbit in a snare. Bludgeoned into my heart by repetition like the rules of arithmetic, I now can't dislodge it. It tends to recite itself when I am trying to settle down to sleep, like a scary, mocking lullaby. It describes listening helplessly to an iterated cry in the woods:

> And now I hear that cry again
> But still I cannot tell from where.

The trite, tragic words made no attempt to describe the sound. I couldn't imagine the noise a trapped rabbit made, but I always strained to hear it: a squeal? a whimper? a screech? The words dully paraphrased the pain, but in the blank spaces between them I eventually overheard the sound I was listening for, a fitful sobbing which didn't bother to dramatise itself as a howl because it knew there was no one to answer it. Having first been warmly nestled in the rabbit skin, I now knew what the rabbit felt like when the skin was torn off. I made a note for future reference: don't get trapped; don't allow yourself to be hurt; imitate the action of the tortoise, impregnable in its shell, not the squirming wailing rabbit.

We can't wait to forget childhood, and fret to recall it again only when it has gone forever. After those first few years of soporific rhymes and nightmarish verses, the rabbits scattered only to pop up again three decades later in the meadow outside Christ Church. When I saw them there, I recognised them: they might have tunnelled diametrically through the earth's core from the other hemisphere, and scraped their way through the rind to resurface, like memories, here in my adult life.

They chose the spot for their second coming with a sure instinct, because the meadow was the place where I could stray out of the quadrangle with its petrified worthies, out of the regime of funereal black gowns and Latin graces, out of my academic chores, and wander clockwise around a world which was always the same and yet always different – the thatched barn with the consignments of junked furniture; the view back across the field of ruminant cows to the equally dreamy spires; the Druidic oak with an atrium beneath its branches, bowing onto the river; the punt, adrift on snarled cables, which should be able to take you over the stream to the path on the opposite bank but can't. The meadow narrated the year to me, like a book of hours, days, seasons in which I was the remorseless, circling clock-hand. The narrative always begins near the end, in autumn: cattle coughing; leaves like a blitzed library on the river; white clumps of mosque-shaped fungus sprouting under the bushes. During winter the trees wither to anatomical diagrams of themselves, the river floods and the meadow listlessly drowns. In spring the birds argue it back to life with their jabbering. By summer it supports an ark-load of creatures: ducks which conduct swimming classes for their offspring, water hens with wobbly houses of grass on roots in the river, swans flexing their necks to trawl green spools of weed from below the surface, the docile longhorn steers embarrassed by their Viking helmets, and an occasional fox, its brush guiltily trailing between its legs as it creeps away from the scene of some crime; but above all the rabbits.

There were three separate colonies, converging from different corners of the meadow. A brown tribe was headquartered around a compost heap of grass clippings near the furniture barn; a yellower family had its own suburb under the pavilion on a cricket pitch; a third group, inky black, occupied a thistle patch in the field where the cattle dozed and moseyed. A year later, the subdivisions had met and interbred. The meadow came out in spots, as if with freckles. They were all the progeny, I suppose, of a few domestic pets, abandoned when they couldn't be house-trained or when the novelty wore off, like those alligators in the New York sewers; they were too guileless to be wild, and I always thought of them as teams of lost children, deserted here and gamely living off the land, though still in their parti-coloured school uniforms.

As I trudged round the circular path like the dutiful pointer on the clockface, I'd pause for as long as the cogs and wheels would allow to admire their playfulness, their endearing irrelevance. Even eating, their only occupation, required no effort. They consumed grass while pretending – upright among the stubble, their ears like twitching stalks – to be grass. The meadow disappeared into them through their nibbling noses as if it were one single continual skein of green, never used up because it grew again as fast as they could ingest it. The combined eating and observation, rearing in profile with one eye keeping watch, bristles testing the air. If I left my

227

appointed path to pace towards them (always in soothing, sleep-walking slow motion), they hopped off almost lazily to their hideouts in the bushes or under the pavilion. It wasn't worth their while to be afraid, because they knew that where they were going I was too old and ungainly to follow.

Every autumn they dematerialised. The meadow – wiped away by fog, denuded when the leaves fell, submerged by the rains – soon afterwards did the same. I returned inside to the company of my rubber, ivory, stone or chocolate substitutes.

Then, one Easter in Lisbon, I was presented with the live, wriggling, clawing, incontinent thing itself: an albino rabbit with amber eyes, bought by Rosalina at a market and carried home thrashing inside a sack. She consented to give it free run of the kitchen, but when after the first few hours it had gnawed a broom to shavings, squirmed into a crevice behind the stove (the gas supply needed to be disconnected before it could be ushered back to safety) and left a fusillade of black pellets in a corner, I had to allow its banishment to the chicken coop, where it promptly established sovereignty over Rosalina's broody hens and nipped the legs of her two crestfallen roosters if they interfered with its access to their food tray.

When it evicted the hens from their nests, I saved it from Rosalina's fury by buying it a clay hutch to live in: a uterine arrangement of pipes, like an earthenware burrow, with a tunnel leading in and a look-out at the top. The chickens perched on the hutch, and bleached the clay with their siftings; the rabbit crouched inside, waiting to vault at the tray of grain and scatter the outraged, gossiping birds.

It proved difficult to love: unlike the effigies on my shelves, it didn't know that rabbits were supposed to be winsome, to pose with one ear drooping, to wear tunics with brass buttons, to dispense cotton wool from their rear ends. I began to suspect rodent traits. Under the fluff, its tail was a flicking appendage like a rat's. The first time I fed it, tweaking its nose with a choice carrot, it clamped the vegetable between its teeth, twisted its head in disdain to relieve me of it, and darted away to finish eating in private. Don't *grab*, I almost heard myself saying. It was my small, belated lesson in filial ingratitude. Worse was to follow. When I picked it up, its flailing hind legs slashed my arm, and narrowly avoided gashing my wrist. I might have been the first person killed by his pet rabbit.

Perhaps I was better off, I thought, with my dummies.

I recalled seeing a toy animal seller barking his wares on the pavement in Petticoat Lane. His fanciest offerings that weekend were some automated bunnies made of pink nylon. They guzzled milk from a baby's bottle in fidgety mechanical jerks, their batteries snarling: it took one jerk to seize the teat, another to worry at it, a third to pull back for a belch. I think their ears wiggled independently as well.

Two cockney youths with boots made for kicking doors down stomped by. 'Are they real or what?' sneered one of them.

'Better than real, lads, better than real,' said the proprietor cheerily. 'They ain't got no feelings. Good for you lot.'

'Up yours,' replied the youths, for want of something wittier to say.

My own postscript was: What about *my* feelings? While considering my options, I struggled to reprieve the rabbit from Rosalina's cooking pot. Every day or so, she proposed him to me as a dish. (We had established his sex by this time: I gripped both sets of protesting paws while Rosalina groped through the white rug for what she delicately referred to as his tomatoes.) She outlined various succulent scenarios: she could lay him out on a bed of rice, she could bubble him up in a stew among all his favourite vegetables, she was ready to bake him in a pie, she would take special pleasure in stuffing him with herbs and bread crumbs, and if only she had known how I'm sure she would have enjoyed grinding him into a pâté. I learned to counter by proposing that she wring the neck of one of her flustered hens.

What rankled was that she could not understand the grounds for my clemency towards him. Like her pig-sticking sister in Mafra, she could conceive of only two uses for animals: either you were breeding them, or you ate them; in both cases, like her chickens, they served some purpose. Since the rabbit was not reproducing for the market and had been spared the pot, she didn't see how his existence could be justified. 'But what *good* is he?' she asked me, genuinely puzzled, when I vetoed the suggestion of a stew. The notion of a pet was as foreign as that of art, because both were self-justifying, supremely useless, made to receive our admiration or our love. I wondered whether I dared to explain the rabbit by citing the devotional objects in the oratory upstairs – all those insipid saints and flights of plaster angels which she dusted so tenderly; but I thought better of it.

Instead I let the rabbit out for a romp round the garden, and relied on him to demonstrate what I meant. He crept out hesitantly, unsure whether the open door led to the oven. Having convinced himself that he was going to live, he sampled some fronds of fern, got his bearings, then set off down the slope. At ground level, I suppose all that mattered to him was the banquet table of grass blades, crinkled weeds and sugary flowers; but from the top of the slope you could see pine trees, the rubber-limbed cactus, the grove of oranges and lemons, while the river shone below.

Just there, before skittering off down the hill, he could be relied on to make a sudden twirling vertical skip of acrobatic joy. He sprung directly into the air, as startlingly as if the ground had exploded beneath him. Once aloft, he seemed to whirl in a circle, and spun like a top. The secret of this leap was the way his hind legs banged together in a kick-start: the shock sent him briefly into orbit. He was a white projectile of pure, capricious energy. Landing again, he hurled himself down the hill as if the earth too bounced and rebounded like a trampoline. The backward spin with which he began never failed to amaze me. It was an exhibition of playfulness, and also a definition of art: Nijinsky said that art meant staying in the air longer than anyone else.

I pointed out the jump to Rosalina, hoping I had proved my case. She looked astonished for an instant, and then reached for the broom she used to shoo him back into captivity. By this time he was already in the vegetable patch, eating his way down a row of cabbages.

After the rabbit, my reconciliation with the great outdoors advanced to embrace a tree.

I had my fortieth birthday that year. Determining not to be downcast by it, I made up my mind to boast about it instead, and bored everyone by telling them it was due, or had just happened. I suppose I expected incredulity. But most of those whom I regaled with the news had been there before me, and couldn't imagine why

I considered the occasion so significant. One of them gave me a sharp-eyed look, making me feel that my sense of having finally reached the age of self-possession was premature. This was Gina, a friend of mine in Lisbon. She had all the knowing assurance of the older woman. When you ate at her house, she summoned the maid between courses by jingling a silver bell the size of a thimble. Perhaps – I always thought – in a previous life as a temple girl she'd had it attached to a finger. All it took was one note: the plates were cleared away as instantly as if they had sprouted wings. That was the kind of effortless command she had. So I crumpled within when she pinned me with that glance and demanded whether I had qualified to turn forty.

'Ah,' she said when I told her about the anniversary which only I thought momentous, 'but have you planted a tree, Peter? They say that you're only properly grown up when you have planted a tree.'

In fact, far from planting a tree, I had been keeping a resentful death-watch on several of them back in London. My predecessor in the house left a withering potted nursery behind her: shrubs in plastic urns on the roof, a nondescript bush in a tray, its leaves speckled with paint, a tangle of weeds grappling up a trellis, some bedraggled vines lapsing from pots on the wall. I threw away the urns on the roof: they made me feel buried, with flowers growing above me. The bush was in an earthenware dish, heavier to move; inertness earned it a reprieve. The trellis, despite the crackling dead ivy and the tufts of soggy moss at its base, at least covered up an air-vent in the wall, blackened with fumes from someone's kitchen. The wall pots I spared because they had impish clay faces: they were satyrs, tanned as terra cotta, with spiky ears and trumpet-shaped crowns in which flowers should have been their wreathing hair. I liked the sight of them scowling on the wall, or leering when a strip of sun cut across. But what grew from their brains of soil – a branching spillage of brown limbs which tumbled over the edge only to think themselves upwards again by sheer force of wishing, turning corners in empty air to grab at the light – did not matter to me.

When the vines finally died off, I decided I would gouge out the pots and let them smirk there emptily. Yet my neglect wasn't enough to deter the thirsting growths. The rain took care of them, keeping them alive just as it punitively fingered for leaks in my house. Who really belonged here, me or this tenacious vegetation, fastening suckers onto the stone?

Almost guiltily, the first morning I was back in London I gave the assorted twigs and tendrils a drink. I had never done so before, and the sense of responsibility which went with the act dismayed me. The creepers in the wall pots needed no more than this dribble of encouragement. Almost at once, like a film speeded up to supply instant gratification, they risked some leaves. The elbow-shaped crook where the arm made its upward turn became tighter and firmer, since it had more weight to support: soon it was waving a handful of buds at the sun. Everything alive reaches imploringly. The gesture of those feelers, inching a little irrigated life down their entire tangled length to the tip, was a hand extended in prayer. A tree – I admitted to myself – would almost certainly be next.

But I didn't plant it. I managed to cheat nature to that extent: planting it would have meant digging up my yard of tiles, delving into the city's nerves of wire and intestines of pipe. The tree arrived already planted, tied to a stick in its own gigantic tub. The stick, twice as tall as the sapling clamped to it, intended to straighten its posture; propped in the middle of the tub, the forked sketch of shoots and green nodes was like an infant made to wear a lumber-jack's boots, on the assumption that after a few decades he would grow into them.

It didn't take the tree that long. Within days, the buds had begun to make copies of themselves. The activity was as fanatical as my own scribbling inside the window – except that the tree produced exact perpetuations of itself, whereas my writing dealt in relics and replicas, figures which deputised for a departed original. A node acquired the notion of becoming a stalk. Having managed that, it signalled success by indulging in a leaf. The leaf, discovering how easy it all was, repeated itself, like a clown unfurling ropes of little flags from his mouth or under his arm. The stalk had changed to a branch, by which time another node half way along it was ventur-ing a stalk of its own, then a leaf, a second leaf, a row of duplicates, until another branch was achieved.

By contrast with this genetic rage, the white sheets of paper on my table were not leaves at all; they didn't deserve the metaphor. I left them to contemplate their own blankness while I went out to tend the tree, swivelling its tub across the yard to follow the passage of the niggardly light. Not being planted or rooted was to its advantage, perhaps: it could dance round in circles (if I turned the pot) and bask on all sides equally. Every week during the summer it seemed to raise another storey, sprout another generation of fronds, advance a little further in its campaign to unite the earth and the sky.

My concern for it became quite foolishly parental. If there was no rain for a few days, I would make nocturnal sorties from Oxford to water it. And when I described it to my parents, they were delighted to discover at last that I possessed an inherited characteristic, and retaliated with snapshots of their wisteria, clematis and hydrangeas. Looking down onto the yard, I saw only a net of wavering leaves, like a fountain stilled as it was drenching the air with green froth. But nothing had been stilled, and the growth was urgent because its time was so short.

I began to dread the autumn, when it would shrivel to a gallows of sticks. But by the time that happened, I had understood the strange instruction issued during the previous winter by the wise woman with the peremptory little bell. Only when you feel that your own death is at least possible do you begin to be concerned for the life of other things. To plant a tree is to acknowledge your own eventual absence from the scene. Having swept up the scurf of withered leaves, I went back indoors to wait for the spring.

9
The Importance of Being Elsewhere

T HE WINDOW HAS FOUR PANES OF GLASS, EACH OF THEM containing a different scene: a wall of grimy brick and a tree shyly uncurling leaves like croziers; next to it the quadrangle with the Greek god, who today is wearing a clown's red nose, strapped in place by a rubber band; the garden buzzing with heat, the lemons aglow, the birds cross-hatching the air; beside that the ballet of cabs, trucks, dogs, gestures and attitudes choreographing itself on the street corner.

A different person wanders through each of the panes. In Oxford there is a figure availing himself of his ancient right to take short-cuts across the barbered grass. The porters once used to shoo him off it, mistaking him for a student; no longer. He is on his way to dinner, in a gown speckled with specimens of institutional meals eaten during the last fifteen years. The gown serves as a black all-over napkin. It is also beginning to come apart at the seams, its threads tangling and frazzling like distracted thoughts. Pathetically, it is the wrong gown: it denotes the rank of BA, not the MA which you are automatically awarded a few years later. The MA gown is a swishier item, with flaps which trail under the arms modelled on some late medieval fashion. I could not avoid getting the degree, but I never acquired the gown. This counted as Peter Pan's refusal to graduate.

The London space is occupied by someone else, reluctantly grown-up whether he likes it or not: the householder who wonders whether he dares to trust this shelter, hears a creak in the floorboards as if it were a snapped bone, treats a pipe which chugs and grumbles as a digestive upset, and transfers all his mortal anxieties to brick, wood and plaster. If it rains will the roof leak, and if it doesn't will the tree die? Sometimes he tries to convince himself not to care: we acquire this need for domestic protection, after all, just at the age when we begin to perceive that it will not last and therefore does not matter. The obsession with permanence accompanies the knowledge of temporariness.

In New York this housebound pot-plant of a person sheds such cares and, having dropped off his bag, loses himself at once in the street. Though I know I have to wait for the elevator and catch up with the doorman's maladies on the way out, I always want to dive directly from the fire-escape and feel the liveliness down there slap and splash and cleave in front of my face like water. I understand why baptism requires total immersion. People gush, flood, cascade along the sidewalk in a flotsam of ripped jeans, gelled hair, power shoulders and aloof, appraising shades; transistors dispense rap, the bell on a fire-engine clangs, and the self-proclaimed psychic lounging on the vinyl banquette in her basement shrills, 'Hey, come get a reading today'. Why not let her invent a future for me?

After all in Lisbon I can reinvent a past for myself. The person I see in that frame of glass is tracking a rabbit through the flowerbeds with the inducement of a carrot and the threat of a broomstick. He seems to be wearing short pants.

Each character in this quadruple life has his own identity, even his own name. To multiply the self is one way of wriggling free from it, suggesting that it is a facet not a face. Remember the adolescent delight in experimenting with signatures? Every twiddle or loop or staccato jerk of the pen sketches a character you might become. What I most favoured at that age was a scrawl which rendered me illegible. It was the announcement, to myself if to no one else, of a mystery.

Before I took over my Oxford rooms, the elderly sign-writer Christ Church employed for these jobs was called out of retirement to letter my name on the lintel of my door. I saw him at work one day when I dropped in to check on the state of the plumbing. He was dabbing away with a curly brush-end, as delicately as if he had been using a feather. He had reached the full stop after my first initial, and was inking it in so thoroughly – the tip of his tongue peeping through his clenched teeth in concentration – that it might have been an infinitesimal black planet he was kneading into shape. I did not dare to tell him it was my name he was inscribing up there. How could I presume that it deserved such treatment? It was ready when I moved in, waiting to see if I would earn the right to succeed the generations of other names – the most recent beginning with REV. – which had been painted over to supply its undercoat.

Mr. P. Conrad.

was what it said; the third full stop looked as ominous to me as a bullet-hole blackening the wood.

On college communications, my middle initial was coughed up to supply me with another identity. In the shorthand of the place, I was PJC. Since we all addressed each other by this code, missives in brown envelopes about bureaucratic problems resembled the proceedings of some boyish secret society. I found myself envying the colleagues who, thanks to a hyphen or a plethora of ancestors, ran to four initials.

I did receive a bonus from the local travel agency. Not wanting to offend, it decided to give me the benefit of its doubt and awarded me a doctorate on the tickets it issued in my name. Once, when a return flight to Australia was delayed for a day, Qantas telephoned my parents to warn them that Dr Conrad had been re-routed. Some time after I arrived, my mother – half in the hope of free consultations, half in annoyance at not having known about the possibility earlier – asked me, 'Are you a doctor then, Peter?' In disappointing her, I disappointed myself.

I had to disappoint All Souls as well when the college librarian, fifteen years after my departure, wrote seeking information for a list he was compiling of Fellows living, dead and quondam (the category to which I then belonged). There were requests for details about county/country of birth ('the latter only if outside *England*') and 'secondary' education. Secondary was cordoned off inside quotation marks to indicate that it was a post-war vulgarism, probably inapplicable since we all attended – didn't we? – public schools, which disdained to recognise this term.

But the trickiest classification was 'paternal status'. I was given a whole hierarchy to choose from, and needed only to delete the stations inappropriate to my personal case: 'nob/bart/kt/doc/esq/ gen/pleb'. It was like being accused all over again by the codified

Jeeves who used to look me up and down when I opened my wardrobe door, deploring my lack of tails, morning suit, shooting stick, etcetera. No, my father was not a noble. Nor was he a bart or a kt. Even I was not a doc (which, according to the questionnaire, 'indicates a doctor in any of the faculties'). Thereafter, now the line-up had declined into the middle class, I began to have doubts. Even the questionnaire conceded that 'in the twentieth century' the last three terms 'may be said to lack definition'. Esquire, for all its indefiniteness, had a lingering after-life in Oxford. Letters were sometimes addressed to me using the obsolete, undeserved order of chivalry. The explanatory note proposed a new definition: ' "esq" might be adopted for members of the professions (but "doc" for doctors)'. Gen I took to mean gent, specifically the kind of tweedy sluggard known as a gentleman of leisure. No thanks.

Which left only pleb, footnoted on the form as referring to 'weekly wage earners'. I still remembered the brown-paper envelope in which my father used to bring home an assortment of notes and coins – promptly passed on to my mother – every Thursday evening. This was the only money which has ever seemed real to me, because it was given in exchange for work and would in its turn soon be exchanged for food; and it was handed over, rather than being mere numbers transferred impalpably between bank accounts. I had no intention of writing my father off as a plebeian. As my eye ran back up the scale of abbreviations, I wondered which term applied to me. None, I hope, of the above.

My London identity is terser, stripped of titles. On the day I took possession I wrote my surname with a marker pen beside the bell at my front door. The intervening years of rain have not smudged its imprint on the metal. Whoever succeeds me there will have a problem dislodging that indelible CONRAD. Actually, I deceive myself. A squirt of ammonia and a minute's scrubbing would probably erase all trace of me.

In New York, I undergo a fourth contraction. 'You the guy from 5-L?' the postman sometimes asks. Once he learned the apartment number, he employed it as a name, which made me feel like a prisoner answering at a roll-call. '5-L, right?' I nod meekly, and extend my hand for the begging letters from Charlton Heston and Elizabeth Taylor.

In the Manhattan telephone book I found my compensation. In

the London directories I had my name to myself; here, however, there were four of me, one of whom announced 'lwyr' after his Park Avenue address. I produced my vestigial middle initial, and relied on it to differentiate me from the three usurpers. An Oxford colleague, unsure of my address, once got all four numbers from the bored sibyl at directory enquiries and – since she had not been warned that one of the Peter Conrads was a Park Avenue lawyer – dialled them all before reaching me. (My stipulation of the J. placed me at the bottom of the list.) One of my homonyms had an answering machine which programmed a selection of favourite big-band tunes for callers. Not my taste, she calculated; not my voice either, asking her to speak after the beep. The next time, whoever answered said brusquely of the Peter Conrad in question 'He left town'. The tone suggested no regrets, and implied that the departure had taken place under a cloud. The lawyer's secretary declared that I was in conference, could not be disturbed, and asked the nature of my colleague's business. Expending the fourth dime, at last she got the right me. 'I can see why you like it here,' she said, exhausted. 'There are *more* of you here than there are in Oxford.'

I didn't let on to her that I sometimes added to the quotient of my selves with a quirk of local pronunciation. I felt uneasy about introducing or identifying myself here as Peter. It sounded phonetically precious, too British. That dental t was the trouble. The New York variant rolled the tongue back from the palate and breathed out the word with a growl which I liked the idea of: Peedah, rhyming more or less with cheetah.

In Lisbon there was a whole verbal family of translations to which I could happily submit. Everyone there had a mouthful of names. The individual was a confluence of clans, all of which had to be credited; there were also the presiding saints – your personal prototypes – to be added into the mixture. Peter on its own was too meagre to mean anything. The forgotten John was again re-activated: to Jorge's parents I was known as Pedro João. And when they knew me better, they coined a diminutive for me, Peterzinho. The z had a soothing buzz, like an adult calming a fractious child. In changing my name, it changed me.

This was not all. As well as a name, I had to have a title, in order to merit the respect of the household help. While I balked at the Oxford definitions of status, I spared myself from having to take offence at the local system. It didn't seem invidious or insulting; like the rest of my life there, it was a game. Jorge's father was already Senhor Doutor, so I could not pretend to that. Jorge himself, being a scientist, was known as Senhor Engenheiro. His brother's retardation meant that he remained Master, never graduating to Mister: he was Menino Zézinho, which sounded even fonder because it rhymed. My first name underwent promotion to a professional rank, and Olga and Rosalina christened me Senhor Peter. A foreign word was anyway honorific in itself. Down the street lived a German woman who was known – like all females from out there – as Madame, though her housekeeper doubled the deference by always calling her Senhora Madame. If only she had been able to produce some academic credential she might even have been Senhora Doutora Madame. Rosalina, who had never seen my name written down, felt free to rewrite it, and if she leaves me a note about a telephone message it is addressed to Senhor Pita, a personification of the envelope-shaped bread. I am content, like Erik Actor and all the other hopefuls, to play as cast.

Each of the window panes contains someone different. Changing longitudes, I move between times or ages. I can recover childhood at will in Lisbon, for the price of a ticket there. Conversely, going back to England means the resumption of responsibilities, of adult cares – sealing the roof, feeding the birds, fertilising the tree, teaching the young, listening to the church clock dole out time. England longs to turn everything into an antique. I groan inwardly each year as I edge further up the seniority league in Oxford. When I was first taken to see the rooms set aside for me at Christ Church, the colleague in charge of such things explained that they had been cunningly manoeuvred away from their former clerical use, and I need not fear eviction by some incoming chaplain. 'They're yours until the retiring age,' he said. He meant to please me, but my heart sank to hear it. I was twenty-five at the time: so *this* was to be it?

But in America the first job/house/wife/nose is not necessarily the last. There was always the chance of exit in that direction, to New York with its adolescent faith that you can be anything or anyone you wish, so long – to quote Miss America – as you feel good about yourself. 'I'm changing my life' is the national creed. It is what the country means, after all. New York keeps alive in me the sense of potentiality.

Returning once to Oxford after a year on leave, I asked one of the college secretaries what had happened while I was away. 'Nothing' she almost snapped, and looked affronted by the very thought of something happening. Then, having got over her irritation, she added, 'Oh, the Queen came to dinner' – though this was a ritual, and therefore did not constitute a happening. It reaffirmed the past; nothing could be less of a novelty. In my rooms, the owl still nodded sagely on its rickety perch.

My first outing in New York is always a survey of what's new: most things are. The city has reconstructed or redefined itself in my absence. The Tex-Mex restaurant across the park is now Burmese, the florist who serenaded his blooms with baroque music has given way to a store selling cowboy boots with a window display of bleached steer skulls, the deli has lunged further down-market and now stocks only the tabloids and not *The New York Times*, the tenement has been reclad as a condominium with post-modern portholes to conceal its wooden water-tank. The dancer across the street has moved on, or is dead. His blinds are pulled up on a bared box which awaits its next transformation. There is a brisk turnover in lives here. The future is always arriving prematurely. The clothes shop dummies wear Bermuda shorts while the last blizzard of winter is scourging the street, and have already adopted flannels in broiling August. After a while, the American acceleration of time alarms me. Can't they see that it is an anticipation of the end? Hence the comfort of retreating to my various safe pasts: Oxford with its gathering dust, Lisbon with the hare-brained rabbit.

They are different pasts. Oxford, like Highgate Cemetery, is the voluminous history we come from and return to. I spend the year there working chronologically through English literature, as the bell clangs above me and the seasons rotate in the meadow. Shakespeare, Sidney and Spenser occupy the autumn. We cough our way through Milton in the winter. The romantic poets arrive in time for the summer – skylarks, nightingales, daffodils, splendour in the grass. In October it all begins over again. The young pass through and are annually replaced. They and the texts remain the same age. Only I get older.

Lisbon is a personal past, a childhood I can live out of sequence, squeezed into vacations from adult existence. However many years pass, I will stay the youngest member of this family. Rosalina, pleading for permission to kill and cook the rabbit, regularly offers to replace it with a new one. It will look just the same, she promises; there are plenty at the market. Perhaps she does just this while I am away. It could be a different rabbit each time, and therefore younger than it was when I last saw it. So long as it is white, would I notice the difference?

Flight was always my ambition, my motive and my motor. Not so much flying as the idea of fugitiveness. During my first trips out of Tasmania to the mainland, I used to watch the plane's propeller jerk, spin, whirl and then vanish into a blur of energy. When it revolved fast enough, it became invisible. As far as I understood it, that was the meaning of flight: it conferred disincarnation.

Or else it was a serial reincarnation, a device for cheating the singleness of our lot, and having several alternate lives. Flight was also, I eventually had to admit, an equivocation: it was irony acted out in space. Just as irony permits you to stand aside from what you have said, so flight allows you to separate yourself from what you have been.

The international date line confirmed this faith of mine. I discovered it when I flew back to Australia from New York, and though I could not have explained quite what it meant, I knew what I felt when crossing it. This perimeter of dots drawn down the empty ocean was the place where the world could be unzipped. It was the seam which showed up the truth about the whole elaborate fiction of parallel lives pasted in strips on the globe. Space was calculated in time. Oxford, all those hours behind me, deemed itself to be five minutes ahead of London, while New York was five hours and several centuries younger than both – and so on until here time ran out of space, reached a brief stop, then began running back in the opposite direction. The line was imaginary, written on water. Yet crossing it became for me what all journeys yearn to be: a rite of passage; the experience of your own death, promptly followed by rebirth.

The joyful trauma happened differently according to the direction. Travelling south, you suffer a triple night. The plane bores and bounces through the dark as if drilling a hole to the bottom of the world. An entire day is somehow lost in an existential hiccup. It is like being in cryogenic storage. Then, with the cramped, exhausted body crying out for release from this suspension, there is finally a dawn. It might be the first dawn of all, and it discovers a life-raft of land in the water: mist boiling from the mountains; a stream which twists as if in delight at escaping from the repetitious uninflected ocean; the oldest, newest continent. Following the curves of the Hawkesbury River, the plane glides towards Sydney Harbour. I am back where I began, where I wish I belonged.

On the return north, time elapses enchantedly, without being marked down to your account. You spend a night, an abbreviated day and another night being moved forward. Still only a few hours separate departure from Sydney and arrival in New York. Your watch can make no sense of this: you live in a time of simultaneous ages rather than consecutive minutes. The stop at Honolulu is for me when the crossover between existences, seasons, hemispheres occurs. It takes place inside a shower room, which you can rent for a few dollars. A wash, a change of clothes, and I have shed one identity and assumed another. I am ready for the next life.

Though travel compounds existences, it is still terrifying – as the ball striped with all those longitudinal hours swivels below, sunning itself like the tree I push round the yard in London – to think about the sheer plenitude of possible lives, and the negligence with which they are distributed among their owners. We land on earth as randomly as raindrops. Why was this the place the raindrop smudged? Only in the crib we pieced together at Christmas in Lisbon is there a guiding, ordaining star. The real reason why the life happened here has more to do with how the wind was blowing. And why did this swimmer rather than another one in the wriggling team reach that particular egg? If you multiply these unlikelihoods by all the generations which precede us, you arrive at the rough sum of our improbability, and the reason for the mismatchments inside us.

No wonder a person is a makeshift assortment of oppositions, of contradictory qualities which we try to reduce to a character. Donne said 'I am a little world', but went on to analyse that microcosm into its warring constituents: a body where four antagonistic elements battled; an angelic spirit which disowned all four. I can only understand myself as a continuing argument between impulses which are forced to share the same skin and must rely on a harassed mind to sort them out or pacify them – diffidence against aggression, a desire to belong against a prickly estrangement, the temptation to drown in a crowd against the solitary tenure of a room with a view of the street, a need for home against disbelief in any such place. Travelling, we are taking the company of selves on tour, allowing each of them its own brief life.

It is just because the fall to earth is so unpredictable and un-designed, like the person falling, that we make a cult of the place where the faller crash-lands. Each spot has its anthem, its boast of centrality. The Londoners after hours in the pub next door to me rowdily warble that maybe it's because they're Londoners that they love London so. Maybe they are right: what other reason could there be? From the *fado* dens in Lisbon you can hear the singers hoarsely chanting the praises of their melancholy Lisboa. In New York, New York, the jingle asserts that it's such a wonderful town they had to name it twice.

These are our noisy protests against coincidence and happen-stance, our dreams of predestination. Life is a long exercise in turning chance into choice, accident into design. Hence those windows which act as frames, pretending that what travels across them is a picture. Hence too the notion of home, with its wishful rearrangement of geography. It decrees a centre, and thus an anchorage. Every love – whether personal or civic – subscribes to the idea of necessity, and entails an illusion of permanence.

When I think of the overnight camp I pitched in my leaky tent on the way round America in 1969 or of the room on 23rd Street, that seems the honest way to live. But you can only live that way when you are that age, and operate on the assumption that time is endless. Soon afterwards, the accumulation of hostages begins: offspring, objects, or perhaps just words. Literature invents a special tense for reciting the present as if it were already past, allowing us to behave as if we can direct time, compose it, transcribe and thus subdue it as musicians do. Home builds a shrine to the hope that nothing will change.

Inside, things hang together temporarily, opportunely. There is no connection between my triple-decker series of birds under the staircase – the cut-out barn owl with the murderous cardboard beak, the seagull with the creaky wooden wings, the migrant

Canada goose on its way to another continent – but they consent to play at being a family. The principle is collage, which holds unlike things in a semblance of belonging. At the bottom of the hill in Lisbon, houses are improvised from crates, planks, scraps of tin, sheets of plastic.

Writing too is an act of salvage. It stakes a claim. No matter who does it, it has the same function as José Manuel's battle against the spasmodic antics of his arm to print out his signature.

Every year my first action is to write my name in a new diary. (I treat myself, shamefacedly, to capitals.) I am then convinced that I will survive to fill it up. Accident is ruled out in advance. I take possession of the year before it begins, by preparing the volume into which the year will be parcelled, and which when the year is complete will be all that remains of it. Each day has its page. Each day *is* a page: unless it is written on or written up, it won't have been experienced. Retroactively I make the day signify something, coax it into telling a story.

A summer evening in Oxford, the usual walk around Christ Church meadow. The wind shaking an earlier rain from the trees, and a sunset which opened across the washed sky like a flower; Magdalen tower streaked with gold; the playing fields across the river waiting unruffled for the next consignment of larking lives to spill onto them; the river itself almost forgetting to flow. It was one of those occasions when you can quite happily deduct yourself from the world, simply because you realise your extreme good fortune in being in it.

In a panel beside this, a stifling April afternoon in New York, another year. I am slogging up Bleecker Street. Between one block and the next, the temperature plunges. Clouds roll in to close over the city. The sun, plummeting faster than usual to hide in New Jersey, lights them from underneath: they are green, swollen, about to burst. A gust of grit slaps my face. Somewhere to the north, a powdery flash detonates in the sky. Then a drum-roll batters the street. A Latino kid with a feather in his hair, worried about the water-tightness of his boom box, says to his friend 'Hey man, is the world gonna end?' It didn't. Not that time.

Or I am crossing Waterloo Bridge at night in a winter gale, wondering whether this is the same city I first saw from here all those years before, and whether I am the same person who saw it then. A skyline of cranes instead of churches, floodlights like banners on the façade of the Savoy, sapphire arcs on top of the Lloyd's Building. The water below is black and choppy. A shame-faced youth asks for money to buy a cup of tea. He came over from Ireland to work on a building site, had his tools stolen, lost his job, couldn't pay his rent, and now dosses down beneath the bridge. 'I'm saving up to go home,' he says, to cover my fussing as I try to calculate how much I need to keep for my bus fare. 'I've been here three years, and I'd like to go back if I could. The way I look at it is, I've seen London.' I walked on, a fellow pilgrim. The city lures us, jumbles us up, and then – accepting no responsibility for the dreams it excites in us – sends us briskly off to our different destinations or destinies. Perhaps it was dangerous to want more than a single life. The city abounded in people you had only just escaped having to be.

And the first time I was asked a question in the street in Lisbon. It must have been ten years ago, at a bus stop. An old woman in the queue – all in black, scarf knotted under her chin, a professional widow – asked me if the bus which was pulling in went to Santos. I understood the question but did not know the answer. At least I was able to tell her in Portuguese that I didn't know. She looked embarrassed, bewildered at having approached a foreigner. Evidence of mental frailty on her part, she probably thought. The strangers, the blow-ins from out there, were supposed to be instantly recognisable. They wore bright colours, carried cameras, and did not travel by bus. What was this one doing in camouflage? Another passenger told her what she wanted to know, and she hauled herself onto the bus with her flagon of olive oil and her strip of dried cod. I was so taken aback at being mistaken for someone who was not a stranger that I didn't realise it was my bus too.

All these days recur, with the aid of a few verbal clues. Representation promises to make what is absent present again, but the reach of words is longer than their grasp. All they can do is catch the trace a body has left in departing.

On my walls in Oxford I have a collection of photographs of New York. They are a double contradiction – of Oxford certainly, but also of New York itself. They confound the local atmosphere of church bells, wan sunlight, footsteps on flagstones, and wheezing organ pipes heard through closed doors; instead they show gutters choked with garbage, streets roofed over by the shaky trellis of the El tracks, tenements ablaze. The photographs are my small act of dissociation. Their ugliness is alluring, simply because it is somewhere else.

Yet they are just as removed from the substance of New York as they are from Oxford. They are images summoned from the air. The Empire State Building shimmers into view along my wall like an exhalation. First it is an idea in the minds of Lewis Hine's steel-workers, who cling to girders a quarter of a mile above the streets and seem to be unfolding the structure from the clouds rather than founding it on the bedrock. Next, now complete, Man Ray sees it glistening in the narrow darkness of Fifth Avenue. For him it is not a building either but a ready-made, a found object, a specimen of useless beauty. Beside this, André Kertész turns the Empire State upside down, plunges it into a puddle, and drives the mark of a car tyre through the reflection. Then Harry Callahan – introducing colour into this lunar city of silver – lines up the blueish shaft of the Empire State, a cream wedge of apartment building, a tumulus of brown brick and the side of an old lodging house painted fire-engine red: the skyscraper now shares the neutral sky with its incongruous neighbours in the bland, permissive visual democracy of Pop.

By changing the building, the photographers make it their own. They treat it as lovingly and as disrespectfully as a toy. To go up the Empire State itself is to appreciate the plucky conceit of this. From on top, the city dwindles to a graveyard of slabs, the citizens to a flurry of transitory dust. What audacity for one of those particles down there to set itself into competition with the pinnacle of steel; to look up at it and, rather than feeling terrified or merely exhausted, to translate it from object to subject – to remake it as a facsimile of itself.

I even found my own building in one of these photographs, and was amazed at my sense of gratification. The building had had its name in the paper when a crime was committed once on the premises, and had featured as well on the late-night television news when a gas explosion across the street caused us all to be evacuated. But these incidents did not validate the building. On the contrary, they suggested its flimsiness. Why was I so elated and comforted to find that it had sneaked into the background of a photograph by Gary Winogrand? The photographer himself had surely not even noticed it. He was compulsively snap-happy, and if he had lived long enough would have photographed every corner in the city, country, world. But what interested him in this case was a girl on a bicycle, with free-range breasts and fluid hair, glowing in the sun as she pedalled downtown, a sprite rejoicing in the hedonistic city of the 1960s. No caption identified the setting, but when I peered at the grainy murk out of which she was riding I recognised the intersection of Christopher and Hudson Streets: on one side a shoddy deli, on the other a shop exhibiting swishily ornate antique furniture. And there, so far back in the network of dots on the paper that it registered only as a shadowy lump not yet honed into form, was what must be the place where I would one day live.

Currently, if I want to persuade myself that the building exists when I am not there, I don't ring the telephone number from England and listen to the non-committal tone at the other end; instead, I look at the photograph. And yet all it will attest to is that the building once was there, at the instant two decades ago when Winogrand's camera-eye, attracted by something else, briefly opened. Do I want to be reassured that things are real, or to confer unreality on them? Before the world can be lived in, it must be described. But no one can inhabit a description.

On the highway north from Chicago – the city which had looked to me like a plantation of twigs in an ice-floe – a gilded pharaoh bestrides the prairie. In himself, this roadside Rameses is an unsurprising sight. To understand him, it will merely be necessary to find out what he is advertising. But no, he has nothing to sell. He is for real; he is standing there on reality's behalf. In the field behind is his pyramid, also made of ingots, which he is too huge to squeeze inside. His owner lives there, though: a Chicago millionaire, prematurely snug in a tomb where he has no doubt installed a jacuzzi. Ozymandias still believes that you can take it with you. Here at least there are no desert sands to blow, shift and disillusion him. Only the whooshing exhausts of the cars, speeding towards a plethora of elsewheres, defy the feet of the pharaoh in their concrete boots.

The insecurity we pave and carpet over sometimes cracks the

surface. In Lisbon one afternoon, I sat through an earth tremor. The windows shivered, jolting the view. Plates in the dressers chattered like nervy teeth. The whole house shuddered, rattled, settled to rest. When the jittery objects calmed themselves, there was a hush. Then every dog in the suburb began to wail. It was a collective dismay, as if all New York's alarmist sirens had sounded off at once. Guardians of property, the snarling Alsatians and slavering Dobermanns needed to have faith in it. This small jerky fit, as the masses in schism beneath bumped the crust, came as a personal affront to them. Richter put the shock at 3.7, we later learned.

What defence is there against such alienation effects of earth, when the floor reminds us that we have no right to tread on it? To forget, until it happens again. Our whole history denies that such things do or should occur. We know we are intruders or strangers here, yet manage the bravado to behave as if we belonged. The pharaoh fixes himself in the field; we feather our nests, congest the staircase with totems and hang up angels around the house.

The other option is to alter our existence, to change what we have been given. Discontent and restlessness dictate our language. There is no poetry without metaphor, and metaphor transforms things into that which they are not: the dregs of a coffee cup into a bleeding neon tear. It is a wand as mercurial as that of the god on his plinth in the Oxford quadrangle. It grants the wish of every noun to be an object other than the one it names, it speeds every verb on its way out of sight; it is imagination's excuse to go walkabout. Despite our burrowing, our home-making, the locks on our doors, it caters to our secret need to shed encumbrances and pass on.

America appeals to me because of the candour with which it admits just this. It contains, compressed, all the worlds that are possible, and reduces them to stage-sets. You can see the wrinkles in the canvas sky, the dents in the cardboard rocks; never mind, the scene soon changes. My other microcosms co-exist in New York. I wander through pockets of Portuguese gossip in Greenwich Village, outside grocery shops run by immigrants from the Azores; further south, on Houston Street, some anaemic figurines beside a church re-stage the appearance of Our Lady – their lady – to the shepherd children at Fátima. Columbus Avenue has its Oxford shops, selling striped blazers and button-down shirts (worn by no one in Oxford) to Wall Street brokers. Two blocks from the tenement I squatted in, 23rd Street manages an excerpt from London in the grim terraced apartment house it calls by that name. All is reversible, relative. Can any place or thing be real if there are so many alternatives to it?

To have more than one life is the craft of the actor, and the dexterity of the traveller. It is also the desire and rage of the artist, who no matter what identity he inherits will long to be different, and no matter what portion of the earth is home to him will want to be elsewhere.

All the same, when summer comes, I sit in the Lisbon garden for a month, happy to be only there.

At first I order myself to worry about the tree I have left to the mercy of the London rains, back in that other occasional world. I can see the faint northern sun swivelling round, to stain the tops of the walls. It switches the tree's shadow on and off, softening it or sharpening it or wiping it out altogether. Clouds pass over, looking like the blotting paper we used at school (which is what, to the earth, they are): edged glaringly white, but damp and fuzzily grey in the middle. In the southern heat, while ants erupt from the ground and bees congregate from the sky, I say a prayer for rain in London.

Gradually I loosen my hold on the tree. It fades, like the features of a dead person erasing themselves from the memory. A thousand miles below that locked yard, here is a world which needs no tending, where life buzzes and flutters and seethes, kills and eats and breeds. The air is as golden as syrup boiling on a stove. The cicadas have made their brief migration to the trees, so the garden trills as they saw their wings together. The sound at first reminds me of the demolition at the top of my London street: the nattering of the jackhammers, the nudging insistence of that great leaden ball thumping the bricks. Except that this is the noise of engendering, not destruction. The whole garden might be a squeaking set of bed springs, enviously overheard upstairs through the ceiling.

The air throbs as if made of strings, from which the cicadas are scraping music. The soil teems: there are craters on the lawn among the flower beds, funnels through which the ants file out to map the world, ruling the garden in militarised straight lines along two-lane highways where there are never any collisions. They bring back a tribute of seeds and crumbs and carcases from outlying districts; they have even found a route into the house, tunnelling through fissures in the masonry to emerge on the kitchen sink in quest of spilled sugar grains. The lanes of traffic are sometimes interrupted by whiffs of insecticide, but the ants soon find new recruits, or contrive a detour. Radiating from the vents in the ground, they travel away to map the world, returning hours later after journeys as epochal and dangerous as those of the navigators down the river and across the ocean. Rosalina, who bars their advance in the kitchen with the spray-can, is their Adamastor. While one line inches to the surface in the garden, another is docilely plodding back into the totalitarian mine beneath. Do they count their daily casualties? Surely not: an ant exists only as a member of a society and an army; since it has no notion of individuality, it must be spared the sensations of separateness and loss. The self in any case is a human invention, of no concern to nature.

Meanwhile, higher up the scale, the lizards have arrived at the idea of leisure. While the ants pave the garden with their dribbling black tarmac, lizards extend themselves on ledges and flicker with pleasure as the rock scalds them. They at least know they exist (which the toiling ants have not noticed yet): hence their genius for pretending not to exist. Their scales disguise them as lichen; coming and going, they alternate between darting leaps like lashed whips and the pretence that not to move is to be unseen, that the observer can escape observation. Along the bottom of the garden, on errands to and from the compost heap where they have their lyings-in, the stray cats operate on the same principle. They pace, slink, then freeze with every hair erect when they realise that I have spotted them; they apply sudden pressure to fire themselves through the hedge just as I reach for something to throw.

Above, the breeze is a mesh of flight paths. Butterflies dither along air-headedly, batting their orange wings as if applauding the cabbages, or themselves. Bees bumble ponderously about their business, and having got a grip on the landing-stage of flowers they dabble in pollen with greedy glee. A wasp hovers like a malicious helicopter. Midges sew the air into a web. The starlings hop, the woodpecker drills. The nightingale sings from inside a cave of branches.

At dusk the swallows shoot into the sky as if from a bow. They have a nest on a whitewashed wall of the house which the doddering fascist President used to occupy: a lump of mucus-bound twigs with stray fringes drooling from it. They make their frantic circuits of the discolouring sky in order to rope it into shape as their domain, before time runs out; once they have defined it with their skimming, soaring loops, they can retreat into that adhesive pocket. Jorge's mother told me during my first summer here that the swallows make only one nest, and if it is invaded they die. I didn't know whether this was true, but I chose to believe it. The story lends a brave vulnerability to the jutting collage of scraps they have pasted onto the stark cliff of the house.

The thought of home matters only when the sun fails. Until then, the patterns continue to scribble themselves on the garden. The ants travel horizontally, the bees and wasps zero in vertically, the birds add spirals and streaking diagonals, while the butterflies free-associate between the leaves and fallen, oozing berries. The air condenses. A nothingness to us, it is a bouncing, buoyant trapeze to these creatures. A spider beside me is climbing the sky. The thread it hangs by has disappeared in the sunlight; it is scrambling up a rope ladder which is not there, a speck of food gripped in its agitated feelers.

Overlaid on the tracery of motions is the thick jangle of sounds – twittering, chuckling, gurgling birds; the vibrant cicadas. The flowers breathe more silently, but in smelling their respiration I am convinced that I can hear it, just as I can see the insensible processes of growth, speeded up by the sun: fruit ripening, roses unclenching.

The wind makes it all happen, stirring things and circulating them. The grasses nod acquiescently, the flowers falter, the trees flex, lemons tremble on their stalks. Every leaf rustles and responds differently to the playful torment, tickled or brow-beaten or gently elbowed. Birds on the branches steady themselves.

Then, ending the daydream, a pine cone fell. The propellers of seed cracked open with the sound of ripped fabric. It thudded to the ground and tumbled like a grenade along the path towards me. The wound where it split from the branch was still sticky with amber gum. The world, like the swallows' nest, has been opportunely glued together.

This was the old tree's cumbersome idea of reproduction – a biological time-bomb, with the seeds in their separate bunkers ready to bail out on the way down, scattering blades across the garden like wreckage from a crashed plane. Where the cone rolled to a halt at my feet, a white butterfly had also flopped down on the flagstones, dead. A day or so out of the cocoon, its eggs laid, its part in the relay race was accomplished. It had been there for only a few minutes, its wings uselessly spread, when a platoon of expeditionary ants was drafted to deal with it. They marched directly from their peep-hole in the wall and occupied the velvety body, which quivered as if in excitement at their prowlings and nibblings. The white wings, deemed indigestible by the ants, held up until there was no more body to connect them.

In the garden that summer, I enjoyed an instant of invisibility – of non-existence, and of pure happiness. I was sitting in the shadow of a tree, dazed by the sun outside it. A butterfly vacillated past. It hesitated, pulsed in the air, trod the wind while reviewing its options. Then it settled on my chest. What had it mistaken me for?

Glancing down, I noticed that I had on a T-shirt daubed with an oily, inky sketch of Sydney Harbour: a yellow sunflower-shaped sun above a pink bridge, with a surf of triangular sails. The butterfly made straight for the painted core of that floral sun, positioned more or less where they say the heart is. I tried to disappear into the mirage I was wearing. I didn't draw breath. It paused there – oh, for seconds: how long *is* a moment? I felt ashamed when my lungs insisted on continuing to work, and the butterfly realised its error.

I don't remember now whether this happened before or after I saw the ants feasting on the hinge of nourishment between those white, grounded wings in the dust.

It could, I suppose, have been the same butterfly.

ABOUT THE AUTHOR

Peter Conrad was born in 1948 in Tasmania, Australia, and since 1973 has taught English literature at Oxford University. His most recent books are *Behind the Mountain: Return to Tasmania* and *A Song of Love and Death: The Meaning of Opera.* He lives in a Greenwich Village apartment, a London flat, rooms in an Oxford college, and a house in Lisbon.